||||||||||||||||||||||||||||||||||||||||||||||||||||||||||||||||||||||||||

A French Aristocrat in the
American West

De Hault de Lassus coat of arms. Notice the motto, *Nul bien sans peine,* "no gain without pain," suggesting a family ethos of industry. Reproduced from Louis de Magny, *Nobilaire universel.*

A French Aristocrat in the American West

The Shattered Dreams of De Lassus de Luzières

Carl J. Ekberg

with a foreword by Marie-Sol de La Tour d'Auvergne

University of Missouri Press ◉ Columbia and London

Cataloging-in-Publication data available from the Library of Congress
ISBN 978-0-8262-1896-4

♾™ This paper meets the requirements of the
American National Standard for Permanence of Paper
for Printed Library Materials, Z39.48, 1984.

Design and composition: Jennifer Cropp
Printing and binding: Integrated Book Technology, Inc.
Typefaces: Minion and Bernhard

For Gloria Ekberg and in memory of Ida Nasatir, two wives who endured much on behalf of Upper Louisiana

Contents

Plans and Maps

Illustrations

Foreword

Pierre-Charles de Hault de Lassus de Luzières was one of a number of French aristocrats who sought their fortune in America during the turbulent times ushered in by the French Revolution. This seismic political and social upheaval reverberated across both Europe and America. Far more French aristocrats invested in land in America than actually settled there. De Luzières's case is exceptional, both because he settled permanently in the Mississippi Valley and because the story is so remarkably well documented. Carl J. Ekberg has skillfully brought to life the frontier struggle of this transplanted Frenchman who courageously adapted to challenging circumstances at a time in life when most men of his age and standing aspired to a genteel retirement on their estates.

De Luzières's arduous journey, which involved uprooting his family in northern France and setting sail for America in 1790 for what he thought would be a 2,000-acre tract on fertile lands on the banks of the Ohio River, proved to be just the beginning of his adventures. He soon discovered that he had been defrauded by the infamous Scioto Land Company. With that dream in ruin, he set about realizing another—creating a vast commercial empire in the Illinois Country, which would extend the entire length of the Ohio River and down the Mississippi from Ste. Genevieve to New Orleans. By this time well in his fifties, he eventually made a name for himself in Nouvelle Bourbon, which he named after the French royal family. This was only fitting because he remained a committed monarchist for his entire life. Although many of de Luzières's vast ambitions were not realized, he showed a remarkable persistence in bringing settlers to New Bourbon, which remained a Francophone bastion in Spanish-ruled Louisiana.

I first came in contact with the region, which witnessed such an influx of my countrymen two centuries earlier, while flying over the flooded Mississippi Valley in 1993. This devastating flood threatened to wipe out every trace of the French presence, dating from the eighteenth century, in that part of the United States. This was the first time I discovered the French presence in the Mississippi Valley, and it made a profound impression on me. As the consul général of France from Chicago and I flew over the flooded Mississippi Valley, I discovered the French settlements at Ste. Genevieve and Kaskaskia (with its remarkable bell, a gift from France). With the immense devastation before my eyes, I realized how impetuous and dangerous this river could be. I thought of the loss of land that the inhabitants suffered in the face of this mighty force of nature. I also imagined the difficulties the early French colonists faced in set-tling this area of vast and imposing wilderness.

Once we landed and visited the communities, I immediately fell in love with the vernacular vertical-log houses with their French influences and their graceful galleries. The houses displayed a unique character having taken on local attributes of the area—but on the inside they were exactly like French country houses, especially the fine Louis Bolduc House restored thanks to the Colonial Dames of the State of Missouri. It was also fascinating to discover the ancient agricultural pattern, which had been transported from France, with its narrow, long fields laid out facing the river, where the *habitants* prac-ticed communal farming. I was briefly transported across time and distance with these evocations of France delineated in the earth right in the heart of America.

Culturally, I felt a poignant emotional jolt, a profoundly moving shock of recognition, when I heard a children's choir from Ste. Genevieve sing, in French, very ancient Christmas songs that we sang at midnight mass during my childhood in my small village in the Berry region of central France. That touching testimony to the French presence as far back as the seventeenth cen-tury reinforced the notion of that shared cultural link, which is today slowly eroding even in our French country villages. That it remained alive in this small Mississippi Valley town was deeply moving. I discovered that many folks in the region were extremely proud of their French origins.

After the great flood, we at the French Heritage Society helped to preserve Ste. Genevieve by awarding a number of restoration grants over the years, but it remains a heritage in peril. Some vertical-log structures, like the Bequette-Ribault House, are in very fragile condition, while others have been much modified by successive waves of owners who lived in them, whether they were English, German, or American. Nevertheless, it is an invaluable and unique heritage, for these houses and villages are a rare testimony of the French pres-ence in America during the colonial period.

The majestic Mississippi River was called the Colbert in the seventeenth century, after Louis XIV's powerful minister, Jean-Baptiste Colbert. He promoted French colonization in America and firmly believed in the opportunities it offered for the economic development of France. He supported Robert Cavalier de la Salle's expedition to the mouth of the Mississippi River in 1682 and urged Louis XIV to promote French settlement in the Mississippi Valley. Colbert is an ancestor of mine on my mother's side, and I am understandably proud of the role he played in the history of North America. We still have in our family château paintings, objets d'art, books, and manuscripts that belonged to Colbert, including a wonderful portrait of him by the seventeenth-century-master Claude Lefèbvre.

I am also proud of the major role played by young French aristocrats during the American War of Independence, who, leading their regiments, came to reinforce and train the American insurgents. Their passion spread to other French aristocrats, and following the example of Benjamin Franklin, inspired them to raise funds and fight for the ideal of a free people. The contributions of the Marquis de Lafayette and the Comte de Rochambeau are well known, but others from all corners of France—her cities, villages, and countryside—also sailed for America, bringing with them professional military knowledge, engineering expertise, and the fighting spirit of a traditional warrior class. One of these was the abbé Paul de St. Pierre, formerly a chaplain in the French expeditionary force, who served as a much-beloved curé in Ste. Genevieve during the 1790s.

I have great hopes for the Illinois Country, which was settled by my countrymen so long ago, to serve as a focal point for interpreting French colonial settlement in North America. I left a part of my heart in Ste. Genevieve on the banks of the Mississippi, but I also left an uncompleted task, which is the proposed establishment of a French Heritage Park in the area. There is still so much to be done in Ste. Genevieve in order for this village to be restored to its eighteenth-century appearance when it flourished along the banks of the Mississippi, its fertile lands supplying the major French city in America, New Orleans, with foodstuffs. It is, for me, a passionate adventure, just as passionate as de Luzières's during his day, though fraught with far less danger than he faced in navigating and settling the American frontier. But it is a challenge suited to our times. And I share with de Luzières that ideal to see the French heritage flourish along the banks of the Mississippi.

In keeping this ideal alive, I must also pay homage to Carl J. Ekberg for his remarkable scholarship in presenting de Luzières's extraordinary letters and journals within the context of his time. Carl's distinguished scholarship and vivid writing bring de Luzières's tale to life in a way that allows us to relive that pivotal period as if we were there—indeed, discovering it for the first time. I can well imagine the emotion that de Luzières must have felt when facing the intimidating currents of the Ohio and Mississippi Rivers, at once his fear and amazement at these awesome forces of nature that led to vast virgin lands in the North American interior. It was the same amazement and awe I felt, tempered with respect for the unbridled river, as I flew over the flooded Mississippi Valley so many years ago, a journey that ultimately brought me into contact with my French roots in the heartland of America.

For that journey I remain grateful, just as I am grateful to Carl Ekberg for bringing that journey, through de Luzières's story, to many others who will discover, as I have, the enduring treasures that bear witness to the French presence in the Mississippi Valley. De Luzières's journey encapsulates so well the adventurous spirit of the settlers who brought their French heritage, culture, and traditions with them to flower and prosper in this fertile land.

Marie-Sol de La Tour d'Auvergne,
President Emeritus, French Heritage Society
Paris, February 9, 2010

Preface and Acknowledgments

I first encountered the extraordinary character Pierre-Charles de Lassus de Luzières back in the early 1980s, when I was working in San Diego with Abraham P. Nasatir's transcriptions from the Archivo General de Indias in Seville. De Luzières's 1797 census of New Bourbon, a community he founded in 1793, caught my eye, and I used this census along with de Luzières's extensive commentary on it when writing my first book about the Illinois Country—*Colonial Ste. Genevieve.*

I then pretty much forgot about de Luzières for a quarter of a century, although occasionally ruminating about the man who had fled Revolutionary France for the Mississippi frontier and who compiled the extraordinary census of New Bourbon. Several years ago, I decided that this census deserved to be published and I began further research on New Bourbon in order to place the census in its historical context. Reading microfilm from the Seville archive at the exceptional Missouri Historical Society in St. Louis, I soon discovered that there was a huge mass of primary source documents by and about de Luzières and the community he founded, materials that had never before been exploited. At this point I decided that a book-length study of de Luzières was in order, and I began to piece together materials from other collections—civil records from colonial Ste. Genevieve, family records from the Delassus–St. Vrain Collection at the Missouri Historical Society, and parish records from northern France and Ste. Genevieve—in order to recreate de Luzières's life between the time he fled France in 1790 and his death in 1806.

Dr. Samuel Johnson opined about biography (*Rambler,* no. 60) that "no species of writing is more worthy of cultivation." Johnson was himself a biographer (*Lives of the Poets*), and of course his own life was the subject of James Boswell's monumental *Life of Johnson,* by consensus the greatest biography in the English language. In mid-twentieth century, biography received some hard knocks, most especially from the Annales School of historiography founded in France. The *annalistes* tended to sniff disdainfully at biography as *histoire événementielle* or *histoire de courte durée,* history of events or short-term history. These historians, such as the brilliant and influential Fernand Braudel, wanted to explore the long term as it was shaped by geography, climate, economic forces, social classes, and so forth. Despite this questioning as to whether biography was a legitimate form of approaching and understanding the past, biography persists as the most widely read form of history writing in the Western World, including France.

It is remarkable how many debts one incurs in accomplishing even a relatively small project, such as a biography—so many generous friends, so many competent librarians and archivists, so many supportive relatives. Larry Franke at the Lindbergh Branch of the St. Louis County Library and Dennis Northcutt at the Missouri Historical Society are precious resources for anyone working on early Missouri history, and their competence and skills are widely known by researchers in that field. But help for me in researching de Lassus de Luzières also came from an unexpected source. Madame Monique Obled maintains the historical museum in Bouchain (the remains of the de Lassus château are just outside of town), and she is a treasure trove of information about local history, including that of the de Lassus family. She provided me with valuable documents, as well as preparing a succulent *tarte aux pommes* to share with my cousin, Christine Knutson-Beveraggi, and me. Christine has chauffeured me around on numerous research trips over several decades, and her adroit driving on French roads has had a calming effect on my naturally excitable disposition.

The Internet and e-mail permitted me to track down Warren J. Wolfe via his son, Phillip J. Wolfe, professor of French literature at Alleghany College. Warren himself is professor emeritus of French literature at Bowling Green University in Ohio, but (more important to me) he is also a leading authority concerning French immigrants to the Ohio River valley during the late eighteenth century. These immigrants were surprisingly numerous, and they of course founded Gallipolis (City of the French) on the north bank of the Ohio River in 1790. Many, including the medical doctor Antoine Saugrain (native of Paris) and the merchant Jean-Baptiste Lucas (native of Normandy), eventually moved on to St. Louis, where they endowed the American frontier city with brains and culture and *savoir faire.* Warren has provided me with numerous written sources about these extraordinary French people, but my conversations with him have been equally important. And these have occurred in memorable, and quite unanticipated places—his elegant apartment near les Invalides in Paris and the inspirational reading room of the Missouri Historical Society library in St. Louis. This biography of de Lassus de Luzières would not have taken shape in its present form without Warren's help.

Morris S. Arnold, Carl A. Brasseaux Helen V. Crist, Anne Johnson, William E. Foley, and Carl Masthay have all read the manuscript in its entirety and, from their different perspectives, have offered numerous suggestions that improved the text. Indeed, Bill Foley has rendered constructive criticism of every book I've written about Upper Louisiana. Indian affairs play a small, though not insignificant, role in this book, and concerning these affairs I have relied on the expertise of Carl Masthay (once again), Michael McCafferty of Indiana University, and Mel Thurman. Cece Myers of St. Louis helped me identify family names on de Luzières's 1797 New Bourbon census, and Bill Potter came through with his usual artisanal cartographic work. Bill recently and tragically died of Creutzfeldt-Jakob disease, and his map in this book is a final testament to his unique skills as a cartographer. Anne Woodhouse, Peter Leach, and I had informative discussions about New Bourbon while overlooking Forest Park from the restaurant at the Jefferson Memorial, and Jim Baker took me to see the picturesque cave south of Ste. Genevieve that de Luzières visited with Manuel Gayoso de Lemos in 1795.

Lastly, copy editor Debbie Upton patiently worked her way through a tangle of text, notes, and source materials to produce a coherent whole.

I am grateful to all these generous folks, who are in no way responsible for the errors that inevitably occur in a book about people who lived more than two hundred years ago.

A French Aristocrat in the American West

Introduction

Pierre-Charles de Hault de Lassus de Luzières was one of very few French aristocrats to emigrate to America, live out his life here, and be buried here—although his grave in the historical cemetery in Ste. Genevieve, Missouri, is unmarked and its exact location unknown. De Luzières had perhaps never heard of the francophone settlements in the Illinois Country when he, his wife, and three of their children fled Revolutionary France in the autumn of 1790. Their destination was the two-thousand-acre tract of real estate situated on the right bank of the Ohio River that de Luzières had "purchased" in Paris in June 1790 from the infamous Scioto Land Company. Arriving in the Ohio Valley late that year, they quickly discovered that they had been defrauded, that de Luzières had bought nothing but meaningless paper from the company's American agent in Paris, Joel Barlow. Effecting a strategic retreat to the Pittsburgh area, the family bought substantial estates there in the spring of 1791 and settled down, apparently with the intention of remaining there for the duration of their lives on the North American continent.

De Luzières's attention was drawn to the Illinois Country by the dream of creating a vast commercial empire, an empire that would extend the entire length of the Ohio River and down the Mississippi from Ste. Genevieve to New Orleans. The basis of this enterprise was to supply Louisiana's capital city with quantities of flour, hardtack, and whiskey, for the population of colonial New Orleans was always dependent on foodstuffs imported from distant locations; the purpose of the plan was to make de Luzières and his two business associates, Pierre Audrain and Bartholémé (his spelling)Tardiveau, wealthy. Promotion of this enterprise impelled de Luzières to move his family to Upper Louisiana and build his house on the hills overlooking the Mississippi River south of Ste. Genevieve. When, for a variety of reasons, this great entrepreneurial scheme foundered, de Luzières turned his attention to advancing his political career, with help from his Flemish countryman, Francisco Luis Hector de Carondelet, governor general of Louisiana (1791–1797).

1

To carve out a political niche for himself within the administration of Spanish Louisiana, de Luzières chose a bold approach. Indeed, audacity was his most pronounced character trait; over and over again he was willing to cast the dice in different directions: from France to the Ohio River valley, from there to Pittsburgh, from there to the Illinois Country, from agricultural to commercial to political schemes. His political initiative—the last, and indeed the most successful, venture of his life—was to erect a new administrative district in Upper Louisiana, a district of which he would be commandant on behalf of the Spanish monarchy. Spanish colonial officials were obsessed with bolstering the population of Louisiana as a means of creating a viable and defensible province. De Luzières would serve the Spanish regime by promoting population growth at New Bourbon, the settlement that he had founded on the west bank of the Mississippi in 1793, and the result of that growth would be the inevitable establishment of a new administrative district.

The strategy worked to perfection. Between 1795 and 1797 de Luzières's recruitment efforts—with Americans arriving from the Ohio Valley and local Creoles abandoning the flood-ravaged old town of Ste. Genevieve—succeeded beyond anyone's expectations. The most powerful evidence of this success is the census of the area that de Luzières compiled in 1797. This census, together with de Luzières's lengthy accompanying commentary, is a rare and important source document for late colonial Louisiana. For his efforts to increase the population of Upper Louisiana, which the Spanish regime desperately wished to do, de Luzières was in 1797 appointed civil and military commandant of the New Bourbon District, created by Governor Carondelet specifically to satisfy his friend's political ambitions.

De Luzières tore up his deep roots in Flanders, took ship across the Atlantic, and transported himself and his family across the vastnesses of North America to the west bank of the Mississippi River. Heroic is the only appropriate word for a man in the sixth decade of his life to have accomplished such a feat. As for his enduring significance, de Luzières's work promoting settlement in Upper Louisiana made him a minor, though not inconsequential, maker of history. But he was also a close observer of the history being made, as he watched the advancing hordes of Americans change the nature of the Mississippi frontier during the last decade of the eighteenth century. His voluminous writings provide an unprecedentedly comprehensive view of this evolving frontier during that critical time period in the colonization of the North American continent.

The mass of de Luzières's correspondence from his hilltop home overlooking the Mississippi Valley is remarkable. His life in France—whether in Valenciennes, Paris, or even his birthplace, Bouchain—had been animated, even hectic. Life on the Mississippi frontier was slow, even sleepy. The only person remotely of his status in the neighborhood was François Vallé II, a man of French-Canadian extraction whose illiterate father by dint of extraordinary effort, and good luck, had lifted the Vallé family to the level of provincial aristocrats. But when de Luzières rode the three miles from his residence at New Bourbon into Ste. Genevieve, where Vallé was commandant, to discuss politics, the latter soon tired of de Luzières's complaints about the fall of the Bourbon monarchy in France and his carping about the necessity of preventing Spanish Illinois from falling into the hands of American vulgarians. De Luzières and Vallé were friends to be sure, but never close friends. They were, *au fond,* simply too different, although they spoke more or less the same French language (neither spoke Spanish though both were important Spanish administrators).

To console himself in his relative isolation, de Luzières wrote—and how he wrote! The hundreds upon hundreds of pages of his correspondence constitute one of the largest bodies of writings ever produced by a French émigré in North America. The most important component of this corpus is his correspondence with Spanish officials in New Orleans and with those in the principal outposts of Spanish Illinois—St. Louis, New Madrid, and Cape Girardeau. Most of this correspondence eventually made its way to the remarkable Archivo General de Indies in Seville; fragments of it are in the Bancroft Library at Berkeley and in the Missouri Historical Society in St. Louis, where de Luzières's son, Carlos de Lassus, was Spanish lieutenant governor during the last years of the Spanish regime in Louisiana (1799–1804).

A second track of de Luzières's correspondence, totally independent of the first, was with a fellow French émigré, Bartholémé Tardiveau. Tardiveau was a highly educated man with a glittering prose style, who corresponded with the famous J. Hector St. John de Crèvecoeur (*Letters from an American Farmer*), during the late 1780s; both men were born and raised in Normandy and both were captivated by America. Tardiveau was first a business associate of de Luzières and then became a close friend. He died at New Madrid in 1801, and his voluminous papers eventually wound up in the Illinois State Historical Library in Springfield.

Part 1 of this volume is a life of de Luzières, from his life in pre–Revolutionary France to his death as a reluctant American citizen in his house in New Bourbon in 1806. Part 2 is a compilation, in translation, of his most important writings. These writings are important but neglected historical sources, for de Luzières has not been the subject of serious study. He is one of those francophone writers in North America (and others exist) who has simply disappeared through the cracks of American historical scholarship. This volume is an attempt to bring this man, both for professional scholars and for students of the Mississippi frontier in late colonial times, back to life and into clear focus.

Part I

From France to the Mississippi Valley

1

Flight from France

Pierre-Charles de Hault de Lassus de St. Vrain de Luzières was councilor to king Louis XVI, treasurer of the province of Hainault, hereditary mayor of Bouchain, commissioner in the royal navy, knight in the royal order of St. Michel[1]—names and titles that evoke an aspiring aristocrat of middling rank, someone who was active in the affairs of his province rather than preoccupied with hunting, carousing, and pursuing women. His remains, along with those of his long-suffering wife, now lie in unmarked graves in the historic cemetery of Ste. Genevieve, a small town in southeastern Missouri, a very long way from their ancestral homes in northern France. They lie there alongside those of a scattering of other Frenchmen, as well as a large number of French Canadians, French Creoles, African slaves, and Indian slaves. How did this all come to pass, how can one explain the strange trajectory in the lives of these French aristocrats?

The Delassus family, though of ancient noble lineage, had been established in northern France (having arrived from western Germany via Lorraine and Champagne) only since the mid-sixteenth century. But by the time of de Luzières's father, Charles-Philippe de Hault de Lassus (1714–1782), the family was deeply rooted at Bouchain, some ten miles southeast of Valenciennes in the county of Hainault, today's district of Nord-Pas-de-Calais. The

1. The Ordre de St. Michel was the first French chivalric order, founded by Louis XI of France in 1469. It was the highest Order in France until it was superseded by the Order of the Holy Spirit in 1578. De Luzières was inducted into this order by Louis XVI himself, at Versailles, on February 16, 1786. See documents in Box 1, Delassus–St. Vrain Collection, Missouri Historical Society, St. Louis (henceforth MHS).

family's ancestral home, the Château de Lassus, was located about a kilometer southwest of the Bouchain and may be seen on the famous Cassini map of mid-eighteenth-century France. The family was of the landed aristocracy but was nevertheless firmly established in town (*bourg*); so in a certain sense it was both noble and bourgeois, this sort of complexity being commonplace during the Old Regime. De Luzières grandfather, Guillaume de Hault de Lassus, was mayor of Bouchain, and the office became hereditary in the family, so that both de Luzières and his father were officially "maires héréditaires" of the town.[2] Northern France had been devastated during the War of the Spanish Succession (1701–1714), and during the following three-quarters of a century the area had to be rebuilt. It is apparent that members of the de Lassus family were not *noblesse fainéante,* idle nobles, but rather were active in promoting the development of agriculture, commerce, mining, and river navigation in their region. The motto on the Delassus coat of arms, *nul bien sans peine* (no gain without pain), reveals this family's code of industry, which ironically smacks of an ethos more Puritanical and bourgeois than Roman Catholic and aristocratic.

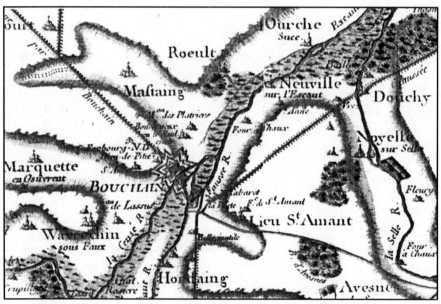

Detail from the eighteenth-century Cassini map of France. Notice Bouchain, de Luzières's native parish, and Noyelle, Governor Carondelet's native parish, in Flanders, province of Hainault. The château of de Lassus is indicated just outside Bouchain. Courtesy of the Library of Congress, Geography and Map Division.

2. Louis Drigon de Magny, *Nobiliaire universel de France: recueil général des généalogies historiques des maisons nobles de l'Europe* (Paris: Archives de la noblesse, 1858), 2:17–24.

Both de Luzières and his wife, Domitille-Josèphe Dumont, were natives of the parish of Bouchain, diocese of Arras, and they were married after Sunday mass in Bouchain's parish church on May 15, 1765, he at age twenty-seven and she at twenty. Domitille's father was deceased but was identified in the marriage record as having been "an entrepreneur of the king's works in this city." This reveals that she came from *haut bourgeois* stock, and that the marriage was a classic example of nuptial quid pro quo—she married into the aristocracy, and he married money. In the twelve years between 1766 and 1788 the couple produced five children, four sons and one daughter, who reached adulthood, which was a remarkable record given the high rate of infant and childhood mortality in a premodern society. As we shall see below, four of these five children wound up living in North America, only the eldest, Pierre-Joseph-Domitil (named after both his parents) never abandoning Europe to pursue his fortune in the New World.[3]

De Luzières was born and married as Pierre-Charles de Hault de Lassus, and the Luzières portion of his long aristocrat handle was added only after, as a mature man, he had acquired an estate by that name. That is to say, Luzières was a *nom de terre*, a name that was attached to a particular piece of real estate that qualified as aristocratic. The same applied, for example, to the estate of Pompadour, which—having been conveyed by King Louis XV to his mistress, Jeanne-Antoinette Poisson, a Parisian bourgeoise—gave this admirable woman the right to the title, marquise de Pompadour. Pierre-Charles Delassus's acquisition of the de Luzières estate occurred sometime between the birth of his fourth child in 1773 and that of his fifth child in 1778—for, for the first time in the parish records of Bouchain, he is identified as "seigneur de Luzières" in the baptismal record of the fifth child. Throughout his adult life Pierre-Charles always included "Delassus" or "de Lassus" in his official signature and usually, but not always, "De Luzières" as well. His descendants, on the other hand, never used the de Luzières name, and are known today as the Delassuses.

In the years just preceding the outbreak of the French Revolution, Delassus de Luzières was a very busy man. He continued to serve as mayor of Bouchain but his responsibilities as treasurer of the Estates of Hainault, the provincial governing assembly of the region, meant that he and his wife, Domitille-Josèphe, lived most of the year in Valenciennes, which was the center of communications, commerce, industry, and art in the region. After King Louis XIV acquired the city from Spain in the Treaty of Nijmegen in 1678, the king's famous engineer, Sébastien le Prestre de Vauban, encircled the place with one

3. The de Luzières's marriage record and the baptismal records of their children may now be found on microfilm in the Registres paroissiaux et des d'état civil communaux, paroisse de Bouchain, Archives départmentales du Nord, Lille, France.

Baptismal record of Pierre-Charles de Lassus, Bouchain, 1738. He later acquired the estate of Luzières and added that *nom de terre* to his name. Copy provided by Monique Obled, reproduced courtesy of the Archives départmentales du Nord, Lille, France.

Baptismal Record of Pierre-Charles Dehault de Lassus

March 9, 1738 I, J.A. Lesure, curé, have baptized the son, born the same day, of the legitimate marriage of Charles-Philippe DeHault, seigneur de Lassus, and Anne-Marguerite-Josephe Darlot, residents of Bouchain. He has been named Pierre-Charles. The godfather is Pierre Darlot, [tax] collector for the royal domains and assistant to the intendant. The godmother is Charlotte-Michelle Taisne, wife of the late Guillaume Dehault, formerly seigneur Delassus and hereditary mayor of Bouchain. They have signed with me.

of his signature star-fort assemblages of bastions, ravelins, and contrescarpes, making it one of the defensive anchors of France's northern frontier. During the eighteenth century, Valenciennes became well known as the birthplace of Jean-Antoine Watteau, an originator of the rococo style in painting, as well as for its production of exquisite linen lace and fine porcelain. Coal mines were discovered in the Valenciennes area in the mid-eighteenth century, and Delassus de Luzières, who on economic matters was a progressive thinker, promoted this new extractive industry.

Pierre-Charles Laurent, marquis de Villedeuil, was a countryman of Delassus de Luzières, both having been baptized and raised in the parish of Bouchain, and they shared first names. In the twilight years of the Old Regime de Villedeuil twice served in Louis XVI's ministry as a financial adviser—first in 1787, and then again a year later. On August 2, 1788, Thomas Jefferson, U.S. minister plenipotentiary to France, wrote to John Adams, U.S. ambassador to Great Britain, from Paris that "the Baron de Breteuil has lately retired from the ministry, and has been succeeded by M. de Villedeuil."[4] In the language of Old Regime France, de Luzières was de Villedeuil's "creature," which is to say that de Villedeuil was his patron and sponsor in Parisian society and in government circles. Surely, de Villedeuil's influence at Louis XVI's court was responsible for de Luzières receiving the largely honorific title of "councilor to the king," which he carried with him to America and of which he was duly proud. And when de Luzières and his wife were in Paris, which they were frequently during the hectic pre-Revolutionary days of 1787–1788, they lived in de Villedeuil's luxurious townhouse on the Place Royale (now the magnificently restored Place de Vosges), right around the corner from the infamous Bastille.[5]

In the nicely calibrated hierarchy of Old Regime France, de Luzières was in turn patron to friends and relatives lower than he in the social-political hierarchy, just as de Villedeuil was his patron. For example, a distant cousin of de Luzières, De Hault *dit* St. Honoré (*dit* = called or nicknamed), was during the late 1780s incarcerated in the prison of St. Lazare on the northern outskirts of Paris. St. Honoré had been a member of a holy order but had been defrocked and thrown in prison for some crime. This was perhaps some sexual delinquency, which St. Honoré described as misconduct (*inconduite*). He wrote to de Luzières from prison, addressing him as "my very dear brother," in the manner of stretched familiarity common among members of extended families at the time, asking that de Luzières help him procure a pardon. The outcome of this case is not known, but de Luzières (via his connection with de Villedeuil) very likely had the power to help out his cousin and gain him the requested pardon. Of course, de Luzières had to judge whether his cousin was a habitual offender (he seems to have been), in which case de Luzières would not have wanted to stick his neck out and risk sullying his own reputation for prudence and good judgment.[6]

Both de Luzières and de Villedeuil were arch-monarchists and were utterly devoted to the Bourbon family and to King Louis XVI; if not more royalist

4. Letter printed in *The Writings of Thomas Jefferson,* ed. Andrew A. Lipscomb and Albert Ellery Bergh (Washington, D.C.: Thomas Jefferson Memorial Association, 1904), 103.

5. Concerning the history of the Place Royale, see Lucien Lambeau, *La Place royale: la fin de l'Hôtel des Tournelles: le camp des chevaliers de la gloire: les duels historiques: la Fronde: la révolution: l'appartement du marquis de Favras: à travers le thèatre: Marion Delorme: les scandals: les amours: scènes ridicules et burlesques* (Paris: H. Daragon, 1906).

6. See De Hault *dit* St. Honoré to Delassus, Paris, October 2, 1788 (Archives de Valenciennes, Valenciennes, France, filed by date in carton 322). I am grateful to chief archivist Guillaume Broekaert for pulling the material pertinent to the de Lassus family.

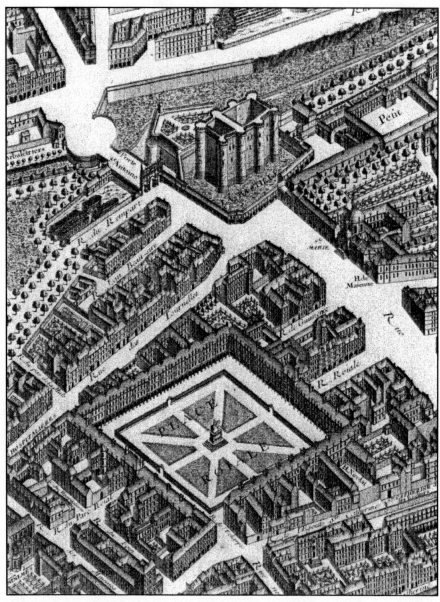

Place Royale (now the Place de Vosges), where de Luzières and his wife resided when staying in Paris. Notice the Bastille prison at the top. Detail of 1739 map drawn by Louis Bretez and engraved by Claude Lucas. Courtesy of the Library of Congress, Geography and Map Division.

than the king, they were as royalist. De Villedeuil wanted no truck with anything that smacked of popular rights or popular sovereignty, and after the States General convened at Versailles in 1789 he fled France for England; political developments that enraptured Jefferson and Lafayette horrified de Villedeuil. He risked death returning to France in 1792 in a futile attempt to save his king, fled to Scotland, returned to France after Waterloo and died in Paris in 1828 in his eighty-sixth year. If de Luzières was in residence in de Villedeuil's townhouse on the Place Royale on July 14, 1789, and he might have been, he could have witnessed the attack on the Bastille, located but a stone's throw from the Place, and seen the revolution's first display of severed heads paraded about on pikes. This sudden eruption of bloody violence may account for his visceral detestation of all anti-monarchical political enterprises, including the republican government of the United States, for the remainder of his life.

By early summer 1790 de Luzières and his wife had seen enough to grasp that France was descending into a maelstrom, the bloody results of which could hardly be imagined. A Parisian mob had invaded the Palace of Versailles in October 1789, killed several guards, and compelled King Louis XVI, Queen Marie-Antoinette, and their children to move to Paris. The royal family was under virtual house arrest in the Tuileries, and, although Louis was still technically king, the Old Regime was coming down around his ears. De Luzières had been deeply committed to this regime, and as it inexorably crumbled he chose to spin the wheel of fortune.

Following the American Revolution, wildly romantic notions sprang up in France about America as a terrestrial paradise—a land of compelling vistas, unimaginable plenitude, and profound innocence. Hector St. John de Crèvecoeur's best-selling *Letters from an American Farmer*[7] helped propagate this vision, as did the very presence in Paris of America's very own noble savage, Benjamin Franklin. Indeed, Franklin's association with Dr. Jacques-Ignace Guillotin led to a little known but extraordinary expedition to the Ohio River valley in 1787–1788, led by Dr. Antoine Saugrain (Guillotin's brother-in-law) and J. N. Picqué.[8] This turned into a literally hair-raising expedition, for Indians (probably

7. J. Hector St. John de Crèvecoeur, *Letters from an American Farmer; describing certain provincial situations, manners, and customs . . . and conveying some idea of the late and present interior circumstances of the British colonies in North America. Written for the information of a friend in England* (London: T. Davies, 1782).

8. See John Francis McDermott, "Guillotin Thinks of America," *Ohio Archeological and Historical Quarterly* 47 (1938): 129–57; H. Fouré Selter, ed., *L'Odyssée Américaine d'une famille française: le docteur Antoine Saugrain* (Baltimore: Johns Hopkins University Press, 1936), 39–40. After this expedition, Saugrain returned to America, and he will reappear sporadically in this book. I am grateful to Warren J. Wolfe for providing me with these articles.

Shawnees) attacked the party, killing and scalping poor Picqué. In any case, no evidence exists that de Luzières was influenced or motivated by prevailing romantic notions about the virtues of America's western wilderness, although such notions wafted tantalizingly through the very air he breathed when he was in Paris. What we know for certain is that de Luzières's loathing of the revolutionary movement in France, as it accelerated during 1789–1790, drove him from his native country to the far edge of Western civilization.

On June 19, in Paris, de Luzières purchased (or thought he purchased) from the infamous Scioto Company for six thousand livres tournois (hard currency) title to two thousand acres of land near where the Scioto River flowed into Ohio from the North; that is, on the right bank of the Ohio. The Scioto Company has been called "the bastard half-sister of the Ohio Company,"[9] from which it was a spin-off. Joel Barlow represented the Scioto Company in Paris from 1788 to 1790, and he set up a real estate office at 162 rue Neuve des Petits Champs,[10] near the Place Vendôme, in the city's traditional financial district. Connecticut-born Barlow was well connected, being a friend of both Thomas Paine and Thomas Jefferson, the latter of whom was serving as American minister in Paris. Moreover, George Washington, the most famous man in the Western World at the time, wrote to France on his behalf. Washington maintained an intermittent correspondence with his old comrade in arms, Jean-Baptist-Donatien, comte de Rochambeau, who had led the French expeditionary force during the American Revolution. Washington took the trouble to write a particular letter to Rochambeau, recommending Barlow as a man of "liberal education, respectable character, and great abilities," and that he was well known "for being the author of an admirable poem."[11] Barlow had developed a considerable literary reputation in 1787 when he published a long and patriotic poem, *The Vision of Columbus*, which Washington

9. Jocelyne Moreau-Zanelli, *Gallipolis: Histoire d'un mirage américain au XVIIIe siècle* (Paris: L'Harmattan, 2000), 39. A curious situation has arisen in American historical scholarship. Moreau-Zanelli's exhaustively researched book is absolutely essential for understanding the complexities of the scene—political, military, and economic—in the Ohio River valley during the 1790s, a critical period in a critical region, and yet the book remains unknown to American scholars. See also Robert F. Jones, *"The King of the Alley": William Duer, Politician, Entrepreneur, and Speculator, 1768–1799* (Philadelphia: American Philosophical Society, 1992), passim. This is a sympathetic biography, emphasizing Duer's attempts to deal fairly with the French colonists arriving in America.

10. Rue Neuve des Petits Champs was later divided into rue des Petits Champs and rue Danielle Casanova. Barlow's real estate office was located at what is now 5–7 rue Danielle Casanova, near where that street crosses Avenue de l'Opéra. I am grateful to Daniel Beveraggi, who lives in that neighborhood, for tracking down this geographical information.

11. Ms. letter Washington to Rochambeau, May 28, 1788, in Letter Book 15: 115, George Washington Papers, Library of Congress.

seems to have read. Historians have not decided whether Barlow was merely an overenthusiastic promoter or was an out-and-out fraud, but he was surely aware that he was playing fast and loose in selling deeds to real estate in the Ohio wilderness for which his company held no clear titles. On the substantial list of those culpable in the Scioto debacle, with all of its attendant dislocation, pain, and suffering, Barlow ranks high.[12]

De Luzières did not simply walk into Barlow's office off the street, cold and ignorant. A surprising number of French aristocrats had already invested in Scioto by the summer of 1790, including Claude-François-Adrien, marquis de Lezay-Marnésia, and Jean-Jacques Duval d'Eprémesnil, both acquaintances of de Luzières.[13] D'Eprémesnil was a Parisian, a member of the Parlement of Paris (the highest law court in France), and was defined by his politics; he was a friend of the famous marquíse de Lafayette, served with him in the Constituent Assembly, and was an advocate of limited, constitutional monarchy. De Lezay-Marnésia was from the provinces (Metz), was an intellectual and sometime author, and contributed the article "Voleurs [Thiefs]" to Diderot's *Encyclopédie*.[14] But he was best defined by a wildly romantic sensibility that led him to believe anything was possible in the virgin territory of the trans-Appalachian American West.

Éprémesnil and Lezay-Marnésia had been charter members of the Société des Vingt-Quatre, the Group of Twenty-Four, a collection of aristocrats who had joined together in early 1790 to promote the Scioto real estate project. Their idealistic thoughts ran to creating an agricultural, patriarchal, benevolent, and Roman Catholic community in the Ohio wilderness.[15] These men were well known in France, and d'Eprémesnil was skewered in a broadside written by the famous Parisian pamphleteer, Camille Desmoulins: "Ships full of fools are about to depart from Le Havre and set sail for Scioto. After a long crossing of the Atlantic, these lunatics will still have 600 leagues to cross before entering the vast wilds of the Ohio and Mississippi. The delicate ladies, who in a fevered delirium have condemned themselves to this fate, will find

12. The Scioto Company had acquired from the U.S. Congress rights of preemption but not proprietary rights to the real estate (see Moreau-Zanelli, *Gallipolis*, 30–32, 127–28; also Jones, *William Duer*, 120–21, 144–45). Both Moreau-Zanelli and Jones lay much blame on Barlow's doorstep. R. Douglas Hurt (*Ohio Frontier: Crucible of the Old Northwest, 1720–1830* [Bloomington: Indiana University Press, 1996], 190–91) is more inclined to lay blame on Barlow's English associate in Paris, William Playfair.

13. Concerning these two men and their involvement in the Gallipolis affair, see Moreau-Zanelli, *Gallipolis*, passim; Phillip J. Wolfe and Warren J. Wolfe, "Prospects for the Gallipolis Settlement," *Ohio History* 103 (Winter–Spring 1994): 50–56.

14. Vol. VIII: 451.

15. Hurt, *Ohio Frontier*, 182–207.

much time to repent."[16] Desmoulins exaggerated distances, if not the difficulties, of the Scioto enterprise in America. It's not clear whether de Luzières was officially a member of the Group of Twenty-Four, but he certainly knew the leaders, was in touch with them, and agreed with their fundamental ideas. Indeed, when de Luzières later founded his community at New Bourbon a few years later it was based on the royalist, conservative, although not necessarily unenlightened, ideas of the group.

Many members of the group, including d'Eprémesnil, never fled France for the Ohio Valley. Had d'Eprémesnil done so he would have avoided the guillotine in April 1794, the same month that Desmoulins, the man who had earlier mocked him, met the same fate. In the last months of the Terror the guillotine was working with gusto on folks of virtually every political persuasion and social status. Other aristocrats, like de Lezay-Marnésia and de Luzières, threw caution to the wind, took sail for America, and attempted to occupy the lands in the Ohio Valley that they had ostensibly purchased in Paris. De Lezay-Marnésia sailed out of Le Havre for Alexandria, Virginia, in May 1790, ultimately became disenchanted with the New World, and returned to France in 1792. In August de Luzières embarked with his family at the same port for Philadelphia, endured an amazing gamut of hardships, and ultimately settled down in the Mississippi Valley, died there and was buried there. Burning his bridges behind him, he took this high-risk gamble when he was well into his fifty-third year, deep middle age for an eighteenth-century person.

Interestingly, we can follow the steps of the de Luzières family rather closely between the summer of 1790 and the spring of 1791, and these steps took the family on a daunting wild-goose chase across the Atlantic Ocean and the face of eastern North America. In July 1790 the French National Assembly officially abolished hereditary nobility, aristocratic titles, and coats of arms. If de Luzières had had any doubts about tearing up his deep roots in northern France, this act of the Revolutionary government in Paris must have dissolved them. Two months after doing business with Barlow in Paris, de Luzières returned north to Valenciennes where he applied to the newly elected mayor and municipal officials for safe passage from France. On August 8, 1790, he, his wife, two sons, one daughter, two domestics, and one female servant were in effect given a passport, being granted permission "to proceed to Le Havre-de-Grâce in Normandy in order to embark for North America where they are going to pursue their affairs."[17] "Affairs" in this instance meant occupation and exploitation of the lands

16. Desmoulins quoted in the *Wikipedia* (French edition), s.v. "Jean-Jacques Duval d'Eprémesnil." Desmoulins vastly exaggerated the distance from the Atlantic seaboard of North America to the Ohio River valley.

17. This curious and precious document may be found in Box 1, Delassus–St. Vrain Collection, MHS.

in the Ohio country that de Luzières believed he had purchased from the Scioto Company. Those brief strokes of a quille pen in Valenciennes's townhall sent de Luzières and his household off on a harrowing journey of 4,000 miles, that endured three years, that proceeded by land, by salt water and by fresh, and that led to much heartbreak, occasional successes, and finally to unmarked graves in a distant land governed by a detested American republican regime.

It may seem odd that elected municipal officials in Valenciennes were willing to cooperate with the flight of an aristocratic family from Revolutionary

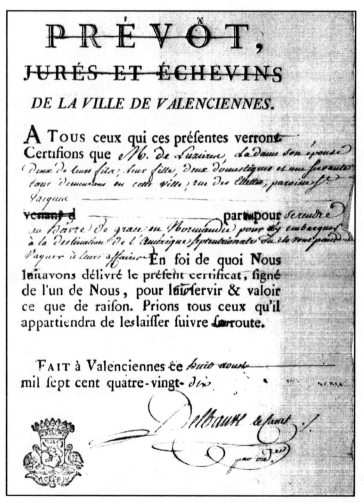

Passport for de Luzières, his family, and his servants, dated August 8, 1790, and signed by the mayor of Valenciennes. The titles of earlier royal municipal officials, suppressed by the Revolution, are barred out. Reproduced courtesy of the Missouri History Museum, St. Louis.

France. A year later, after the royal family's unsuccessful attempt to flee France in June 1791, this cooperation would not have been forthcoming. But in the late summer of 1790 a man with de Luzières's deep roots in the province of Hainault still possessed some clout in Valenciennes, and the municipal officials, even in a newly revolutionary city government, had not yet cast off all respect for the traditional local aristocracy.

Once they had received their passport in Valenciennes, de Luzières, his family, and their servants moved quickly, or as quickly as was possible in that day and age, to reach Le Havre and find passage to America. Their convoy that rumbled and growled across the face of Revolutionary France during the early autumn of 1790, from the flat grain and poppy fields of Flanders to the undulating orchards and pastures of Normandy, must have been a strange apparition to the peasants who saw it pass as they harvested their crops. In addition to the human cargo, the convoy carried a harp, belonging to de Luzières's only daughter, and smart millstones—for de Luzières intended to pursue serious wheat production in North America, and French composite millstones (assembled from multiple, finely cut stone components bound together with an iron band) had a reputation for being the best in the Western World.[18] Harp and millstones would successfully make the trip across the Atlantic and the face of eastern North America all the way to the Mississippi River valley.

De Luzières had planned everything down to the last detail—and had good luck to boot—and the trip proceeded like clockwork.[19] Two weeks and two days after having left Valenciennes (assuming they left the same day that their passport was issued), de Luzières and his entourage embarked (August 24) at Le Havre-de-Grâce on the ship "Cytoiens [sic] de Paris," *Citizens of Paris*.[20] Surely it galled de Luzières that he was forced to find passage on ship with a patently revolutionary name, but no doubt exists that he wanted to get the hell out of France as quickly as possible on any ship available. It's curious that when he described this fateful embarkation nine years later he could

18. On eighteenth-century French millstones, see Steven L. Kaplan, *Provisioning Paris: Merchants and Millers in the Grain and Flour Trade during the Eighteenth Century* (Ithaca, N.Y.: Cornell University Press, 1984), 221–44.

19. This and the following six paragraphs are based on de Luzières's appeal to the U.S. Congress asking for land along the Mississippi River in the Northwest Territory in compensation for having been defrauded in the Scioto real estate scam. March 29, 1799, Papeles de Cuba, legajo 216B, Archivo General de Indies, Seville (henceforth this collection will be cited simply as PC [Papeles de Cuba] followed by the legajo number). No evidence exists that the Congress paid any attention to this appeal from a European aristocrat living in Spanish Louisiana.

20. Moreau-Zanelli (*Gallipolis*, 271) claims that de Luzières embarked on August 21, but he claimed August 24 (see Part 2, document, no. 33).

not avoid the Freudian slip of misspelling *Citoyens*—de Luzières despised everything related to the revolution, including the new title given to persons whom he still considered to be *subjects* of their monarch by divine right, King Louis XVI. Just before embarking at Le Havre-de-Grâce a glitch cropped up: the passport prepared in Valenciennes on August 8 specified that de Luzières would be leaving France accompanied by *three* servants, but he showed up dockside with *eight*. Either through bribery, cajolery, or the carelessness of port officials this anomaly was overcome, and the voyage across the north Atlantic to Philadelphia went smoothly and relatively quickly. So far, so good.

2

The Ohio River Valley

As the lighthouse at the entrance to Le Havre's harbor slipped out of sight, de Luzières, gazing back over the taffrail of *Citoyens de Paris,* knew that this would be his last mortal glimpse of France, for he had solemnly decided to forsake the ancient compost heap of Europe for the virgin soil of America.

De Luzières's journey, by land and sea, from Valenciennes to the East Coast of North America went smoothly, but his headaches began as soon as he arrived at the docks in Philadelphia on October 15, 1790, even before he and his family could disembark; and to a large degree they never let up until death gave him his ultimate relief just before Christmas 1806 in New Bourbon, the community he had founded thirteen years earlier. In his rush to board ship and flee France in August; de Luzières had not ironed out the details regarding expenses with the captain and the outfitter of the *Citoyens de Paris* before the ship sailed out of Le Havre-de-Grâce. In Philadelphia the captain refused to let de Luzières disembark without paying a surcharge of 3,159 livres tournois, apparently for the goodly size of his entourage and his astonishing mass of material possessions. It's also possible that the captain was personally devoted to the French Revolutionary cause, and when he had an aristocrat in his clutches he took advantage of the situation to extort a large chunk of cash from him.

Philadelphia became temporary capital of the American republic in 1790, but in the early 1790s the city was gorged with thousands of French refugees (numbering perhaps as much as 15 percent of the city's total population)[1]

---

1. Allan Potofsky, "The 'Non-Aligned Status' of French Emigrés and Refugees in Philadelphia, 1793–1798," www.transatlantica.org/document1147.html. These refugees included

in flight from the republican revolution in France. Once de Luzières's substantial entourage managed to disembark at the foot of Lombard Street, they were met by a representative of the Scioto Company, one Colonel David S. Franks. Franks tried to be helpful, and his dedication reveals that the company was not merely an elaborate fraud but also one whose benevolent (if also greedy) intentions were overwhelmed by the scope of the enterprise, a few irresponsible individuals, and the contingencies of events on the ground. Colonel Franks, who had served in the American Revolution, was one of many American soldiers who appreciated France's support during that revolution. De Luzières later complained that Franks had not served him well, but Franks was a serious and competent person, and he tried his level best to be of assistance to the French immigrants, most of whom could not speak a word of English.[2]

During the spring of 1790, American organizers of the Scioto Company recognized that the company had no valid title to lands on the north bank of the Ohio River, something that Barlow in Paris had not wished to recognize. The company's contract with the U.S. Congress provided for a preemption right, an option to buy, rather than a fully consumated purchase. The Scioto Company therefore purchased from the Ohio Company of Associates (whose contract with Congress went beyond preemption to purchase) an alternative site upon which to settle the French Scioto colonists, some of whom were already en route.[3] A crew of husky woodcutters from western Massachusetts was brought in to build log cabins and blockhouses for defense; the threat of Indian attack in the Ohio River valley at this time period was real and persistent. Major John Burnham, yet another veteran of the American Revolution involved in the Scioto affair, commanded this crew, and they worked throughout the summer and autumn of 1790. They were apparently assisted by an experienced woodsman from the region—Daniel Boone—who at the time was settled close by near the mouth of the Kanawha River (the present location of Point Pleasant, West Virginia).[4]

This was a tumultuous, dangerous, and complicated time in that part of North America, for the Ohio Country had not yet been "pacified." In late

the famous, or infamous, Charles-Maurice de Talleyrand-Périgord, who paraded on the streets of Philadelphia with his black mistress on his arm.

2. Concerning Franks, see Jocelyne Moreau-Zanelli, *Gallipolis: Histoire d'un mirage américain au XVIIIe siècle* (Paris: L'Harmattan, 2000), passim, esp. 289–91.

3. Moreau-Zanelli, *Gallipolis*, 30–32, 127–28. See also Robert F. Jones, *"The King of the Alley": William Duer, Politician, Entrepreneur, and Speculator, 1768–1799* (Philadelphia: American Philosophical Society, 1992), 120–21, 144–45.

4. Moreau-Zanelli, *Gallipolis*, 130–31, 348. Reuben Gold Thwaites, *Daniel Boone* (New York: D. Appleton and Co., 1902), chap. 14.

October 1790, General Josiah Harmar led an expedition to take on the Indians (mostly Miamis, Shawnees, and Potawatomis) of the Northwest Territory for the purpose of making the region safe for white settlement. But the Miami war chief, Little Turtle, inflicted a serious defeat on Harmar's ragtag force of ill-trained regular soldiers and undisciplined Kentucky militiamen near the headwaters of the Maumee River, present-day Fort Wayne, Indiana. Harmar was forced to retreat—tail between his legs—back to the sanctuary of Fort Washington (Cincinnati), his nose bloodied and his career in tatters.[5]

De Luzières wisely decided not to loiter in Philadelphia, not to socialize with the masses of Frenchmen in temporary residence there, not to visit Independence Hall, symbol of the detested (in his mind) republican government, not to try to settle his various financial grievances. Rather he struck out immediately overland for Pittsburgh (or Fort Pitt, as it was often still called). Pittsburgh was the major jumping-off point for westward American migration during the early 1790s, and the road there from Philadelphia was well worn if not exactly easy-going. This trip required two to three weeks at that time

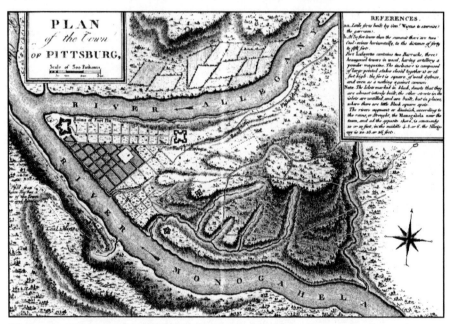

Pittsburgh, 1795, drawn by Charles Warin, engraved by Pierre-François Tardieu, and reproduced from Georges-Henri-Victor Collot, *Journey in North America*. De Luzières's estate would have been at the bottom-right, on the south bank of the Monongahela River.

5. R. Douglas Hurt, *The Ohio Frontier: Crucible of the Old Northwest, 1720–1830* (Bloomington: Indiana University Press, 1996), 105–11.

and provided de Luzières and his family with their first exposure to life on the American frontier.[6]

Several months before de Luzières, his friends Claude (father) and Albert (son) de Lezay-Marnésia had taken the same route across Pennsylvania. And half a century later, Albert remembered overnighting in a log cabin owned by one Mr. Skiner, "who was so strange I haven't forgotten him." Skiner provided the sophisticated Frenchmen a supper of beef jerky ("boeuf salé et desséché"), black bread, and raw whiskey ("détestable eau-de-vie de grain"); sleeping, or some semblance of it, was accomplished on the ground spread with animal pelts, and was communal, "with all those who happened to stop in."[7] These French aristocrats, most especially Madame de Luzières, must have begun to wonder whether the French Revolution would have been easier to face up to than the American frontier.

De Luzières's party seems to have arrived in Pittsburgh sometime during the first week in November and immediately engaged flatboats and crews.[8] Eager to occupy and improve the two thousand acres he believed he had purchased from the Scioto Company, he did not linger long in Pittsburgh but led his group down the Ohio River to "Bufalo Crick" (Wellsburg, West Virginia), and then on downriver for a reunion with his friend de Lezay-Marnésia, who was holed up at Campus Martius.[9] This camp was the fortified portion of the embryonic settlement of Marietta, Ohio (situated at the confluence of the Ohio and Muskingum Rivers), and the name reveals the passion for the Roman Republic at that moment in American history. Bizarrely, to our eyes, the path from the Muskingum River up the hill to the fort even had a Latin handle, the Via Sacra, the Sacred Way.[10]

6. Several years later, Georges-Henri-Victor Collot made the trip between Philadelphia and Pittsburgh in fourteen days but he was not burdened with de Luzières's large entourage. See Collot, *A journey in North America, containing a survey of the countries watered by the Mississippi, Ohio, Missouri, and other affluing rivers*, ed. Christian Bay, 3 vols. (Florence: O. Lange, 1924), 1:23. In July 1788, Dr. Antoine Saugrain traveled on horseback from Pittsburgh to Philadelphia in the remarkably short time of ten days (H. Fouré Selter, ed., *L'Odyssée Américaine d'une famille française: le docteur Antoine Saugrain* [Baltimore: Johns Hopkins University Press, 1936], 66–70).

7. Albert-Magdelaine-Claude de Lezay-Marnésia, *Mes souvenirs à mes enfants* (Blois: Dézairs, 1851), 13. I am indebted to Warren J. Wolfe for providing me with this very rare text.

8. Likely the letter that de Luzières sent to d'Eprémesnil on November 6, 1790, was posted from Pittsburgh, or conceivably Buffalo Creek (see Moreau-Zanelli, *Gallipolis*, 291 n. 76).

9. Collot claimed (*Journey in North America*, 1:54–55) that there were twenty-eight to thirty houses at Buffalo Creek in 1795. Concerning Lezay-Marnésia, see Moreau-Zanelli, *Gallipolis*, 314.

10. Hurt, *Ohio Frontier*, 180–83. See also Rowena Buell, ed., *Rufus Putnam and Certain Official Papers and Correspondence Published by the National Society of the Colonial Dames of America in the State of Ohio* (New York: Houghton, Mifflin and Co., 1903), 105.

Rather than venturing any further down the Ohio so late in the season, de Luzières decided to winter over in the safety of Campus Martius. Despite the Roman names, the fort was quintessentially American frontier in style, consisting of four, corner blockhouses of hewn timbers with residential quarters forming the curtain walls between the corners. By 1795 Campus Martius had been abandoned, but Georges-Henri-Victor Collot claimed that some French families, "victims of American land speculators," still lived at Marietta.[11] The quality of life on the Ohio frontier was a very rude shock for folks accustomed to the polished existence of pre-Revolutionary aristocrats. Not only were creature comforts in short supply, Harmar's recent defeat had left the entire Ohio frontier, even forts, vulnerable to Indian attacks at that time. Adding insult to injury, de Luzières's hired hands, his *engagés,* who had been with him since his departure from Valenciennes five months earlier, deserted him that bitter winter.[12] It must be wondered whatever became of this handful of French laborers, all nameless and none speaking English, cast adrift in the wilderness of the Ohio River valley. One is permitted to hope that their descendants are now flourishing in that rich and verdant valley.

While Harmar was engaged in his futile Indian campaign during the autumn of 1790, the first French settlers—hopeful, anxious, exhausted—disembarked at the clearing that had been carved out of the forest on the north bank of the Ohio River by Burnham's lumberjacks. This fateful disembarcation probably occurred on October 17, after an astounding trip (via Le Havre, Alexandria, Winchester, Cumberland, Redstone Bluff [today Brownsville, Pennsylvania], and Pittsburgh) of some 5,000-odd miles. The site was dubbed "Gallipolis," although by whom no one knows for sure. Settlements with French names dotted the banks of the Ohio River in the late eighteenth century—Marietta, named after Marie-Antoinette; Louisville, named after King Louis XVI; and Gallipolis, City of the French. William G. Sibley, himself a descendant of French colonists, composed a prose-poem evocation of the arrival of the first settlers at Gallipolis:

11. Collot, *Journey in North America,* 1:70–71.

12. This according to de Luzières (see Part 2, document no. 33). It seems to have been the habit of the *engagés* of the more-or-less wealthy Frenchmen to take flight and find their personal freedom in America. The *Virginia and Winchester Gazette* (microfilm in the Stewart Bell Jr. Archives, Handley Regional Library, Winchester, Virginia) for September 1, 1790, contains a notice submitted by "Malartie" (obviously, vicomte de Malartic) offering a reward of $18.00 for help in retrieving three French indentured servants who had fled his service. Concerning Louis-Hippolythe-Joseph de Maurès, vicomte de Malartic, see Moreau-Zanelli, *Gallipolis,* passim, esp. 362 n. 82; also Phillip J. Wolfe and Warren J. Wolfe, "Prospects for the Gallipolis Settlement," *Ohio History* 103 (Winter–Spring 1994): 49–50.

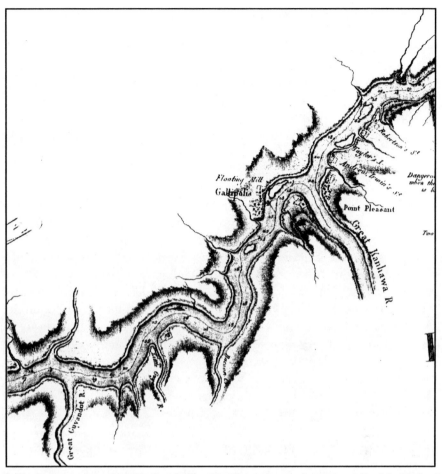

Gallipolis (City of the French), founded by French immigrants in 1790 on the right bank of the Ohio River, was de Luzières's original destination, although he never settled there. Drawn by Charles Warin, engraved by Pierre-François Tardieu, and reproduced from Georges-Henri-Victor Collot, *Journey in North America.*

Down the river they floated in sunlight and moonlight, until at last they arrived at Gallipolis. Scrambling up the high, steep bank their gaze fell on the rectangular clearing in which stood the eighty log cabins that were to be their homes, and the block houses on the corners designed for their refuge and times of peril. Surrounding all sides except the river front stood the lofty trees of the virgin forest, mute and impressive sentinels of unviolated creation.[13]

13. William G. Sibley, *The French Five Hundred* (Gallipolis: Gallia County Historical Society, 1933), 50–51.

Gallipolis was only the third substantial non-Indian community founded in what became the Ohio Territory, the first two being Marietta (Fort Harmar) and Cincinnati (Fort Washington). Each settler was to receive two town lots and a four-acre outlot beyond the village limits.[14] The French colonizers were not peasants, hardened by constant physical labor, but mostly city-dwellers—artisans, lawyers, merchants, even doctors, along with a handful of aristocrats—ill-adapted to subsistence agriculture, not merely in a rural region but in a primordial wilderness. During their first two years at Gallipolis the lot of them nearly perished.[15]

De Luzières and entourage, and de Lezay-Marnésia and entourage, spent two frustrating winter months at Campus Martius, pretty much penned up for fear of being bushwhacked by Indians. They did venture forth enough to examine the prehistoric Indians mounds ("monuments énigmatiques") in the area, until the discovery of a cadaver, "tomahawked and scalped" drove them back into the safety of the fort.[16] De Luzières later complained that the two months spent at Marietta cost him 1,460 livres tournois for food and lodging.[17] In late winter, de Luzières led what was left of his group back up the Ohio River to Pittsburgh, arriving there in mid-February 1791. He immediately dashed off an alarming letter to General Arthur St. Clair, governor of the Northwest Territory, who was in Philadelphia consulting with President Washington's cabinet about the Ohio Country: "You will have read the details, most touching, of a new scene of horror committed by the savages in the environs of Buffalo [Creek]. Since then they have multiplied upon all points of the Ohio. . . . I believe it my duty to inform you, my general, that one is not even without inquietude in this town."[18] Pittsburgh was never in fact threatened, but the Ohio Country remained a dark and forbidding land for some years to come.

In Pittsburgh de Luzières connected with one Pierre Audrain, a French trader who had been established there for at least a decade, spoke English, and knew the lay of the land. During his trip West a few months earlier, de Luzières had likely met Audrain, for Pittsburgh was a frontier community in

14. Moreau-Zanelli, *Gallipolis*, 348–49; *American state papers: documents, legislative and executive, of the Congress of the United States, Public Lands* (Washington, D.C.: Gales and Seaton, 1832–1861), 1:24 (hereafter *ASP, PL*).

15. Moreau-Zanelli, *Gallipolis*, 353–87; Sibley, *French Five Hundred*, chap. 7.

16. Lezay-Marnésia, *Mes souvenirs à mes enfants*, 15.

17. See Part 2, document no. 33.

18. Letter dated February 20, 1791, printed in William Henry Smith, ed., *The St. Clair papers; the life and public services of Arthur St. Clair, soldier of the Revolutionary War, president of the Continental Congress, and Governor of the North-Western Territory, with his correspondence and other papers* (Cincinnati: Robert Clarke and Co., 1882), 2:199.

1790–1791, and the number of Frenchmen living there was very small indeed. Nevertheless, during the spring of the year 1791, three intelligent, educated, and energetic Frenchmen—de Luzières, Audrain, and the marquis de Lezay-Marnésia (who had also retreated from the Ohio Valley) were all living in or near Pittsburgh.[19]

These three men became fast friends, the marquíse, given the circumstances, not being offended by rubbing shoulders with Audrain, a rank commoner. When these three men got together for a glass or two, which they frequently did, they engaged in phantasmagoric conversations about the American West and the prospects that that region might hold for émigré Frenchmen. De Lezay-Marnésia, despite his initial wild enthusiasms for the virgin American wilderness, became discouraged and decided to return to France, but Audrain and de Luzières stayed on, casting their fates with the New World and eventually finding their graves there. The destinies of these two Frenchmen would be tightly intertwined for the next five years as each, in his own respective way, attempted to fashion a brighter future in North America.

Four years after the de Luzières family arrived in Pittsburgh, the French officer and putative spy Georges-Henri-Victor Collot[20] described the town thusly:

> Pittsburgh formerly called Fort Duquesne, constructed by the French when they were masters of Canada, is situated on a slip of land which separates the waters of the Alleganies [sic] and those of the Monongahela. At this point the Ohio takes its source and its name. This town contains, at the utmost, one hundred and fifty houses, some of which are built of brick, and the rest of wood. . . . Placed at the source of one of the noblest rivers in the world, navigable as far as the ocean, after flowing eleven hundred miles, through the finest and most beautiful countries on the surface of the globe; this town, when the Indian frontier is thrown back, and the roads are rendered practicable, will certainly become one of the first inland cities of the United States.[21]

19. Concerning these three men in the Pittsburgh area, see Moreau-Zanelli, *Gallipolis,* 314, 403–5; Howard C. Rice, *Barthélemi Tardiveau, A French Trader in the West* (Baltimore: Johns Hopkins University Press, 1938), 41–47; Warren J. Wolfe, "The First American Citizen of Detroit: Pierre Audrain, 1725–1820," in *Detroit in Perspective* (Winter 1981): 45–47.

20. Collot had been sent on this trip to the Mississippi Valley by Pierre-Auguste Adet, French minister to the United States. Concerning Collot's sojourn in North America, see Abraham P. Nasatir, ed., *Before Lewis and Clark: Documents Illustrating the History of the Missouri, 1785–1804,* 2 vols. (St. Louis: St. Louis Historical Documents Foundation, 1952), 2:383 n. 1.

21. Collot, *Journey in North America,* 1:37–38.

Audrain guided de Luzières around the area surrounding the forks of the Ohio and was a facilitator when de Luzières purchased real estate near Pittsburgh on April 1, 1791. De Luzières bought two tracts of land from Widow (of William) Catherine Thompson situated in Mifflin Township, Allegheny County, and lying along the left bank of the Monongahela River a few miles above Pittsburgh proper.[22] One parcel called "Liberty" contained 266 ⅜ acres, for which de Luzières paid 399 pounds, 7 shillings, and 3 pence, and the other "Hamilton Hall" contained 2,873 acres, for which was paid 431 pounds, 2 shillings, and 4 pence. The witnesses in both transactions were Audrain and Henry H. Brackenridge, the latter being the father of the Henry Jr., who would soon be sent off to Ste. Genevieve to learn the French language and civilized etiquette. Henry Jr. would later render remarkable accounts of his life in the exotic (to the young Brackenridge) French Creole colonial village situated on the west bank of the Mississippi.[23] Henry Sr. was doubtless inspired by the polish and good manners of the Frenchmen he met in Pittsburgh to send his son to Ste. Genevieve for schooling. It is worthwhile ruminating over the likelihood that small, remote francophone Ste. Genevieve was more cultivated than Pittsburgh during the 1790s, for so it seems to have been.

The fact that each parcel of land purchased by de Luzières was graced with a name, and that each parcel was conveyed with "appurtenances," indicates that they contained buildings, perhaps in fact dwelling houses. But the properties contained nothing good enough for a former councilor to King Louis XVI of France, and de Luzières "had a house built at great expense, using funds acquired by selling part of our silverware."[24] De Lezay-Marnésia described de Luzières's estate on the bank of the Monongahela as "a large and rich plantation, with his wife, his sons, and his daughter, charming and talented, who is married to an educated, honest, and likeable young man. . . . He has had a house built there—not magnificent, but pleasant and agreeable, which serves the needs of a man who is wealthy but not too particular."[25] De Luzières's estate would have marked him as a man of substance in frontier Pittsburgh, and the trouble and

22. Allegheny County Real Estate Records Office, Deedbook 2: 324–27, Pittsburgh.

23. See James Baker, "Le Petit Anglais: Henry Marie Brackenridge and the Vital Bauvais Family of Ste. Genevieve," *Le Journal, Center for French Colonial Studies* 21 (Winter 2005): 1–8; also Henry Marie Brackenridge's two volumes: *Views of Louisiana: together with a journal of a voyage up the Missouri River, in 1811* (Pittsburgh: Cramer, Spear and Eichbaum, 1814); *Recollections of persons and places in the West*, 2nd ed. (Philadelphia: J. B. Lippincott and Co., 1868).

24. This was de Luzières's comment in a memorial he sent to the U.S. Congress in 1799 requesting a large land grant near the mouth of the Illinois River (see Part 2, document no. 33).

25. Claude-François-Adrien de Lezay-Marnézia, *Lettres écrites des rives de l'Ohio* (Paris: chez Prault, 1800), 141. I am indebted to Warren J. Wolfe for providing me with this letter.

expense he bore to build a house there strongly suggests that he had no precon-
ceived plan to move on and settle in the Mississippi River valley, that he and his
wife were planning on living out their lives in western Pennsylvania.

Pierre-Charles Bourguignon Derbigny,
who married the de Luzières's daughter, Jeanne-Félicité, at Pittsburgh in
1790. Derbigny went on to serve briefly
(1828–1829) as governor of Louisiana.
Reproduced from Alcée Fortier, *History
of Louisiana.*

The nice young fellow whom de Lezay-Marnésia identified as Luzières's
son-in-law was Pierre-Charles Bourguignon Derbigny—a dashing, intelligent, well-educated young man originally from Laon, site of a towering medi-
eval cathedral and birthplace of another, more famous, Frenchman who also
immigrated to America and died there, Père Jacques Marquette. It is not clear
precisely where Derbigny hooked up with the de Luzières family, but it seems
likely that he sailed from France to Philadelphia on the same ship. In any event,
de Luzières himself, for lack of a proper Roman Catholic priest, married his
only daughter, Jeanne-Félicité, to Derbigny in Pittsburgh in the fall of 1790.[26]

26. Jean-Baptiste Lucas, another French immigrant, also happened to be in Pittsburgh
at the time of the marriage, and de Luzières invited him to the wedding (see invitation in
Lucas Collection, Box 1, Missouri Historical Society, St. Louis). Unfortunately, the only
date on the document is 1790. Lucas eventually became a wealthy and influential citizen
of St. Louis (see William E. Foley, *The Genesis of Missouri: From Wilderness Outpost to
Statehood* [Columbia: University of Missouri Press, 1989], passim; Frederick A. Hodes,
Beyond the Frontier: A History of St. Louis to 1821 [Tucson: Patrice Press, 2004], passim).

The couple's first child was born in Pittsburgh in August 1792, baptized there provisionally in the absence of a priest, and formally baptized (Charles-Zénon-Bauroisgnay) on June 6, 1795, in Ste. Genevieve.[27] After settling for a time with de Luzières at New Bourbon, Derbigny and his wife moved to New Orleans in 1796, where he went into politics and served, in turn, as judge of the supreme court, secretary of state, and governor (1828–1829) of the state of Louisiana before getting killed in a freak carriage accident. When Derbigny was in Washington, D.C., during the winter of 1804–1805, representing the city of New Orleans concerning legal issues raised by the recently concluded Louisiana Purchase, Napoleon's minister to the United States, Louis-Marie Turreau, described Derbigny as "young still, with wit, ready expression, and French manners, I believe him to be greedy of fortune and fame."[28] Derbigny and his wife appear frequently in de Luzières's correspondence from New Bourbon during the 1790s.

27. See Ste. Genevieve Parish Records, Baptisms 1786–1820, p. 59. Microfilm available at the St. Louis County Library, Lindbergh Blvd. Branch.
28. Turreau quoted in Henry Adams, *History of the United States of America during the First Administration of Thomas Jefferson* (New York: Charles Scribner's Sons, 1903), 406. See also Charles Gayarre, *History of Louisiana* (New York: William J. Widdleton, 1867), 4:654.

3

The Grand Enterprise

During the last two decades of the eighteenth century, Pittsburgh was the principal jumping-off point for travelers heading west; for it was at Pittsburgh that the waters of the Allegheny and Monongahela Rivers merged to create the Ohio (Belle Rivière to the French), which was the principal avenue into the heartland of North America. Two years before the de Luzières family arrived in Pittsburgh, another Frenchman, Bartholémé Tardiveau, had come to town and stayed over as a houseguest *chez* Pierre Audrain.

Tardiveau was born circa 1750 in Nantes, a major commercial city on the lower Loire where as a youth he would have encountered both sailors and merchants with tall tales to tell about the New World. He was formally educated, and his prose was intricate, elegant, and suffused with Gallic irony. During the 1780s, he conducted an extensive correspondence with Hector St. John de Crèvecoeur, author of the much admired *Letters from an American Farmer*.[1] Tardiveau is the only French writer I have encountered in the colonial Mississippi Valley to use the imperfect subjunctive tense as a matter of course. He had arrived in Philadelphia in 1778 and apparently was employed there for a time as a schoolmaster. But anyone knowing the least little bit about the man understands that he was not cut out for a sedentary life in the classroom—far

---

1. *Letters from an American Farmer: describing certain provincial situations, manners, and customs, not generally known, and conveying some idea of the late and present interior circumstances of the British colonies in North America* has gone through numerous editions, in both French and English, since it was first published in London in 1782. See the fascinating correspondence between Tardiveau and Hector St. John de Crèvecoeur in Howard C. Rice, *Barthélemi Tardiveau, A French Trader in the West* (Baltimore: Johns Hopkins University Press, 1938), passim.

from it. Before the end of the American Revolution he moved westward over the Alleghenies and had become a trader and entrepreneur, first in Kentucky and then at Kaskaskia, the largest settlement in what became the Northwest Territory of the United States of America in 1787.[2]

Kaskaskia, founded in 1703, had been the metropole of the Illinois Country under the French regime. It had become a British possession with the Treaty of Paris in 1763, and in 1783, with yet another Treaty of Paris, had become part of the United States. Throughout these dizzying political upheavals, it had remained a thoroughly francophone community in which Tardiveau would have been at ease, if perhaps a bit distressed with its remoteness. He did business with the Chouteaus and Charles Gratiot in St. Louis and in Kaskaskia with his friend and neighbor, Pierre Ménard; indeed Tardiveau was one of the witnesses when Ménard married Thérèse Godin in Kaskaskia in June 1792.[3] Ménard, a recent immigrant from Canada, would go on to fame and greatness, becoming the first lieutenant governor of the state of Illinois and leaving to posterity his superb vertical-log house, an architectural treasure to rival the Frank Lloyd Wright houses in Illinois. A life-sized bronze statue of Ménard stands near the statehouse in Springfield. His friend and trading partner, Tardiveau, however, would die in penury and obscurity at New Madrid on the west bank of the Mississippi River in 1801.

On a flier on July 17, 1792, Tardiveau dashed off a long letter to Baron Francisco Luis Hector de Carondelet, Spanish governor general of Louisiana, who presided over the immense (indeed of unknown immensity) province from his office in New Orleans.[4] It may strike one as outrageously presumptuous for a minor merchant, of humble French origins, living in the Northwest

2. Concerning Tardiveau and his far-flung business activities, in addition to Rice, *Barthélemi Tardiveau*, passim, see Rice, ed., "News from the Ohio Valley as Reported by Barthélemi Tardiveau in 1783," *Bulletin of the Historical and Philosophical Society of Ohio* 16 (October 1958): 266–92; also Clarence Walworth Alvord, *The Illinois Country, 1673–1818* (Springfield: Illinois Centennial Commission, 1920), 369–71, 396, 404.

3. See Rice, *Barthélemi Tardiveau*, 86 n. 62.

4. Louis Houck, ed., *The Spanish regime in Missouri; a collection of papers and documents relating to upper Louisiana principally within the present limits of Missouri during the dominion of Spain, from the Archives of the Indies at Seville, etc.*, translated from the original Spanish into English, 2 vols. (Chicago: R. R. Donnelley & Sons Company, 1909), 1:360–66; also printed in Lawrence Kinnaird, ed., *Spain in the Mississippi Valley, 1765–1794* (Washington, D.C.: U.S. Government Printing Office, 1949), 3:60–66. On Carondelet's tenure as governor general, see Charles Gayarré, *History of Louisiana, With city and topographical maps of the state, ancient and modern,* 3rd ed. (New Orleans: A. Hawkins, 1885), vol. 3, chap. 6; Abraham P. Nasatir, ed., *Before Lewis and Clark: Documents Illustrating the History of the Missouri, 1785–1804*, 2 vols., passim; Abraham P. Nasatir, ed., *Spanish War Vessels on the Mississippi* (New Haven, Conn.: Yale University Press, 1968), passim.

Territory of the United States to write, out of the blue, to the aristocratic governor of Spanish Louisiana. But Carondelet himself had been born French, indeed had been a virtual neighbor of de Luzières when the two of them were growing up in the province of Hainault (western Flanders) in far northern France. Moreover, educated men with ambition and energy made up but a small coterie in the Mississippi River valley of the late eighteenth century; within this group no one was too particular about another's origins or too fastidious about breaching European standards of etiquette so long as serious business was on the table. And Tardiveau had a plan that squarely confronted the fundamental existential issue of Spanish Louisiana, a plan that might save Carondelet's province from the "Long Knives" and "Whiskey Boys," those rambunctious, aggressive, and volatile Americans who had already reached the Mississippi River (Kentucky had become a state on June 1, 1792) and were just itching to lunge across it into a trans-Mississippian West of limitless free land and boundless possibilities.[5]

Since the American Revolution ended in 1783, Spanish statesmen had understood that the young republic, a new player in the complex and competitive geopolitics of the greater Mississippi River valley, represented a serious threat to Spanish possessions. At that time, Count Pedro de Aranda, longtime Spanish ambassador to France and an acquaintance of Benjamin Franklin's at the court of Louis XVI, sat down at his desk in his rococo chambers in Paris to analyze the consequences of the emergence of the United States, remarking that "this federal republic is born a pigmy.... The day will come when she will be a giant, a colossus formidable even to these countries [France and Spain], ... and will think only of her own aggrandizement."[6] Spanish administrators in Louisiana were fully aware that they faced a fundamental demographic problem: they absolutely had to build up a substantial population on the west side of the Mississippi River or they would lose their colony to the barbarians, as American frontiersmen were generally viewed from Ste. Genevieve and St. Louis, the principal communities in Spanish Illinois.[7]

5. Bonnevie de Pogniat, an acquaintance of de Luzières, used the English expression, "Whiskey Boys," to characterize American frontiersmen in his 1795 "Mémoire sur la Louisiane," Dépôt des fortifications des colonies, Louisiane 26–30, Centre National des Archives Nationales d'Outre-Mer, Aix-en-Provence.

6. Aranda quoted in Houck, *History of Missouri*, 1:303.

7. "Spanish Illinois" was a placename invented by Herbert Bolton and his graduate students at Berkeley back in the 1920s to distinguish the area west of the Mississippi and north of the Arkansas rivers from British, and then American, Illinois on the east side of the Mississippi (see Abraham P. Nasatir, "The Anglo-Spanish Frontier in the Illinois Country During the American Revolution, 1799–1783," *Journal of the Illinois State Historical Society* 31 [October 1928]: 291 n. 1).

Spanish Illinois (now Missouri) was governed by the lieutenant governor residing in St. Louis. The settlements remained overwhelmingly francophone during the Spanish regime in Louisiana. Map drawn by William L. Potter.

The bait, therefore, that Tardiveau cast out in his audacious letter to Caron-delet of July 1792, was a plan to recruit settlers for Spanish Louisiana in such numbers that the province would be populous enough and vigorous enough to confront the threat presented by the aggressive, adolescent United States of America. As Tardiveau put it in stark terms, "I have no need to waste time showing the great interest that will result to Spain from establishing a nu-merous population on the western bank of the Mississippi. . . . We're dealing not only with giving value to a hitherto uncultivated country, for the central and urgent issue is to oppose the rapid developments of the Americans in the West and to erect a barrier between this bold people and the Spanish posses-sions [in the southwest]."

Tardiveau put his finger squarely on the issue over which Spanish officials obsessed during the last decade of colonial rule in Louisiana. He also believed that he had close at hand a perfect pool of settlers to attract to Spanish Il-linois, specifically the five hundred or so French men, women, and children who had settled on the right bank of the upper Ohio River in 1791 and named their community "Gallipolis," City of the Gauls.[8] These poor settlers had been duped into paying for lands to which they were given no clear titles, were re-puted to be fed up with America and American swindlers, and were therefore ready to flee the United States for Spanish Louisiana. At the end of his long missive, Tardiveau gilded the lily by claiming he was in touch with an expert millwright possessing the skills required to build a first-class mill in Illinois that could supply New Orleans with a steady supply of fine flour. Creoles in Louisiana's capital were scornful of cornbread (maize being reserved for live-stock and slaves) and demanded good wheat flour.

Abraham P. Nasatir, who understood Carondelet's mind better than any other American scholar, past or present, remarked of him that he was "a strat-egist of wide view and agile combinations, . . . [with] a prophetic vision of the magnitude of the issues at stake."[9] Tardiveau could hardly have thrown out his bait to a more receptive mind, and Carondelet rose eagerly to it. From in his office on La Plaza de Armas (or La Place d'Armes, now Jackson Square) in New Orleans Carondelet responded to Tardiveau on September 24, 1792, claiming that he was "truly pleased" to have received Tardiveau's letter and in-sisting that the latter should betake himself on downriver to New Orleans as soon as possible to discuss his proposals for bringing settlers to Louisiana.[10]

8. Concerning Gallipolis, see Jocelyne Moreau-Zanelli, *Gallipolis: Histoire d'un mirage américain au XVIIIe siècle* (Paris: L'Harmattan, 2000); William G. Sibley, *The French Five Hundred* (Gallipolis: Tribune Press, 1901); Phillip J. Wolfe and Warren J. Wolfe, "Prospects for the Gallipolis Settlement," *Ohio History* 103 (Winter–Spring 1994): 41–56.

9. See Nasatir, ed., *War Vessels,* 29.

10. Illinois State Historical Library, Tardiveau Papers (hereafter ISHL, TP), no. 153.

Carondelet continued that he already decided to admit to Louisiana French, Germans, Dutch, and Flemings—but no Americans, for, of course, they might very well carry with them the insidious republican political ideas that were at that very moment devastating Carondelet's homeland, France. The governor was, however, prepared to grant total liberty of conscience (he was apparently thinking about German and Dutch Protestants, well known as good farmers) but with no right to public worship. Families of six or more would receive 400 square arpents (roughly 340 acres) of land, whereas single men owning at least two black slaves would receive 240 arpents (204 acres). Carondelet obviously wanted large families and/or prosperous men to immigrate to Louisiana. He concluded his letter expressing his delight that Tardiveau intended to have built a state-of-the-art ("based on grand principles") flour mill in Illinois.

While Tardiveau's mind was feverishly spinning with projects in Kaskaskia, his friend out in Pittsburgh, Pierre Audrain, was also ruminating about ventures in the greater Ohio-Mississippi-rivers corridors. Audrain and de Lezay-Marnésia had often discussed such ventures during the year or so (early 1791 to early 1792) that the latter spent in the Pittsburgh area. De Lezay-Marnésia had returned to France but nevertheless still entertained romantic dreams of returning to America and establishing a colony far out in the virgin West.

On August 18, 1792, Audrain responded to a letter he had recently received from de Lezay-Marnésia and picked up on their earlier discussions: "I shall not send you the proposal for the settlement that you requested, for you are more capable than I am of drawing it up. However, when friend Tardiveau arrives, we shall put our ideas together on this matter and I will send you the result. . . . I am most grateful for the interest you take in establishing a business speculation in the Illinois lands." In a postscript to this letter, Audrain noted that "M de Luziere has received news from his son. His affairs in France are in desperate shape. God only knows how this worthy man will be able to extricate himself from the embarrassing straits that he'll be in by next spring. I tremble for him."[11] Interestingly, nowhere in this letter did Audrain connect de Luzières with any discussions concerning westward colonization or wide-ranging commercial schemes. As of August 1792, de Luzières and his family were settled down in their new residence on the bank of the Monongahela River just outside Pittsburgh on an apparently permanent basis, whatever their trying circumstances. All this would change dramatically within a

11. See letter in Wolfe, "Audrain," 48–50. In a personal communication, Professor Wolfe supplied me with this letter's important postscript. Moreau-Zanelli (*Gallipolis,* 405 n. 59) also comments on Audrain's letter but mistakenly places him in Philadelphia rather than Pittsburgh.

matter of several months, but how it changed must be pieced together with fragmentary evidence and reasonable inferences.[12]

Tardiveau, in his seminal letter of July 1792 outlining for Carondelet his plan for bringing French settlers from the Ohio River valley to Spanish Louisiana, had mentioned that "one of my friends . . . has written me to know whether I am ready to take an interest in this enterprise." Almost certainly this friend was none other than Pierre Audrain, whom Tardiveau had visited in Pittsburgh in 1789 and who was familiar with the French settlers living at Gallipolis on the Ohio; indeed, he would have encountered many of them as they passed through Pittsburgh on their way down the Ohio River valley. Obviously, Tardiveau and Audrain had been corresponding since Tardiveau's visit to Pittsburgh in 1789, and we have seen above that Audrain and de Luzières became very close once the latter had arrived there in the late winter of 1791.

In the early autumn of 1792, when in Pittsburgh Audrain began discussing Tardiveau's grand plans with de Luzières, the latter had a quite wonderful bit of information to add to the discussions: the recently appointed new governor of Louisiana, Carondelet, was in fact his countryman, having been born and raised at Noyelle, less than ten miles distant from Bouchain and the château of Delassus in the province of Hainault in far northern France. Although Carondelet was ten years de Luzières's senior, it seems likely that the two provincial aristocrats would have encountered each other during their youths and that they were acquaintances if not indeed friends. The facts that de Luzières became a councilor to a French king and that Carondelet had joined the army of a Spanish king meant absolutely nothing in mid-eighteenth-century Flanders. Louis XIV had taken the region from Spain only a century earlier, and strong Spanish influences remained (still do remain in some of the architecture) in the area. Moreover, cousins of the same Bourbon family ruled in both France and Spain. For a young Flemish aristocrat with military or political ambitions deciding whether to serve France or Spain was like deciding whether to dress one's artichoke with drawn butter or olive oil—either would do just fine. De Luzières's own son, Charles (Carlos) de Hault de Lassus, had, like his older neighbor Carondelet, gone into the Spanish service and would, within six years, become Spanish commandant in St. Louis. And of course all of these Flemish aristocrats in the royal service of either France or Spain were allies in their fear and hatred of republican revolutionaries, whether they were of the American or French stripe.

When Pierre Audrain—sitting with de Luzières in his new residence overlooking the Monongahela River, whose waters flowed unfettered across the

12. No known correspondence between de Luzières, Tardiveau, or Audrain exists for the period between August 1792 and April 1793.

continent to New Orleans—heard that his new aristocratic French friend had a close personal tie to Governor Carondelet he must have bolted straight out of his chair. Suddenly everything jelled in Audrain's inventive brain—Tardiveau's plans, as expressed in his letter to Carondelet, to recruit settlers for Spanish Illinois and build a flour mill there; the direct river links between Pittsburgh, Gallipolis, the Illinois Country, and New Orleans; and finally and serendipitously de Luzières's homegrown association with Governor Carondelet.

Late in the autumn of 1792, Audrain persuaded de Luzières to throw over all his efforts of the preceding eighteen months, during which he had purchased estates and built a house near Pittsburgh, and throw in with the grand plans of Audrain and Tardiveau. De Luzières was apparently not altogether happy with his new place of residence, and, moreover, he repeatedly exhibited a streak of audacity that bordered on the reckless. He was not an aristocrat who had led cavalry charges, but he nevertheless possessed something of the warrior spirit of the ancient *noblesse de la race.* De Luzières decided that he would descend the Ohio River with Audrain, rendezvous on the Mississippi with Tardiveau in the Illinois Country, proceed on down to New Orleans, and lay before Carondelet a business scheme of breathtaking audacity and geographical scope.

Late in 1792 (probably mid-November), de Luzières and Audrain left Pittsburgh in a river vessel (more likely a pirogue than a *bateau* because they were traveling light and fast) and proceeded down the Ohio River. Some one hundred miles downriver they would have stopped and visited the French settlers at Gallipolis, many of whom de Luzières knew and upon whom turned much of his grand strategic plan for populating Spanish Illinois. Ice floes would have constantly challenged the adventurers' boatmen, but at that early time of year they could likely have ridden the high, spuming water right over the slate ridges at Louisville, more commonly called "the Falls of the Ohio." De Luzières had not contemplated such adventures when he fled Flanders in August 1790.

In 1793 the right bank of the Ohio River, although held under U.S. sovereignty (at least in white men's opinion), was unorganized Indian territory, where Shawnees and Miamis held sway. Less than two years earlier, these Indians nearly annihilated the American army (and in 1791 there was, for all intents and purposes, but one American army) under General Arthur St. Clair in the worst defeat ever inflicted by red men upon white men in the history of the New World. Interestingly, history books have never been able to agree on a name for this Indian victory, other than the pallid "St. Clair's defeat," and a startling defeat it surely was. Three years later, General ("Mad")

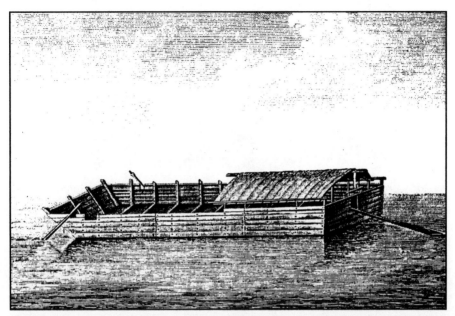

Eighteenth-century riverboat (*bateau*) of the kind that carried goods and passengers between New Orleans and the Illinois Country. Drawn by Charles Warin, engraved by Pierre-François Tardieu, and reproduced from Georges-Henri-Victor Collot, *Journey in North America*.

Anthony Wayne's army crushed a smaller force of numerous allied tribes at Fallen Timbers, the white man's victory receiving a memorable name in history textbooks. This defeat largely ended Indian resistance to white settlement in what became the Ohio Territory in 1799.[13] In any case, with a bit of luck, de Luzières and Audrain would have reached the mouth of the Ohio within six weeks. There, they turned upstream on the Mississippi and headed for Ste. Genevieve and Kaskaskia, with the last leg of the trip entailing the most arduous paddling.

Carondelet's response to Tardiveau's July 1792 letter, sent from New Orleans on September 24, would likely have arrived in Kaskaskia in late December. In early January 1793, Tardiveau was in Kaskaskia getting his affairs in order in preparation for his trip down the Mississippi to meet with Governor Carondelet, as the governor had urged. This would be the most important mission of Tardiveau's life, a mission he hoped would transform him from small-time trader into grand entrepreneur, even, as Carondelet's collaborator, a provincial statesman of sorts. About the same time, de Luzières and Audrain

13. For an account of travel on the Ohio River at this time, see Part 2, document no. 6.

Shawnee Indian, Upper Louisiana, late eighteenth century. A large village of Shawnees lived in the New Bourbon District. Drawn by Charles Warin, engraved by Pierre-François Tardieu, and reproduced from Georges-Henri-Victor Collot, *Journey in North America.*

arrived in the Illinois Country from Pittsburgh, and the three men spent several months in and about Kaskaskia and Ste. Genevieve strategizing about how they would approach Carondelet with a plan that would appeal to him and would, eventually, make all of them rich and famous. Moreover, de Luzières reconnoitered the region and decided that he would uproot his family once again, bring them all out to the Mississippi Valley, and create a new colony in Spanish Illinois on the hilltops just south of Ste. Genevieve.[14]

In the spring of 1793, captain of the Spanish army Don Pedro (Pierre) Rousseau, commanding officer of the armed galiot *La Flecha,* was descending the Mississippi after having conducted a water-borne reconnaissance of the Illinois Country. Astonishingly, Spanish freshwater war vessels based in New Orleans patrolled the Mississippi all the way upriver to the mouth of the Wisconsin River (Prairie du Chien) during the 1790s.[15] Spain was evidently serious about keeping a grip on the full extent of its province of Louisiana if at all possible. On March 6, Rousseau encountered just below Écores à Margot (Chickasaw Bluffs [upstream from Memphis along the left bank of the Mississippi]) "an American barge loaded with furs coming from Cas aux Illinois [Kaskaskia], having on board three French passengers who were coming from the United States of America [and were] going to New Orleans; [the] names of the three Frenchmen were the Chevalier de Luzières, of the Comté d'Allegène [Allegheny County]; Mr. Bartholomé Tardiveau, of Kaskaskia, Illinois; . . . [and] Pierre Audrain, of Fort Pitt, all in the States of America."[16] This record permits us to pinpoint de Luzières's precise location in North America for the first time since Audrain had located him at Pittsburgh in August 1792.

Captain Rousseau obviously boarded this barge, inspected the cargo, and demanded that the passengers identify themselves. The Treaty of San Lorenzo (Pinckney's Treaty), which gave Americans unrestricted navigational rights on the Mississippi River, was still more than two years off. This meant that this barge was subject to being stopped and inspected during its river voyage and its cargo subject to controls and duties in New Orleans.[17] Tardiveau likely finessed this encounter with Rousseau and his war galiot by waving Governor Carondelet's cordial letter from the previous autumn, a letter urging Tardiveau to get himself on down to the governor's office in New Orleans as soon as possible.

When Captain Rousseau encountered the Frenchmen on the Mississippi south of Chickasaw Bluffs in early March 1793 all three were now in Tardiveau's *bateau,* which was loaded with furs that had come from Tardiveau's trading post in Kaskaskia. On the river trip between New Madrid and New Orleans, which would have taken less than a month, Tardiveau and de Luzières

14. Tardiveau, who assisted de Luzières with his reconnaissance, drafted a crude but invaluable map of the Ste. Genevieve vicinity at this time (see map p. 52).

15. See the indispensable study edited by Nasatir, ed., *Spanish War Vessels.*

16. Nasatir, ed., *Spanish War Vessels,* 178–79.

17. See Arthur P. Whitaker, *The Spanish-American Frontier, 1783–1795* (Boston: Houghton Mifflin Co., 1927).

became fast friends, and this friendship, one of de Luzières's closest in the New World, endured until Tardiveau's death in New Madrid in 1801. By early April, our three sojourners were in New Orleans pounding on Governor Carondelet's door, or rather impatiently cooling their heels in his antechamber while awaiting an audience that would reshape their lives. Perhaps they passed the time watching spit-and-polish Spanish regulars parade in the Plaza de Armas, for, of course, General Andrew Jackson's statue did not yet grace that elegant urban space facing New Orleans' embarcadero. De Luzières would have been thinking about his son, Carlos Delassus, who was at the time serving in a Spanish Walloon regiment in Europe.

New Orleans was in the early 1790s the third largest (after Montreal and Quebec City) francophone city in North America. A small group of Spanish administrators and soldiers spoke Spanish, and an even smaller group of British and American merchants spoke English, but overwhelmingly the language of the city was French. De Luzières would have felt perfectly at home on the streets and in the taverns of New Orleans, although he would surely have been taken aback by the very large numbers of blacks, both slaves and freemen, who casually rubbed shoulders with the whites. Forty years later, Tocqueville was likely referring to widespread interracial sexual relations in New Orleans when he remarked that "we saw the French of Canada; they are a calm people, moral, religious. We left behind in Louisiana quite different Frenchmen, restless, dissolute, lax in all things."[18] De Luzières may well have put up in the residence of Berthe Grima on Conti Street, Grima being the financier of Sephardic Jewish background who served as banker in New Orleans to many Illinois Country merchants (including the Vallés and Chouteaus) and who often hosted important out-of-town visitors to New Orleans.[19] But de Luzières was not in town to socialize or sightsee, and, unlike his successor Tocqueville, he left no known record of his impressions of the city.

The month (early April to early May 1793) that de Luzières remained in New Orleans was devoted in large measure to business, and that business got done in spectacular fashion. Surely at the first audience with Carondelet, the governor and de Luzières chatted a bit about their childhoods in the Scheldt River valley in the province of Hainault. But these civilities were brief, what with the momentous negotiations at hand. In discussions lasting several weeks, de Luzières, Tardiveau, and Audrain persuaded Governor Carondelet to sign on to a breathtakingly bold enterprise intended to place the three

18. Tocqueville quoted in André Jardin, *Tocqueville: A Biography,* trans. Lydia Davis with Robert Hemenway (New York: Farrar, Straus and Giroux, 1988), 170.

19. See Carl J. Ekberg, *Colonial Ste. Genevieve: An Adventure on the Mississippi Frontier* (Gerald, Mo.: Patrice Press, 1985), 157, 172–73, 408.

Governor Francisco Luis Hector de Carondelet, who was born and raised in Flanders, as was de Luzières. Carondelet created the New Bourbon District and made de Luzières commandant of it. Reproduced from Louis Houck, *The Spanish Regime in Missouri.*

projectors in control of a large share of the commerce of the Mississippi and Ohio River valleys.

The proposed enterprise was not something for timid souls, and its grand scope and boldness, even recklessness, suggests that the Frenchmen who hatched it in New Orleans had been breathing the heady air of the American frontier where anything was deemed possible: The French community at Gallipolis would be moved en masse to a new community to be developed near Ste. Genevieve that would be named New Bourbon, to which de Luzières would move his family and where he would make his home. Carondelet wrote that he had decided upon this august dynastic name, but in fact it had been first suggested by de Luzières, Tardiveau, and Audrain.[20] Attaching the Bourbon name to the new community would honor the ruling family in Spain (Borbón in Spanish), would memorialize the recently (January 21, 1793) executed Bourbon king of France, Louis XVI, and would serve to warn off all those who were not committed monarchists, who may have become infected with the new-fangled, toxic republican ideas that were circulating in both France and the United States: the name of the mighty Bourbon dynasty, whose history ran back nearly one thousand years, was endowed with virtually magical qualities.[21]

The farmers brought west from Gallipolis would produce wheat for a state-of-the-art flour mill to be built at Ste. Genevieve. Another like mill would be built at New Madrid, below the mouth of the Ohio River, which mill would be fed not only by the farms surrounding this community but also by wheat coming from the increasingly productive Ohio Valley. Ever since serious arable agriculture had developed around the villages of the Illinois Country in the early eighteenth century, milling the abundant grain harvests into flour had been a persistent problem. Experiments with water and wind power had generally failed, and at the end of the colonial era horse mills continued to be the principal device for milling flour in the area. Bake ovens and distilling facilities (bourbon was already being produced from locally grown maize in Bourbon County, Kentucky) would also be added at New Madrid, creating the first industrial complex in the Mississippi Valley. This extraordinary group of eighteenth-century Frenchmen dreamed as big as future Texas oilmen.

Carondelet, who at the time was both governor and intendant (i.e., chief financial officer) of Louisiana, committed the Spanish crown to providing financial support, to the tune of 11,500 piastres (dollars), for this mind-boggling plan.[22] He sincerely, and credulously, believed that it had the potential to solve most of the major problems he faced as governor of Louisiana. It would increase the population of the province with a mass of new immigrants, it would boost agricultural production, and it would provide the wheat flour that was chronically in short supply in New Orleans.

20. See correspondence concerning this issue in Houck, ed., *Spanish Regime*, 1:376, 392.

21. News of Louis XVI's execution had not yet arrived in Louisiana when the decision was made to attach the Bourbon name to de Luzières's proposed settlement, but the entire Western World knew that it was only a matter of time before the deposed king would be guillotined.

22. Houck, ed., *Spanish Regime*, 1:374.

The solution of these discrete problems would in turn solve the transcendental problem facing Spain in Louisiana—protecting the province against the hordes of barbarous Americans, who were already lining up along the east bank of the Mississippi and who gave every evidence of aiming to wrest control over the greater Mississippi River valley from a decadent Old World monarchy. Carondelet had to be, absolutely was forced to be, interested in a plan, no matter how seemingly far-fetched, that had any potential of providing all these benefits to his regime in Louisiana. He was, however, cautious enough to demand that the wealthy New Orleans merchant Jean-Baptiste Sarpy should agree to secure against loss the funds supplied by Carondelet out of Spanish coffers.[23]

Carondelet was bursting with an enthusiasm unusual for a bureaucrat when on April 26, 1793, he wrote to Diego de Gardoqui, Spanish minister to the United States, in Philadelphia: "I have just concluded a transaction the consequences of which will form an epoch in the annals of the province and of North America."[24] Five days later, de Luzières, flush with the success of the negotiations, drafted a lengthy memorandum (Part 2, document no. 2) for Carondelet in which he laid out all that needed to be done in the Illinois Country to improve the area and strengthen it in the face of threats from Americans as well as Indians. De Luzières was moving the discussion well beyond mere considerations of commerce; this was a sweeping, comprehensive bill of particulars dealing with everything from agriculture, to politics, to religion, and even to medicine (the Ste. Genevieve-New Bourbon area desperately needed a doctor and a midwife). De Luzières, an aristocrat of the Old Regime and a devoted royalist, presented Carondelet with a plan that would have delighted almost any *philosophe* of the Enlightenment. If one were to place de Luzières within an eighteenth-century European school of politics, the textbook niche that would best suit him would be that of Enlightened Despotism, progressive on many issues but certainly not liberal about politics.

Carondelet's triumphal letter to Gardoqui was likely dispatched to Philadelphia on the same brigantine that carried Audrain, who embarked in New Orleans toward the end of April en route to Pittsburgh, by sea to Philadelphia and then overland to the forks of the Ohio. He complained from Plaquemine, as his ship wended its way through the curves of the lower Mississippi en route to the Gulf of Mexico, that the passengers were packed in "like herrings in a barrel," but his passage back east was in fact remarkably easy and swift. He arrived in Philadelphia on May 20, right at the time that the American capital

23. Sarpy had a brother, Sylvester, in St. Louis.
24. Houck, ed., *Spanish Regime*, 1:374.

city was in a veritable frenzy over Edmond-Charles Genêt, the French Revolutionary government's new minister plenipotentiary to the United States. Toasts were offered, salvos were fired, and the "Marseillaise" was sung as radical republicans in the city rejoiced over the presence of a flesh-and-blood French Revolutionary.[25]

Audrain seems to have paid no heed to the celebratory mood in Philadelphia but rather forged straight on to Pittsburgh, arriving there on June 2.[26] He had made amazingly good time, his brigantine obviously having been blessed with favorable winds during the New Orleans–Philadelphia leg of the trip. If Audrain had attempted to get to Pittsburgh via the rivers, up the Mississippi and then the Ohio, the trip would have consumed five or six months. Audrain wrote that he was not reporting on de Luzières's family, which remained in Pittsburgh, because Madame de Luzières and son-in-law Pierre Derbigny would themselves communicate on that topic; that he was forwarding some gazettes[27] carrying news from the Atlantic seaboard, and that he was sending his post via Fort Washington (adjacent to embryonic Cincinnati), where General Anthony Wayne was assembling his troops. Literate folks in the Illinois Country were always starved for news from the East and eagerly awaited the arrival of printed materials from Pennsylvania. Wayne was just beginning his campaign against the Shawnees and their allies (Ottawas, Miamis, Wyandots, and Potawatomis) that would climax with his decisive victory at Fallen Timbers in August 1794. Audrain made no mention of any progress recruiting the settlers at Gallipolis for a mass immigration to New Bourbon, although this recruitment was ostensibly to be his principal contribution to the grand strategy the three partners had agreed upon in New Orleans.

For the remainder of his life, de Luzières would remember the glorious month he spent in New Orleans during the spring of 1793, his one and only sojourn in the capital of his adopted province. He, Tardiveau, and Audrain had left New Madrid during a driving March sleet storm and arrived at New

---

25. President George Washington was much less pleased with Genêt than were the street crowds in Philadelphia. Indeed, Washington was infuriated with Genêt's presumption and eventually demanded that the French government replace the fiery minister. See Eugene R. Sheridan, "The Recall of Edmond Charles Genêt: A Study in Transatlantic Politics and Diplomacy," *Diplomatic History* 18 (Fall 1994): 463–68; Harry Ammon, *The Genet Mission* (New York: Norton and Company, 1973), 98–109.

26. ISHL, TP, no. 168.

27. Audrain preferred the *Federal Gazette* compiled in Philadelphia by Andrew Brown and subscribed to it using funds from his partnership with de Luzières and Tardiveau (ibid.). Concerning Brown and his newspaper, which, despite its name, leaned Republican rather than Federalist, see David Paul Nord, *Communities of Journalism: A History of American Newspapers and Their Readers* (Urbana: University of Illinois Press, 2001), chap. 9.

Orleans in early April, when the scent of flowers hung heavy in the humid spring air. The negotiations with Carondelet had gone swimmingly, and de Luzières could say, at least to himself, that his personal association with the governor had been the key to success. As, one by one, every component in the grand plan to revolutionize commerce in the Mississippi and Ohio river valleys eventually crumbled, he would look back upon the high hopes evinced during that exhilarating month. In early May (probably the tenth) 1793, de Luzières and Tardiveau departed New Orleans and headed up the Mississippi toward the Illinois Country. Once there, they were to prepare a welcome for the settlers due to arrive from Gallipolis and get started overseeing the building of gristmills at New Madrid and Ste. Genevieve. As damnably difficult as this upriver journey was, they were in great good humor as the trip began, and they reported on their progress from Natchez and Nogales (Walnut Hills to Americans).[28]

De Luzières and Tardiveau arrived at New Madrid on August 1, 1793, after having spent not quite three months on the Mississippi, the usual duration of such an upriver journey.[29] The second half of the trip had gone less well than the first half, at least for de Luzières, who, according to Tardiveau, had been ill for six weeks. De Luzières's spirits were surely not lifted by a ghastly object that washed up on the bank of the Mississippi while he and Tardiveau were at New Madrid—the bloated body of Tardiveau's nephew, hands bound behind him and with a badly bruised back. This nephew had only recently arrived from France, was new to the Mississippi frontier, and had been awaiting the arrival of his uncle from New Orleans. Indians (no tribe given, but likely Shawnees) had captured the young man along with five Americans; the Indians had forthwith scalped and dismembered the Americans in front of the dazed and disoriented young Frenchman. Tardiveau speculated that, although his nephew had been beaten, he had been spared a gruesome death because the Indians had noticed that he was not an American, for which variety of white man they reserved special loathing. Further speculation had it that the nephew, fearing far worse treatment than he had already received, had flung himself into the river and thus perished. The young man had perhaps escaped the guillotine by fleeing Revolutionary France only to die a gruesome frontier death in the American West.

It's at least worth speculating that this adroit little massacre of Americans was encouraged, if not in fact engineered, by Louis Lorimier, commandant at Cape Girardeau, mentor and councilor to the groups of Shawnees and

28. Letters of June 1, 2, 17 in ISHL, TP, no. 164.
29. Letter of August 9, 1793, ibid., no. 165.

Delawares living in the area, and bitter foe of Americans, all Americans.[30] François-Marie Perrin du Lac remarked at this time that "Shawnees are distinguished by their bravery and their hatred of Americans."[31] During the American Revolution, Lorimier had used his influence, which was substantial, to keep the Indians in the greater Ohio River valley on the British side of the conflict, and after the revolution had fled American control of the Northwest Territory. General Collot commented in 1795 that Lorimier's "talents and great influence with the Indian nations" were very important to the Spanish colonial regime in Upper Louisiana.[32] Tardiveau was an acquaintance, if not a friend of Lorimier, and the fact that his nephew had gotten tangled up in this bloody episode was just one of those unfortunate quirks of fate that characterized the Mississippi frontier in colonial times. If Lorimier was in fact behind this affair, his fine hand would never have been revealed to anyone but his *métisse* (half-Shawnee) wife.[33]

On a brighter note, Tardiveau reported that he was eager to dive in, start reconnoitering to locate the best place to build a flour mill at New Madrid, and find laborers to get the project started. He was also receiving favorable reports about the quality of wheat being produced in Kentucky, which would make admirable grist for the new mill once it was completed. So far so good, everything seemed to be on track, at least in principle. De Luzières's physical condition soon improved enough at New Madrid so that he could proceed on upriver to Ste. Genevieve. His family—wife, two sons, pregnant daughter, and son-in-law—were scheduled to leave Pittsburgh soon and run the gauntlet of the Ohio River through Indian country (the same country in which Tardiveau's nephew had met his grisly fate) in order to rendezvous with him at Ste. Genevieve. De Luzières was justifiably terrified at the prospect of his family's impending trip.

30. Ironically, President Thomas Jefferson appointed Lorimier's sons, Louis Jr. and Augustus, to West Point in 1804 (George W. Cullum, *Biographical Register of the Officers and Graduates of the U.S. Military Academy at West Point, N.Y.* [New York: Houghton, Mifflin and Company, 1891], 1:76).

31. François-Marie Perrin du Lac, *Voyage dans les deux Louisianes* (Lyon: Bruysset aîneì et Buynand, 1805), 178.

32. Georges-Henri-Victor Collot, *A journey in North America, containing a survey of the countries watered by the Mississippi, Ohio, Missouri, and other affluing rivers,* ed. Christian Bay, 3 vols. (Florence, O. Lange, 1924), 1:219.

33. On Lorimier, see the extended notes in Abraham P. Nasatir, ed., *Spanish War Vessels on the Mississippi* (New Haven, Conn.: Yale University Press, 1968), 71–72, 297–98. When I was working with Nasatir in California during the early 1980s, he repeatedly opined that Lorimier was terribly important to the Spanish colonial regime as an intermediary with the Indians and that he deserved a full-scale biography. Nasatir regretted that he never got a chance to visit the graves of Lorimier and his wife, which overlook the Mississippi River from the historic cemetery in Cape Girardeau.

Tardiveau next wrote from Kaskaskia, whence he had gone to close out his personal affairs before moving permanently to New Madrid. He informed Audrain that de Luzières was having difficulties getting settled in, that he was living at François Vallé's home in Ste. Genevieve, and that he was still afflicted with fevers. Tardiveau admonished Audrain "not to mention the issue of his family,"[34] in his correspondence with de Luzières, for the man was consumed with worry about his family's impending journey down the valley of the shadow of death, through which ran the Ohio River.

François Vallé was during the 1790s head of the wealthy and powerful Vallé family that had been at the center of life in Ste. Genevieve virtually since the town's founding circa 1750.[35] He was soon to be appointed Spanish commandant in Ste. Genevieve, and would remain one of de Luzières's closest friends until his death in 1804, just two years before that of de Luzières. The hospitality that Vallé extended to the ill Frenchman in his newly built house in the new town of Ste. Genevieve brought de Luzières into the Vallé family's political ambit, where he remained until the Louisiana Purchase put an end to the colonial regime in Upper Louisiana. This regime change substantially reduced the influence of the Vallé family (and of course of de Luzières himself), which had dominated politics in Ste. Genevieve for nearly half a century.[36]

34. Letter of August 26, 1793, ISHL, TP, no. 165.
35. See Carl J. Ekberg, *François Vallé and His World* (Columbia: University of Missouri Press, 2002), passim.
36. Ibid.

4

At Home in the Illinois Country

André Michaux, the intrepid French botanist, sometime political agent, and travel writer, was in Pittsburgh in August 1793 and met Audrain there. Michaux remarked that Audrain had been in North America for fourteen years, that his business was shipping flour to New Orleans, and that he was said to be in partnership with "one Louisière or Delousière. . . . This Louisière is at present absent from Pittsburgh."[1] Absent indeed, for when Michaux commented about him de Luzières was in faraway Ste. Genevieve where he had the specific responsibility of getting a first-class flour mill up and running. He seems never even to have begun this task. His letters to Tardiveau, who was in New Madrid overseeing the mill-building project there, during the autumn of 1793 are full of pathos and sadly lacking in energy. His intermittent malarial fevers were compounded by other illnesses, both physical and mental. "My situation is frightful, persistent diarrhea and stomach problems, and I'm getting weaker every day. Moreover, my sad and dark ruminations are not conducive to getting better."[2]

De Luzières's mood was not lightened by the arrival in Upper Louisiana of the news of Louis XVI's execution. De Luzières was extremely proud of his honorific title, "councilor to the king," and he never wavered in his loyalty to

1. See André Michaux's "Journal," in *Early Western Travels, 1748–1846,* ed. Reuben Gold Thwaites (Cleveland: A. H. Clark Co., 1904), 3:31. On Michaux's sojourn in North America, see *Dictionary of Canadian Biography,* s.v. "André Michaux," by J. F. M. Hoeniger. Michaux had met Edmond Genêt before heading for the Ohio River valley.
2. De Luzières, letter of September 30, 1793, Illinois State Historical Library, Tardiveau Papers (hereafter ISHL, TP), no. 177.

the Bourbon family, which via Spain ruled Louisiana at the time. On October 2, 1793, Lieutenant Governor Zénon Trudeau wrote from St. Louis to Carondelet that de Luzières had conveyed to him the news of Louis XVI's death, "which affected all the old French people here."[3] Surely this gloomy news descended on de Luzières with more weight than anyone else in the region, but in the autumn of 1793 he did not have spare time to "sit upon the ground and tell sad stories of the death of kings."

De Luzières was especially worried that his new residence, which was rising very slowly on the hills above the plowlands of Ste. Genevieve's Grand Champ (see map, p.59), would not be completed when his family arrived, and, as it turned out, it was not. "Everything here is talk and promises but nothing ever gets done," he complained.[4] Trudeau wrote to François Vallé in Ste. Genevieve informing him that de Luzières was "terribly upset [*une inquiétude infinie*]" about the prospect of his family arriving from Pittsburgh and finding no proper house in which to live.[5] A building boom was in full swing in the region as the move from the old town of Ste. Genevieve to the new town was being accomplished, however, and skilled craftsmen were in short supply.[6] Eventually, black slaves belonging to the wealthy Ste. Genevieve residents, Vallé and Jean-Baptiste Pratte, were put to work on de Luzières's house.[7] This case suggests that many of the fine residences erected in the new town of Ste. Genevieve during the 1790s—including the still-standing Nicolas Janis, Louis Bolduc, Vital St. Gemme Bauvais, and Jean-Baptiste Vallé houses—were built largely by anonymous black craftsmen, trained in the local vernacular style of vertical-log construction.

"Merde, les américains arrivent, les américains arrivent" were words that surely reverbrated through all serious conversations in the francophone communities (and they were uniformly francophone) of Spanish Illinois for about four months, from the autumn of 1793 to the late winter of 1794. Rumors were rife and they were wild. The gist of them was that George Rogers Clark

3. Trudeau's letter in Papeles de Cuba, legajo 211, Archivo General de Indies, Seville (henceforth this collection will be cited simply as PC [Papeles de Cuba] followed by the legajo number). See Trudeau's official service sheet ("good application, capacity and conduct") in Jack D. L. Holmes, ed., *Honor and Fidelity: The Louisiana Regiment and the Louisiana Military Companies, 1766–1821* (Birmingham, Ala.: privately printed, 1965), 153.
4. ISHL, TP, letter of September 22, 1793, no. 176.
5. Trudeau to Vallé, October 4, 1793, Box 1, François Vallé Collection, Missouri Historical Society, St. Louis (henceforth MHS).
6. Concerning this move from old town to new town, see Carl J. Ekberg, *Colonial Ste. Genevieve: An Adventure on the Mississippi Frontier* (Gerald, Mo.: Patrice Press), chap. 13.
7. Louis Vandenbemden to Tardiveau, March 16, 1794, ISHL, TP, no. 200.

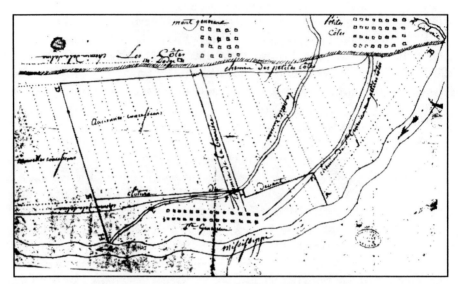

New settlements at Ste. Genevieve in the spring of 1793. Mont Généreux would soon be re-named Nouvelle Bourbon, and Petites Côtes would become Nouvelle Ste. Geneviève. Map drawn by de Luzières's colleague, Bartholémé Tardiveau. Reproduced courtesy of the Archivo General de Indias, Seville, Spain.

was going to rouse himself out of his alcoholic stupor,[8] and that with finan-cial support from Edmond Genêt, minister from the French Revolutionary government to the United States, Clark would lead a savage attack on Upper Louisiana, smashing the Spanish colonial regime and instituting some sort of republican government based on French and American revolutionary ideals.

Clark, of course, was remembered as the leader of the Virginia militia-men who had "liberated" Kaskaskia from the British in 1778. But he was also known as the fiery redhead who practiced frontier warfare *à l'outrance,* no holds barred and no quarter given, the most vicious of the "Whiskey Boys"— as when he had had a half dozen Indian captives tomahawked in the public square at Vincennes, he perhaps swinging the instrument of death on at least one occasion, basking in the scarlet spray of brains and blood.[9] Official corre-spondence between Spanish Illinois and New Orleans concerning the Clark-

8. In 1795, General Collot reported that Clark was "often found lying in a state of stupi-fied drunkenness." Georges-Henri-Victor Collot, *A journey in North America, containing a survey of the countries watered by the Mississippi, Ohio, Missouri, and other affluing rivers,* ed. Christian Bay, 3 vols. (Florence: O. Lange, 1924), 1:153.

9. Richard White, *The Middle Ground: Indians, Empires, and Republics in the Great Lakes Region, 1650–1815* (Cambridge: Cambridge University Press, 1991), 374–77.

Genêt threat fills hundreds and hundreds of manuscript pages, and de Luzières was one of the principal correspondents (see, for example, Part 2, document no. 5).[10] Indeed, de Luzières was frantically concerned with this curious sidelight to American history because it just happened to coincide with his family's daunting river journey from Pittsburgh all the way down the Ohio and up the Mississippi to Ste. Genevieve during the winter of 1793–1794.

The story of de Luzières's family's journey down the Ohio River during the winter of 1793–1794 ranks as one of the more extraordinary tales in the history of westward expansion in North America. In preparation for the trip, Domitille-Josèphe, Madame de Luzières, sold off, with help from Pierre Audrain and Pierre Derbigny, the family's large real estate holdings near Pittsburgh on November 3, 1793. The two properties brought roughly 50 percent more than de Luzières had paid for them two and a half years earlier.[11] Real estate prices in the Pittsburgh area were certainly rising at this expansionary period in the town's history, but the greater value of the de Luzières properties was certainly a consequence of the large new residence that de Luzières had had built to house his family, including his daughter and her husband, Derbigny. The young couple's first child was born in this residence in August 1792. Widow Catherine Thompson, who had sold the land to de Luzières, was apparently attracted by this house and willingly bought back the properties at their substantially increased value.

By the end of November 1793, the de Luzières family—led in principle by Madame—with its extraordinary entourage was about ready to push off into the waters of the Allegheny and Monongahela Rivers as they converged to form the Ohio River, just at the tip of the peninsula where European settlement had originated in the area—first as Fort Duquesne, then after the French and Indian War as Fort Pitt, and finally after the American Revolution as Pittsburgh.

Derbigny, the newest member of the extended de Luzières family, was in fact in charge of the expedition, rather than Madame de Luzières or one of her sons. This may have been because Derbigny was better educated and knew some English, because he had a more forceful personality, because he was father to the only de Luzières grandchild, because he already had traveled in the Ohio River valley, or most likely a combination of all these reasons. Audrain wrote from Pittsburgh on November 30 that "Sieur Derbigny will leave on Wednesday with the de Luzières family. He'll be carrying this letter with

10. See Frederick Jackson Turner's classic essay on the Clark-Genêt affair, "The Origin of Genêt's Projected Attack on Louisiana and the Floridas," *American Historical Review* 3 (July 1898): 650–71; also Ammon, *Genêt Mission.*
11. Allegheny County Real Estate Records Office, Deed Book 3: 341–42, Pittsburgh.

him as well as the gazettes that I've accumulated since Sieur [Pierre] Ménard's departure."[12] No one headed down the Ohio River from Pittsburgh in the late eighteenth century without a bundle of gazettes (most printed in Philadelphia, capital of the United States) for the news-famished Illinois Country; news from the greater Atlantic world came more quickly to Ste. Genevieve and St. Louis via Pittsburgh than via New Orleans.

As it turned out, the de Luzières party did depart on a Wednesday but it was on December 11, 1793, rather than the fourth as Audrain had predicted (Part 2, document no. 6). The departing convoy was a sight to behold.[13] The main *bateau* was huge, perhaps forty-five feet long and twelve wide, described by de Luzières as being driven by twenty-four oars. Although consistently called a *berge* (i.e., barge), suggestive of a flat-bottomed boat, this vessel boasted of a more complex architecture, with a skeleton (probably of oak) consisting of keel and ribs. Tethered behind it, cow-and-calves fashion, were two smaller, although still substantial, flat-bottomed vessels, sometimes called "Kentucky boats," each driven by eight oars.[14] Passengers on the large boat included Madame de Luzières, two of her unmarried sons (Jacques-Marcellin-Léon and Philippe-François-Camille), her pregnant daughter, Jeanne-Félicité-Odile, Jeanne's husband, Pierre Derbigny, future governor of the state of Louisiana, the Derbignys' fifteen-month-old son (Charles-Zénon), and Antoine Soulard, a former French naval officer who would acquire fame, and some fortune, as a surveyor in St. Louis. There, a street, a park, an outdoor market, and a historic neighborhood still bear the Soulard name, for de Luzières's protégé is much better commemorated than de Luzières himself. Assorted domestics, including one named Albert, accompanied Madame de Luzières on the large boat, as did a curious American, who was an outsider in the overwhelmingly native-French group. Henry Green, a millwright, had been recruited in Pittsburgh by Derbigny to migrate to Spanish Illinois to help construct the proposed flour mill at New Madrid.[15]

12. Audrain to Tardiveau, November 30, 1793, ISHL, TP, no. 188.

13. Concerning the composition of this party, see Part 2, document no. 6, as well as de Luzières to Tardiveau, January 4, 1794, ISHL, TP, no. 192.

14. Concerning the various types of riverboats that plied the Ohio River during the 1790s, see Collot, *Journey in North America*, 1:32–33; also St. Martial to Carondelet, February 8, 1793, PC, Leg. 210, in which St. Martial explains that the boat of Madame de Luzières had a "quille," whereas his was flat-bottomed.

15. Green appears as an unmarried man on the 1797 New Madrid census (see Louis Houck, ed., *The Spanish regime in Missouri; a collection of papers and documents relating to upper Louisiana principally within the present limits of Missouri during the dominion of Spain, from the Archives of the Indies at Seville, etc.*, translated from the original Spanish into English, 2 vols. (Chicago: R. R. Donnelley & Sons Company, 1909), 2:393, 398).

One of the smaller, trailing boats carried three nuns of the Order of St. Clare, along with their chamber maid, a "young negresse," two additional domestics, and of course the *engagé* (hired) oarsmen. De Luzières claimed that the nuns rode in a separate boat so that they would be more comfortable during the arduous trip, but he would later learn that the three were so difficult, so capriciously contentious, that they had likely been segregated in order to maintain a modicum of comity within the group. The second trailing boat carried Cruzel de St. Martial, "former doctor to the king," and his small entourage of domestics. If any boating party more exotic than this one has ever descended the Ohio River from its source to its mouth, it remains unknown.

The midwinter trip down the Ohio to the Mississippi was difficult and occasionally hair-raising, but not a total nightmare.[16] The unsung heroes of the trip were the three *patrons,* the skippers of the three boats. St. Martial, who, as self-described "former doctor to the king," was a bit of a snob, later wrote that "I have nothing but good to say about Joseph Senequier, my skipper. . . . His conduct and feelings [*sentiments*] were quite superior to his station in life during my entire voyage."[17] Madame de Luzières's skipper remains unknown, but Senequier may have been the anonymous author who chronicled this amazing trip down the Ohio River; portions of this chronicle appear in translation below.[18]

The right bank of the Ohio was still very much Indian territory, and many Indian groups within the region remained volatile and hostile to white men. They had destroyed an American army led by General Arthur St. Clair in 1791 and had not yet been put down, hard, by General ("Mad") Anthony Wayne at Fallen Timbers in August 1794. The de Luzières party never experienced an Indian attack, but each night sentinels were posted and little sleep was got for fear of one. Because it was the dead of winter ice flows were a constant hazard, especially those grinding and churning out into the Ohio from its south-flowing tributaries like the Muskingum. Salted pork, flour, and perhaps peas would have been stored in barrels on the *bateaux,* but fresh food (other than the chickens that skampered freely about the boats, providing eggs and some fresh meat) was difficult to come by, for the Frenchmen in the group were maladroit as hunters, usually returning from the woods empty-handed. They discovered that hunting for food in the primordial American forest was not the same thing as sport-shooting in a deer park back in France. Fresh milk was occasionally purchased from settlements along the river, for Madame de

16. Part 2, document no. 6.
17. St. Martial to Carondelet, February 8, 1793, PC, Leg. 210.
18. Part 2, document no. 6.

Luzières, American wilderness or not, would have her café au lait, if not crois-
sants, for her breakfast!

Madame de Luzières's party made two extensive layovers on terra firma
during their watery journey westward, the first, appropriately, at Gallipolis.
This community was composed of French immigrants who had been swin-
dled in the famous Scioto land scam. The Scioto Company, with a branch
office in Paris, had sold tens of thousands of acres of land in the Ohio country, land to which the company held no title. Several hundred French strug-
gled westward cross-country from Alexandria, Virginia, and in October 1790
settled, essentially squatted, on the right bank of the Ohio River a few miles
downstream from the mouth of the Kanawha River. The trials and tribula-
tions of Gallipolis (which did survive and still exists) cannot consume much
space in this volume, but the community does play a small role in the story of
de Lassus de Luzières—first because he bought (or thought he bought) land
from the Scioto Company in Paris in the summer of 1790 and second because
of his involvement in a scheme to move the residents of Gallipolis en masse to
Spanish Louisiana; this scheme is dealt with below.

The de Luzières's party arrived at Gallipolis on December 24, 1793, and departed January 6, 1794. Collot described the community in 1796 as containing
"ninety or ninety-five men and from forty to forty-five women, a community
formed of the wreck of the Scioto Company. The Congress granted seven
acres of land to each family, which is not sufficient for their subsistence, and
therefore they are extremely miserable."[19] Nevertheless, Madame de Luzières's
party was happy to lay over at Gallipolis for two weeks, some of the folks
(such as Madame herself) lodging in town and some remaining on the boats.
On December 25 the finer folks dined at the commandant's house, he having
been an officer in the Queen's Regiment of the French royal army, and on January 1 a huge bonfire was lit to celebrate the coming of the New Year. Despite
Collot's disparaging remarks about the misery of Gallipolis, when Madame
de Luzières's brave party pushed off the bank into the icy Ohio River in early
January they took with them a load of flour, whiskey, cider, and apples.[20]

"Louisville contains about sixty or eighty houses, built for the most part
of wood," remarked Victor Collot in 1796. Three years earlier an anonymous
observer claimed that Louisville had "very pretty houses, well-built, all located on a beautiful street and all aligned just like in Philadelphia."[21] Lou-

19. Collot, *Journey in North America*, 1:80. See *American state papers: documents, legislative and executive, of the Congress of the United States, Public Lands* (Washington, D.C.:
Gales and Seaton, 1832–1861), 1:23–24; 2:358.

20. Part 2, document no. 6.

21. Collot, *Journey in North America*, 1:149; see also below, document no. 6.

isville was smaller and less cultured than Lexington in the early 1790s, but Madame de Luzières's party was happy to spend a week there, taking advantage of the hospitality of Michel Lacassagne. Lacassagne was one of many odd and interesting characters to be found in the Ohio River valley during the late eighteenth century. French-born, he became a wealthy merchant and was one of the principal citizens of Louisville at the time. Madame de Luzières and company dined *chez* Lacassagne, and for after-dinner entertainment Derbigny and Lacassagne competed in displaying their repertories of French songs. The contrast between life on the river—coursing through the vast American wilderness with its innumerable dangers, both natural and human—and a formal dinner in Louisville with fine food, sophisticated conversation, and a French-song fest was as dramatic as any to be found on the continent of North America.

Lacassagne had no deep attachment to the American republic, and he was sympathetic to the Spanish regime in Louisiana. He was in contact with Governor Carondelet in New Orleans, and was apparently party to the wild-eyed schemes to sever Kentucky from the United States, creating an independent state allied to Spain.[22] Dinner at Lacassagne's had a spicy element of political intrigue, and he was very likely the spy at the Falls of the Ohio (i.e., Louisville) whose letter Madame de Luzières carried to the authorities in Spanish Illinois.[23] Trudeau, lieutenant governor in St. Louis, had his own spies in the area as well, and they likely made contact with Derbigny, who was charged with gathering intelligence in the Ohio Valley.[24] Georges Rogers Clark was rumored (falsely as it turned out) to be stopping and impounding all river craft on the Ohio as he prepared his much-vaunted invasion of Spanish Illinois, and Derbigny wanted to know everything possible about American dispositions in the region.

Two days (January 25–26) were required to jockey all three boats through the Falls of the Ohio, but it was carried off without a hitch; it bears repeating—the skippers of these boats were very able men indeed. Descent of the lower Ohio went quickly and more-or-less effortlessly; the weather improved, there was lots of sun, and the spirits of those on board the riverboats rose noticeably. River traffic increased greatly as they approached the Mississippi, and on several occasions our French travelers treated American boatmen and

22. See Lacassagne to Carondelet, October 1, 1794, in Lawrence Kinnaird, ed., *Spain in the Mississippi Valley, 1765–1794* (Washington, D.C.: U.S. Government Printing Office, 1949), 3:348–54; Whitaker, *Spanish-American Frontier*, 195.

23. See Louis Lorimier's letter from Cape Girardeau to Thomas Portell at New Madrid, February 16, 1794. PC, Leg. 2363.

24. Lorimier to Thomas Portell, February 16, 1794, PC, Leg. 2363.

Indians to gulps of raw whiskey, sometimes as early as 7:00 A.M. Whiskey constituted a sort of passport employed to facilitate travel down the Ohio River, and Madame de Luzières's party was generous in pouring it out when the occasion required it. François-Marie Perrin du Lac, who also traveled down the Ohio River in this early period, was impelled to discuss American use of "Wisky, which is distilled from both rye and maize. This liquor, the most disagreeable of any I've ever tasted is also the worst in its effects. The sort of drunkenness it provokes when it is taken in excess is disgusting. Grug [grog] is simply a mixture of this liquor with water. It's the people's favorite, and they consume it with abandon."[25] Fiery frontier corn liquor was only for Indians and vulgar Americans, and certainly the Frenchmen on this voyage down the Ohio River confined themselves to more refined alcoholic beverages.

Our travelers arrived at the mouth of the Ohio on February 3, 1794, turned right out of the relatively clear waters of the Ohio into the turbid waters of the Mississippi, and began the slow upstream ascent toward Ste. Genevieve. Then, unexpectedly, moving quickly downstream came a welcome sight. François Vallé and Louis Lorimier had arranged for a pirogue to descend the Mississippi, meet the de Luzières party, load the immediate family into the pirogue, and bring them up to Cape Girardeau in relatively expeditious fashion. This was the family's first experience with travel in a well-manned Mississippi-River-valley pirogue, and they would have been astonished by the strength and skill of the Creole boatmen. Vallé and Lorimier no doubt dispatched their best men (and they had the best in the Mississippi Valley) on such a mission of relief for a French aristocratic family; these men of French blood both born in North America harbored lingering loyalties to the Bourbon dynasty that de Luzières had passionately served right on into the first stages of the Revolution.[26]

At the Cape a delirious Pierre-Charles de Lassus de Luzières awaited the advent of his family, delirious with his persistent intermittent fevers as well as with happiness at being reunited with his wife, daughter, and sons after more than a year of separation. The sight of his noticeably pregnant daughter, Jeanne-Félicité, to whom he must have lent a hand as she clambered out of the pirogue onto the muddy west bank of the Mississippi River must have come nigh on to overwhelming him. De Luzières's wife, Domitille-Josèphe, at forty-nine years of age had survived the trip from Pittsburgh and would remain a resident of Upper Louisiana—under Spanish, French, and American rule—until her death in 1806, never returning to her homeland and never even visiting New Orleans.

25. *Voyage dans les deux Louisianes* (Lyon: Bruysset aîneì et Buynand, 1805), 131.
26. Vallé to Trudeau, February 14, 1794, PC, Leg. 209; Lorimier's "Journal," February 7, 1794, Houck, ed., *Spanish Regime*, 2:69.

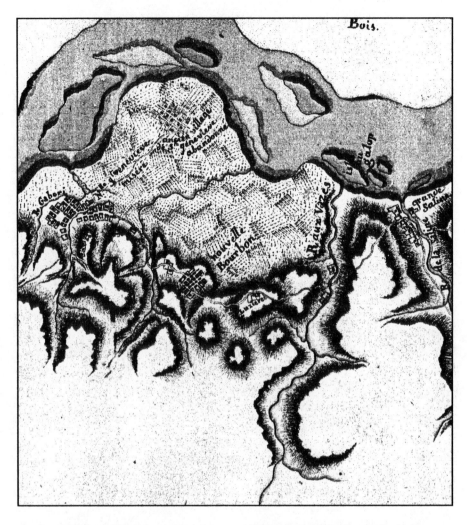

Detail of Nicolas de Finiels's superb 1797 map of Upper Louisiana. Notice de Luzières's estate just south of Nouvelle Bourbon and the cluster of houses at the "grande Saline." Reproduced courtesy of the Service historique de la Défense, Château de Vincennes, France.

On February 27, 1794, de Luzières wrote his friend and business associate, Tardiveau, who was in New Madrid working on their flour-mill project, that his family had arrived "safely and in good health, despite the fatigues of a journey that had taken nearly three months."[27] As for de Luzières himself, he had been confined to his room for three weeks with a bad cold. This letter was

27. ISHL, TP, no. 194.

dated from Ste. Genevieve, where the entire de Luzières family was apparently still enjoying the hospitality of François Vallé, likely seconded by his brother, Jean-Baptiste, who had just completed his fine new vertical-log house at the corner of La Grande Rue and Rue à l'Eglise, a house that still stands at what is now the corner of Main and Market Streets in Ste. Genevieve.

Black slaves belonging to François Vallé and Jean-Baptiste Pratte were still working on de Luzières's house at New Bourbon during the early spring of 1794,[28] and on March 15 de Luzières wrote from New Bourbon that "we're still camped out [campés], and God only knows when our thatched cottage [chaumière] will be liveable." Reading between the lines, it would appear that the de Luzières family had moved into their still-uncompleted house during the first weeks of March 1794, and that the general crudeness of the living conditions qualified them as tantamount to camping out. Furthermore, it's very unlikely (although conceivable) that the house was in fact thatched, and more likely that de Luzières was using "chaumière" as a metaphor for "rude and rural." Houses of the Illinois Country were by the late eighteenth century generally roofed with split white oak or chestnut shingles (bardeaux rather than chaume).

Providence smiled broadly on the reunion of the de Luzières family when Jeanne-Félicité happily gave birth to her second child, a "big boy," on March 31, 1794.[29] She was assisted in the delivery by one Madame La Caisse, a midwife, who was one of several French settlers from Gallipolis who did in fact migrate to Spanish Illinois, first to New Bourbon and later on to St. Louis.[30] This son, Jean-Baptiste, was officially baptized in June 1795 along with his older brother Charles-Zénon (godfather was Lieutenant Governor Zénon Trudeau), who had been born and informally baptized in the de Luzières residence outside Pittsburgh in August 1792.[31] As spring arrived in the Illinois Country in 1794, de Luzières must have been thinking that his decision to flee the Old World for the New had been, despite the extraordinary hardships that he and his family had had to endure, the correct decision after all.

28. Louis Vandenbemden to Tardiveau, March 16, 1794, ISHL, TP, no. 200; de Luzières to Tardiveau, March 15, 1794, ibid., no. 199.
29. De Luzières to Carondelet, printed below, document no. 9.
30. See Ekberg, Colonial Ste. Genevieve, 265–66.
31. Ste. Genevieve Parish Records, Baptisms 1786–1820, pp. 59–60. Microfilm available at the St. Louis County Library, Lindbergh Blvd. Branch. Lay baptisms in the absence of a priest are efficacious but usually followed up by an official baptism.

5

The Grand Enterprise Collapses

As the eighteenth century progressed, the politics of the greater Mississippi River valley became increasingly complicated, and in the decade preceding the Louisiana Purchase they were as intricate as they would ever be. In the final stages of the French and Indian War, France had cut away the albatross of Louisiana from its own neck and hung it around that of Spain (secret Treaty of Fontainebleau, November 13, 1762). The province had never paid its own way, and the Bourbon government of King Louis XV hoped that the Borbón government of King Carlos III could prevent Louisiana from falling into British hands—the worst of all possibilities from the French perspective. Spain in turn had accepted the lands of the Mississippi Valley to provide a buffer of safety for its North American territories in the Southwest.

After the American Revolution, however, Spanish officials in Upper Louisiana were feeling pressure from four quarters: American threats from right across the Mississippi River; British commercial incursions from outposts like Detroit, Michilimackinac, and Prairie du Chien, places that Great Britain had not yet relinquished to the United States; the indomitable Osages to the immediate west, who were never pacified during the colonial era; and finally Revolutionary France's aspirations, which included the irredentist impulse to repossess Louisiana. Spanish officials took all of these threats seriously, which is why the rampant rumors of a Franco-American invasion caused so much consternation in the Illinois Country during the autumn of 1793 and the early winter of 1794.

Fortifications were hurriedly begun at New Madrid, southern gateway to Spanish Illinois; a fort was built at Ste. Genevieve on the hill overlooking South Gabouri Creek; a river war galiot, La Flecha (The Arrow), was dispatched to cruise the Mississippi River between Natchez and New Madrid; and spies were posted at Vincennes on the Wabash and at the Falls of the Ohio. The Spanish colonial regime in Louisiana was fragile and ultimately would not survive, but most of the officers and administrators of this regime were serious, sober, capable men. If George Rogers Clark had ever mounted an expedition against Spanish Illinois, he would have had his hands full, for Lieutenant Governor Zénon Trudeau in St. Louis was fully capable of organizing a general defense of his colony. And at the local level, the males in the de Luzières family would have gladly manned the parapets of Ste. Genevieve's stockaded fort against a mob of Americans who were seen as uncouth and unclean, drunken and violent, Protestant and dangerous, possessing no civilized, or civilizing, virtues whatsoever. The Indians of the Ohio River valley and the white colonists (French, French Canadian, Spanish, Creole) who inhabited Upper Louisiana were of one mind when it came to Americans—the very best Americans were dead Americans.

But the much-vaunted invasion never amounted to anything more than wild rumors. American possession of the trans-Mississipian West was to be acquired through inexorable pressure generated by weight of numbers, by a veritable demographic revolution, rather than by armed conquest. French minister Genêt's agents in the Ohio River valley, Auguste la Chaise and Charles de Pauw, simply did not have the resources to gin up an invasionary army, and President Washington's government in Philadelphia was adamantly opposed to all such hare-brained schemes. Washington had made many French friends when Louis XVI's army, commanded by General Rochambeau, helped him defeat the British at Yorktown in 1781, effectively ending the American Revolution. But Washington was not at all keen about the French Revolution, and when the reserved American president finally met Genêt he thought the fiery Frenchman was a person of such levity and impetuosity that he demanded he be replaced as minister to the United States.

In the meantime, Secretary of State Thomas Jefferson wrote to Kentucky governor Isaac Shelby, warning him about the French agents and expressing hope that "the citizens of Kentucky will not be decoyed into any participation in these illegal activities." Jefferson even provided physical descriptions of La Chaise (5'5" [French measure] in height, long face, well built) and De Pauw (5'9" in height, a bit blond, pale faced), for whom Shelby was to be on the lookout should they gain any traction in raising an American army to invade Spanish Louisiana.[1] Jefferson used even stronger language face to face with

1. See Jefferson's letter in Thomas D. Clark, ed., *The Voice of the Frontier: John Bradford's Notes on Kentucky* (Lexington: University Press of Kentucky, 1993), 275–76.

Genêt, telling him that any Kentuckians who committed hostilities against Spain, "a nation at peace with the U.S., would assuredly be hung."[2]

But even as Jefferson wrote the Clark-Genêt threat was fast evaporating. By the end of January 1794, Lieutenant Governor Trudeau in St. Louis could confidently report that his spies in Vincennes and at the Falls were assuring him that the American frontier was not mobilizing to attack Louisiana. Indeed, the "Long-Knives" in Kentucky and the Ohio Country continued to be preoccupied with Indians until after the Battle of Fallen Timbers in August 1794. Then, in mid-February, Madame de Luzières and her entourage arrived at Ste. Genevieve, and Pierre Derbigny, the madame's son-in-law, resoundingly confirmed the spies' reports. Throughout his trip from Pittsburgh (December 1793 to February 1794) he had been on the lookout for signs that an invasionary force was gathering in the Ohio Valley, for it was in that eastern gateway to the Illinois Country where, indubitably, it must have gathered. Derbigny had seen nothing, absolutely nothing, to suggest that Clark's army was coalescing. By the end of February 1794 the scare in Spanish Illinois had dissipated as quickly as early morning mist over the Mississippi River. In St. Louis Trudeau relaxed a bit and pulled in his spies, while at Ste. Genevieve the fort, a curious artifact of the convoluted history of the Mississippi frontier, was abandoned forever, becoming a forlorn reminder of the Spanish colonial presence in the area.[3]

The three French nuns of the Order of St. Clare, who had been part of Madame de Luzières's entourage on her trip down the Ohio River from Pittsburgh during the winter of 1793–1794 (see Part 2, document no. 6), arrived in Ste. Genevieve belatedly and in bad humor—and things did not improve during their brief sojourn in Spanish Illinois. They had been confined to their smallish *bateau* (relative to Madame's grand vessel), and they had not enjoyed the exhilarating pirogue trip up the Mississippi from the mouth of the Ohio to Ste. Genevieve—this had been reserved for immediate members of the de Luzières family. These were not minor insults in view of the fact that two of the sacred sisters came from ancient and renowned French aristocratic families—La Marche and La Rochefoucauld.

A month after the nuns arrived in Ste. Genevieve, de Luzières enthused that they were "truly beyond any praise I could render them. . . . Our commandant,

2. Jefferson's minute of his conversation with Genêt in *Annual Report of the American Historical Association for the Year 1896* (Washington, D.C.: U.S. Government Printing Office, 1897), 1:985.

3. Part 2, document no. 7. Concerning Derbigny's reconnaissance in the Ohio Valley, see also François Vallé to Trudeau, February 14, 1794, PC, Leg. 209. The archeological remains of this fort off the north side of Seraphin Street on the hill overlooking South Gabouri Creek in present-day Ste. Genevieve represent a time capsule waiting to be opened.

Monsieur [François] Vallé, is making every effort to find them provisional board and room, and all the residents are terribly eager to get them settled here."[4] Vallé himself found the nuns "very decent and enlightened," and that they could be a "precious asset for the colony."[5] The genteel ladies, it seems, were a bit less pleased with Ste. Genevieve than Ste. Genevieve was with them, for within a matter of weeks they had decamped for St. Louis. Lieutenant Governor Trudeau was at first just as taken with them as de Luzières had been and decided that they should remain in St. Louis. De Luzières had apparently already seen enough of the nuns and wrote disingenuously to Governor Carondelet that "despite the eagerness that I and my entire family have to live in close proximity to these estimable persons, I cannot but agree with Monsieur Trudeau."[6] Carondelet, however, for his own reasons, wanted to establish the nuns in the Ursuline Convent in New Orleans and suggested that the nuns be sent down river;[7] the governor perhaps wanted an infusion of fresh French blood into this venerable but flagging institution.[8]

The nuns were soon back in Ste. Genevieve from St. Louis preparing to depart for New Orleans, and de Luzières felt obliged to provide Carondelet with a confidential warning about their respective personalities: "Dame Chevalier seems to have maintained the principles of a truly religious woman, and she will surely be happy in the Ursuline Convent. The same might be said about Madame de la Marche if she would stop letting herself be directed and governed by Madame La Blond [de la Rochefoucauld]. As for this last one, it would be difficult to find a person more gossipy and indiscreet, more autocratic and stubborn. . . . I repeat, Monsieur le Baron, what I'm saying here is confidential."[9]

The grandiose commercial plan of de Luzières and his business associates, Audrain and Tardiveau, was three-legged—bring the French settlers at Gallipolis en masse to Spanish Illinois; build large, water-driven mills for both flour and lumber at New Madrid and Ste. Genevieve; and corner the grain and flour trade in the Ohio and Mississippi River valleys. This grandiose plan, they hoped, would make them rich. But because it would also buttress and preserve the Spanish colonial regime in Louisiana they would acquire political power as well.

4. De Luzières to Carondelet, March 15, 1794, PC, Leg. 210.

5. Vallé to Trudeau, February 24, 1794, PC, Leg. 209.

6. De Luzières to Carondelet, April 6, 1794, PC, Leg. 208A.

7. Carondelet to Trudeau, May 16, 1794, PC, Leg. 21.

8. See Emily Clark, *Masterless Mistresses: The New Orleans Ursulines and the Development of a New World Society, 1727–1834* (Chapel Hill: University of North Carolina Press, 2007). Curiously enough, no record apparently exists indicating that these nuns ever entered the convent in New Orleans (personal communication, Emily Clark).

9. De Luzières to Carondelet, September 1, 1794, PC, Leg. 210.

The first component of the plan to collapse was the Gallipolis initiative, the plan to move that francophone settlement, like a piece on a chessboard, from the Ohio River valley to the Mississippi River valley. When Pierre Audrain returned to Pittsburgh from New Orleans in the late spring of 1793, he was supposed to take the lead in recruiting the Gallipolitans. But no evidence exists that he ever traveled down the Ohio to Gallipolis from Pittsburgh to attempt to effect this recruitment. On December 16, 1793, Audrain wrote a bit cryptically to Tardiveau, his friend and associate, that "our Mister V. will give you a report on the Gallipolis affair, and I won't get into any of its details. What you've told me about it certainly does seem extraordinary."[10] "Mister V." was surely Louis Vandenbemden, a Flemish engineer who had settled at Gallipolis in 1790, and at the time Audrain wrote to Tardiveau was about to depart for the Illinois Country to enter the employ of the Spanish government. During the 1790s Vandenbemden worked as an engineer throughout Spanish Illinois (on a fort at Ste. Genevieve, on the circumferential fortifications at St. Louis, and on the flour mill at New Madrid).[11]

But the news that Vandenbemden carried down the Ohio River during the winter of 1793–1794 had nothing to do with mundane engineering work; it was hotly political. French minister Genêt's agents were in the Ohio River valley working to persuade the Gallipolitans to sign on for the proposed Clark attack on Spanish Illinois. La Chaise and De Pauw were telling the French settlers at Gallipolis that if they supported the Clark-Genêt invasion plan vast quantities of trans-Mississippian lands would be theirs for the having. Once Vandenbemden arrived in Ste. Genevieve from Gallipolis (sometime during the late winter or early spring of 1794) he sat down and discussed this issue with de Luzières. The latter then wrote to Governor Carondelet that La Chaise and De Pauw had met with no success at Gallipolis, that the French settlers there, who had fled the French Revolution, would have nothing to do with the hare-brained scheme being promoted by a French Revolutionary operative, namely Genêt. Some Gallipolitans had already moved to Spanish Illinois as de Luzières insisted (indeed, at least two had, Madame La Caisse, the midwife, and Vandenbemden himself), and that more would follow when the coast was clear, when the invasion scare had evaporated.[12]

10. ISHL, TP, no. 191.
11. See Nasatir, ed., *Spanish War Vessels*, 96, 225, 293–94, 335; Finiels, *Account of Upper Louisiana*, 3, 4, 60–61. Jocelyne Moreau-Zanelli (*Gallipolis*, 271) claims that Vandenbemden sailed from Le Havre on the same ship as de Luzières, *Citoyens de Paris*, which seems entirely plausible. Vandenbemden and his wife appear on the 1797 Spanish census of New Madrid as small-time farmers owning four slaves (Houck, ed., *Spanish Regime*, 2: 393).
12. De Luzières to Carondelet, April 6, 1794, PC, Leg. 208A.

De Luzières, however, told a rather different story when he wrote to Tardiveau the same week he wrote to Carondelet.[13] De Luzières complained that the solicitous letters he had addressed to the citizens of Gallipolis, and most especially to Sieur Le Moine, the surgeon whom he desperately hoped to recruit for New Bourbon, had never been delivered. De Luzières's proposals had been distorted in the minds of the Gallipolitans, his intentions had been nefariously perverted. The French settlers on the Ohio had been told that de Luzières had in effect sold them to Spain for his own profit. This charge did contain a kernel of truth because some of Carondelet's 2,500-piastre subvention for the immigration project had indeed been paid out to de Luzières for his expenses in promoting it. The French aristocrat was scandalized that his motives had been impugned and his honor sullied, and he had a good idea who had done it (la Chaise and de Pauw). Addressing Tardiveau directly, de Luzières wrote "this, my good friend, is a new embarrassment that I wish to bury secretly in the bosom of our friendship." That is, please, please don't tell Carondelet. Whether or not the Gallipolitans believed the worst about de Luzières's motives will never be known, but in any case the machinations of la Chaise and de Pauw worked well enough to preclude any mass immigration from the Ohio Valley to Spanish Illinois.

And Audrain, upon whom de Luzières had so much depended when he arrived in Pittsburgh as a greenhorn in 1791, was proving unreliable—or possibly even worse. Reports reached Carondelet in New Orleans that Audrain was a vile republican at heart, that he had even hosted parties at his home in Pittsburgh where toasts were raised to the French and American republics.[14] When de Luzières heard these rumors he acknowledged to Tardiveau that Audrain's "fickleness, vanity, and egotism" were well known, but de Luzières really couldn't believe that Audrain was capable of the "baseness and knavery" of which he had been accused.[15] The fact of the matter was that Audrain was an honest participant in the grand plans that had been laid to make money from the grain trade in partnership with the Spanish colonial regime. But he had absolutely no ideological interest in propping up an old-fashioned monarchical regime in Louisiana, which was a cause into which de Luzières was pouring his heart and soul. When the possibility of turning a handsome profit disappeared, so did Audrain, who slipped off to become a U.S. Government clerk in Detroit after the British turned that outpost over to the Americans

---

13. De Luzières to Tardiveau, April 3, 1794, ISHL, TP, no. 125.

14. Howard C. Rice, *Barthélemi Tardiveau*, 46; "Correspondence of George Rogers Clark and Edmond Genêt," *Annual Report of the American Historical Association for the year 1896* (Washington, D.C.: U.S. Government Printing Office, 1897), 1096.

15. De Luzières to Tardiveau, June 11, 1794, ISHL, TP, no. 216.

in 1796.[16] His knowledge of both French and English was essential in a community whose population remained overwhelming French Canadian. De Luzières dryly noted in February 1797 that "it's reported from Vincennes that our former associate, Audrain, has been appointed clerk in Detroit."[17] In any case, the Gallipolis initiative was effectively dead by the spring of 1794, although de Luzières preferred that Carondelet not know it immediately.

In a postscript to his letter to Tardiveau, de Luzières discussed issues that affected his quotidian existence in his new house at New Bourbon: One of the crates that Tardiveau had forwarded upriver to him from New Madrid contained bottles of refined honey, rather than the (olive?) oil and orange syrup that de Luzières had ordered; furthermore, he still had not received a "case of wine with the long corks," that is to say, the good stuff, the high-quality clarets from Bordeaux.[18] Life on the trans-Mississippian frontier could have been worse.

But not much. All through 1794, de Luzières's letters are loaded with descriptions of various illnesses, mostly malarial fevers, but also diarrhea and upper respiratory infections.[19] In April he positively believed that he was dying and set about putting his "spiritual affairs in order."[20] In June his youngest son (Camille) had been ill for five days, and his three *engagés* had had three degrees of fever for fifteen days. The only person able to help out with the bedridden and the two grandchildren was the family's only black slave, a female.[21]

In July de Luzières himself was finally feeling better, but his house had "metamorphosed into a hospital," Madame de Luzières was struck down with a fever for twelve days, and Camille and all the engagés were still ill.[22] In September (a bad malaria time) de Luzières claimed that out of his household (i.e., family members, engagés, and the one black slave) of twelve persons eleven had been laid low with "violent and persistent fevers."[23] These persons included de Luzières himself, his wife, his son Camille, son-in-law Pierre

16. Great Britain relinquished the Northwest fur trading outposts to the United States as prescribed in Jay's Treaty (November 19, 1794). See J. Leitch Wright Jr., *Britain and the American Froniter, 1783–1815* (Athens: University of Georgia Press, 1975), 95–99.

17. De Luzières to Tardiveau, February 2, 1797, ISHL, TP, no. 335. Concerning Audrain's life in Detroit, see Warren J. Wolfe, "The First American Citizen of Detroit: Pierre Audrain, 1725–1820," in *Detroit in Perspective* (Winter 1981): 45–47.

18. De Luzières to Tardiveau, April 3 and 4, 1794, ISHL, TP, no. 204.

19. Concerning malaria in Spanish Illinois, see Ekberg, *Colonial Ste. Genevieve*, chap. 8.

20. De Luzières to Tardiveau, April ?, 1794, ISHL, TP, no. 206.

21. The sickle cell gene, which is much more common in Africans than Europeans, provides some protection against malaria.

22. De Luzières to Tardiveau, July 9, 1794, ISHL, TP, no. 223.

23. De Luzières to Tardiveau, September 1, 1794, ibid., no. 234.

Derbigny, two engagés (the third?), and this time even the female black slave, despite the fact that Africans resisted the malarial parasite better than whites. De Luzières either forgot to mention his daughter, Jeanne-Félicité or conceivably she somehow was the one member of the family who escaped the malarial plague. With two children under the age of two years, plus the ill adults in the household, Jeanne would have had her hands full functioning as medical nurse, as well as nursing mother. And she didn't have much to work with. According to her father the family was holed up in their house at New Bourbon "without care, without succor, without appropriate food, and without medications; you [Tardiveau] can not possibly imagine a similar situation."[24]

Given these dire conditions, all hope of building a water mill in the New Bourbon–Ste. Genevieve area was abandoned. Rather, all resources, human and material, would be thrown at the mill project in New Madrid. Tardiveau was already in residence there,[25] and in the autumn of 1794 he was joined by Vandenbemden and Derbigny, the former as engineer and the latter as organizer. The New Madrid project was already a year behind schedule. During the autumn of 1793 and early winter of 1794, the area's resources had been requisitioned for preparing the defenses of Upper Louisiana against the anticipated George Rogers Clark assault. As Tardiveau explained, in his arch, ironic prose, to Governor Carondelet: "The measures required to defend the colony against our enemies have dictated to the commandant of this post [Thomas Portell] the imperious law to use all manpower available, thus taking from me all the workers whom I had brought here for the construction of our mills. Since this sacrifice was necessary for the public good, I accepted it with joy."[26] Tardiveau's Gallic irony often slid across the line into biting sarcasm, which likely did not endear him to Spanish officials, Carondelet included.

And then, of course, the issue of gudgeons arose, an absolutely essential issue, for which subject we must digress a bit from our story in order to delve briefly into the technology of eighteenth-century water mills. A gudgeon was the cross-shaped metal component that fitted into the slots on the upper stone of gristmills and was attached to the lower end of the vertical shaft that carried the power to the mill head; a gudgeon was a component of a mill that had to be made of cast iron, for it was required to absorb the full torque of the turning shaft as it engaged the top millstone.

24. Ibid.
25. Tardiveau appears on the 1797 Spanish census of New Madrid (Houck, ed., *Spanish Regime*, 2:393) as a small-time agriculturalist, unmarried, owning two slaves.
26. Tardiveau to Carondelet, January 27, 1794, ISHL, TP, no. 183. On Portell's career in the Spanish army, see Nasatir, ed., *Spanish War Vessels*, 56 n. 65, as well as Jack D. L. Holmes, ed., *Honor and Fidelity*, 164.

It was noted above that a member of Madame de Luzières's entourage that accompanied her down the Ohio River during the winter of 1793–1794 was a millwright named Henry Green. Before leaving Pittsburgh in December 1793, Green, a meticulous technician, had left in Audrain's hands wooden models of the gudgeons to be forged in cast iron at Pittsburgh before being sent on out to Spanish Illinois; the technology to do this forging simply did not exist in Upper Louisiana. Audrain wrote to Tardiveau in March 1794 that "I've finally received the millstones and am sending them to you in good order, along with some pieces of iron; we're still missing what are called gudgeons in English [Audrain apparently was not familiar with the French word, *goujon*, from which the English word obviously derives] . . . I was going to have them made at Messieur Belen's forge, but because his furnace is not yet fired up I sent the models over to Cumberland County to have them made there."[27] It must be noted that Cumberland County lies westward from Pittsburgh, half-way across Pennsylvania. Three months later, Audrain wrote, "with mounting vexation," that he had still not received the cast-iron gudgeons from Cumberland County,[28] and it's not known whether in fact he ever did receive them. This little episode reveals how devilishly difficult it was in the late eighteenth century to assemble on-site in Spanish Illinois the components necessary to build a state-of-the-art water mill, and this of course compounded the mounting frustrations of de Luzières and his associates.

With de Luzières's blessing, Tardiveau decided that he had better head down the Mississippi to New Orleans, get some flour and hardtack[29] delivered in accord with the associates' contractual obligations to the Spanish government, explain the difficulties of the situation to their benefactor, Governor Carondelet, take ship to Philadelphia, cross overland to Pittsburgh, jack up Audrain, and finally complete what was becoming a well-traveled circuit by descending the rivers to New Madrid to work on the mills. Tardiveau departed New Madrid the last week in July 1794 in a *chaland* (a flat-bottomed, keelless cargo vessel) loaded with hardtack and flour destined for the Spanish garrison in New Orleans. Audrain wrote Tardiveau on June 6 that "I'm sending you a superb bateau containing hardtack, flour, and whiskey."[30] These products had come from the valley of the Monongahela, southeast of Pittsburgh, for it was there that bountiful harvests of grain, both wheat and maize, brought forth these necessities of frontier life. It's worth noting, incidentally, that it was in

27. Audrain to Tardiveau, March 15, 1794, ISHL, TP, no. 198.
28. Audrain to Tardiveau, June 6, 1794, ibid., no, 214.
29. "Hardtack" seems an appropriate translation for the French "biscuit" in this context. One might also use "ship's biscuit."
30. ISHL, TP, no. 214.

the summer of 1794 that the Whiskey Rebellion broke out in the Mononga-hela Valley.[31] Tardiveau loaded only the hardtack and flour on his *chaland* at New Madrid, for the soldiers at the Spanish garrison there were delighted to assure a happy fate for the corn liquor.

Disaster overtook Tardiveau's expedition near the mouth of the St. François (now the St. Francis) River, where Helena, Arkansas, stands today. A ferocious summer storm had blown up, and Tardiveau had had his crew tie up the chaland in a protected cove. An hour before daybreak on July 30, Tardiveau awoke to find the boat swamping. When he pulled back his buffalo robe and crawled out of bed, he found himself ankle-deep in water. No exact cause for the disaster was ever determined, but Tardiveau speculated that the vessel, rocking in the wind, had been breached by an undetected snag beneath it.[32] He roused the rest of the crew, which worked desperately to save the cargo. They managed to salvage most of the hardtack and all of the flour, but within half an hour the boat had filled with water and was lost for good.[33]

Tardiveau dug deep into his substantial store of resourcefulness, managed to hire another *bateau,* get the salvaged cargo loaded, and proceed on down to New Orleans. Back upriver in New Bourbon, however, de Luzières had picked up some news that unsettled him enough to comment on it. He had received no letters from Tardiveau but he had heard from one Sieur Grenon, who had recently seen Tardiveau in Natchez, that the latter did not appear to be in good health.[34] Indeed, Tardiveau was slowly dying of syphilis, for which there was no cure in the eighteenth century. As he explained from New Orleans (see Part 2, document no. 12) he was using mercury, the traditional treatment for syphilis, but the mercury itself was devastating him. Tardiveau never did complete the circuit (round about to Pittsburgh and then back to New Madrid) as planned, but remained in New Orleans for more than two years. Perhaps he found a physician there who, with careful, prudent use of mercury, prolonged his life, for he survived until 1801, dying at age fifty-one.[35]

31. See Thomas Paul Slaughter, *The Whiskey Rebellion: Frontier Epilogue to the American Revolution* (New York: Oxford University Press, 1988).

32. De Luzières in New Bourbon heard that the unfortunate incident had been caused by a careless crew member (De Luzières to Tardiveau, October 1, 1794, ISHL, TP, no. 242.

33. Tardiveau to Monsieur (Vandenbemden?), August 7, 1794, ibid., no. 230.

34. De Luzières to Tardiveau, November 22, 1794, ibid., no. 256.

35. Mercury as a heavy metal is of course toxic, but it was used by responsible physicians for treating syphilis right into the early twentieth century, see William Allen Pusey, *The principles and practice of dermatology, designed for students and practitioners, by . . . with fifty-four plates and four hundred and sixty-six text illustrations* (New York and London: D. Appleton and Co., 1917), 680–90.

With Tardiveau laid up in New Orleans, Vandenbemden made a valiant effort to take over direction of the mill-building project in New Madrid, but he
was almost immediately struck down with malarial fevers and confined to his
bed for six weeks. The workers weren't making much progress, but they were
of course nevertheless consuming provisions. Vandenbemden considered that
it would be best to acquire some black slaves, "at least eight, a blacksmith and
either a wheelwright or a mason, plus six *bruts*." *Brut* meant untrained Africans, in a natural state, just as brut champagne is natural, unmodified, with
nothing added—sugar in the case of champagne, training in the case of slaves.
Believing that Tardiveau was going to return to New Madrid via Pittsburgh,
Vandenbemden urged him to buy a set of millstones there, as well as the tools
for the black blacksmith.[36] A week later, still recovering from his debilitating
fevers, Vandenbemden added supplies he had forgotten to enumerate in his
first missive: "a strong chain, a cable of fifteen ligues [*sic*] diameter, a good
wagon, and complete harnesses for two horses."[37] The extensive correspondence regarding the fitting-out of water mills reveals just how destitute of
basic materials and skills the Illinois Country was in the late colonial period.
Vandenbemden's correspondence, predictably, came to naught, for Tardiveau
never sailed to Pittsburgh from New Orleans, where he was holed up nursing
his syphilis.

De Luzières customarily referred to himself and his business associates as
"Our Enterprise [Notre Société]," and it was becoming evident by the spring
of 1795 that this enterprise was in free-fall toward total collapse. Early in the
year they lost to the multitudinous and random hazards of the Mississippi River
yet another chaland headed for New Orleans with a precious load of flour and
hardtack. De Luzières found this news "la plus affligeante," the most distress-
ing.[38] Back home in his native province of Hainault, de Luzières had served
as financial manager for the provincial governing assembly, and he doubtless
considered himself a man of the utmost probity and the best judgment when
it came to money matters. The unraveling of his financial initiatives in Louisiana caused him severe psychological as well as financial distress.

A French aristocrat with a keen sense of honor and responsibility, Governor
Carondelet continued to insist that his decision to back the plans of de Luzières, Tardiveau, and Audrain was fundamentally sound and had served the
best interests of the Spanish regime in Louisiana. "The hazards of war; the expedition projected by the French for attacking Louisiana by way of the Ohio;

36. Vandenbemden to Tardiveau, November 1, 1794, ISHL, TP, no. 251.
37. Same to same, November 6, 1794, ibid., no. 254.
38. De Luzières to Tardiveau, March 20, 1795, ibid., no. 289.

the opposition and hindrances that the Kentuckians have thrown up"[39] were all unforeseen contingencies that had thwarted the grand plans laid down at New Orleans in the spring of 1793. Nevertheless, all was not lost. Carondelet argued that the gristmill at New Madrid was up and running, and that it could be expected to produce three thousand barrels of flour for the Spanish garrison in New Orleans during the year 1795. Even if this expectation of flour production was fulfilled (unlikely),[40] this modest success was not good enough to provide de Luzières's "Society" with funds to reimburse the monies fronted by the Spanish crown. Jean-Baptiste Sarpy, guarantor of the loan, was forced to pay up in the spring of 1796,[41] and de Luzières and Tardiveau remained in debt to this New Orleans merchant for much of the remainder of their lives.

De Luzières's hope that the Spanish monarchy would invest further in his commercial schemes was utterly unrealistic, though he clung to these hopes for several years. Once the Treaty of San Lorenzo, or Pinckney's Treaty (October 27, 1795), gave American farmers and merchants the right to transport their products on the Mississippi and unload them at New Orleans,[42] flour coming down out of the Ohio River valley on American flatboats largely solved subsistence problems in Louisiana's metropole. The Spanish colonial regime therefore no longer had reason to inject government resources in rather far-fetched proposals to increase the flour trade.

39. Carondelet to Francisco Rendon, August 27, 1795, Houck, ed., *Spanish Regime*, 2:405–8.

40. On July 16, 1798, Tardiveau wrote de Luzières that 600 piastres would be required to get the mills (apparently one for flour and for lumber) at New Madrid up and running, and that he had no idea where the funds might come from (ISHL, TP, no. 359).

41. Ibid., no. 408.

42. See Arthur Preston Whitaker, *The Spanish-American Frontier: 1783–1795* (repr., Gloucester, Mass.: Peter Smith, 1962), 200–222.

6

Americans Recruited

His grandiose commercial schemes in utter disarray, de Luzières reoriented his efforts. Beginning in early 1796, he threw himself into the task of recruiting colonists for Spanish Illinois. This initiative he hoped, correctly as it turned out, would gain him favor with Spanish officialdom and redound to his own political benefit. The development of a productive population in Louisiana had been a preoccupation of officials in New Orleans, both French and Spanish, since the province's earliest days. De Luzières himself had been encouraging settlement at New Bourbon since 1793, and he had had some success. General Collot reported in 1795 that "two miles to the south-east of St. Geneviève, on the height, is an increasing settlement, called Lusières."[1] But the issue of increasing Louisiana's population took on urgency as American settlements marched down the Ohio River valley during the later 1790s. These flourishing settlements provided concrete evidence for all to see that the Spanish colonial regime might be swamped, not by military force but by a demographic tidal wave.

One alternative was to induce Americans themselves to settle in Louisiana, hoping to turn them into loyal Spanish subjects. This possibility, however, aroused deep anxieties in Spanish administrators, not least because of religious considerations. Protestants had been prohibited from settling in Louisiana by the French Black Code, and the interim Spanish governor, General Alejandro O'Reilly (1769–1770), wished to adhere to this prohibition. His instructions for the governance of Upper Louisiana specified that any immigrant wishing to settle in the territory had to obtain written permission from

1. *Journey in North America*, 1:253–54.

the governor general in New Orleans.[2] Such a draconian restriction could hardly have been enforced, but in any case it reveals O'Reilly's intention of maintaining a safe population in Louisiana.

Under Governor Esteban Miró (1784–1791) religious policy in the province, which bore directly on the issue of American immigration, was liberalized. Protestant churches, worship, and preachers remained outlawed, but immigrants were not *compelled* to become communicants in the Roman Catholic Church.[3] At l'Anse à la Graisse (soon to be New Madrid) in November 1789 fourteen Americans swore allegiance on the Holy Gospels to "His Catholic Majesty," the king of Spain, but the text of the loyalty oath contained no prescriptions about religious practice.[4] A sort of de facto liberty of conscience therefore prevailed in Upper Louisiana during Miró's tenure as governor, and during the final years of his regime many Americans settled in Ste. Genevieve's environs if not in the nuclear village itself.

The issue of American immigration to Louisiana trapped Spanish colonial officials in a serious dilemma, however: increase the colony's population or lose it to hostile invasion and internal atrophy; but populate the colony with Americans (most of whom were Protestant) and lose it to cultural submersion or political and religious subversion. From the Spanish point of view it was therefore best to encourage immigrants of Roman Catholic European stock to settle in Louisiana; this, of course, had been the basis for de Luzières's Gallipolis initiative.

Henri Peyroux de la Coudrenière, French born and raised, was commandant of Ste. Genevieve from 1787 to 1794, but before he arrived in Upper Louisiana he had been active recruiting dispossessed Acadians to settle in Spanish Louisiana. An enterprising fellow, he traveled to Philadelphia (via New Orleans going, and Pittsburgh returning) in 1792–1793 in the hope of persuading refugees from the French Revolution living there to resettle in Louisiana. In the U.S. capital he met, among others, Thomas Jefferson, who was serving as President Washington's secretary of state at the time. In any case, those few Frenchmen whom he did manage to recruit for settlement in Louisiana did not please Governor Carondelet, who wrote with palpable scorn: "Of all the settlers you've sent me, very few are appropriate for bolstering the population

2. Louis Houck, ed., *The Spanish Regime in Missouri; a collection of papers and documents relating to upper Louisiana principally within the present limits of Missouri during the dominion of Spain, from the Archives of the Indies at Seville, etc.,* translated from the original Spanish into English, 2 vols. (Chicago: R. R. Donnelley & Sons Company, 1909), 1:82.

3. Concerning Miró's policies as governor, see Caroline Maude Burson, *The Stewardship of Don Esteban Miró* (New Orleans: American Printing Company, 1940).

4. Houck, ed., *Spanish Regime,* 1:319.

of this colony, which needs farmers and useful laborers rather than actors, wigmakers, musicians, and so forth, who are for the most part persons of bad morals."[5]

Immigration was on everyone's mind in 1793, and in August Jacques Clamorgan, a thoughtful trader from St. Louis, penned a searching memorandum concerning Louisiana and its population.[6] His basic argument was that the colony desperately needed people, especially agriculturists, in proportion to its vast area. Clamorgan advocated recruitment of immigrants of continental European stock, especially German farmers. Those who had settled at the famous Côte des Allemands (German Coast) on the right bank of the Mississippi River in Lower Louisiana in 1721 had proven exemplary colonists. Above all, Clamorgan did not want Louisiana populated with Americans, for he correctly foresaw that demographic changes inevitably precipitate political changes—a Louisiana populated with Americans would eventually be absorbed by the United States, which had vaulted westward to the Mississippi River as a consequence of the American Revolution. Carondelet replied, noting that he agreed with the thrust of Clamorgan's arguments and emphasizing that "true wealth is to be found only in agriculture, and this requires a competent population."[7]

Since becoming governor general of Louisiana in 1792, Carondelet had had profound reservations about permitting Anglo-Americans to settle in the colony. When a group of Americans settled on the upper Meramac River (today the Big River) west of Ste. Genevieve, Carondelet ordered Lieutenant Governor Trudeau to roust them before they seized any land, even suggesting—remarkably—that if necessary he might call in some Indians to harass the Americans.[8] Carondelet was more concerned with the cultural and ensuing political consequences than with religious principles. In his September 1792 letter to Tardiveau the governor advocated recruiting Western Europeans of many stripes (Frenchmen and Germans, Dutchmen and Flemings) rather than Americans, and he was prepared to grant them total liberty of conscience—although

5. Carondelet to Peyroux, September 24, 1792, Papeles de Cuba, legajo 205, Archivo General de Indies, Seville (henceforth this collection will be cited simply as PC [Papeles de Cuba] followed by the legajo number).
6. Clamorgan to Carondelet, October 4, 1793, Lawrence Kinnaird, ed., *Spain in the Mississippi Valley, 1765–1794* (Washington, D.C.: U.S. Government Printing Office, 1949), 3:208–11; on Clamorgan's life and career in Upper Louisiana, see Abraham P. Nasatir, ed., *Before Lewis and Clark: Documents Illustrating the History of the Missouri, 1785–1804*, 2 vols. passim.
7. Carondelet to Clamorgan, July 22, 1794, *American state papers: documents, legislative and executive, of the Congress of the United States, Public Lands* (Washington, D.C.: Gales and Seaton, 1832–1861), 8:234.
8. Carondelet to Trudeau, June 8, 1792, PC, Leg. 18.

of course no right to public worship ["culte extérieur et public"].[9] Protestants from Europe were preferable to Americans as long as they kept their religious ideas to themselves. When Carondelet drafted his military report on the state of Louisiana's defenses in November 1794, he reiterated his objections to Americans, "a new and vigorous people, hostile to all subjection, advancing and multiplying . . . with prodigious rapidity."[10]

But Carondelet's hope of blocking the advance of the swarming Americans was in effect dashed by the Spanish government, for San Lorenzo, the treaty that gave American boatmen unfettered access to the Mississippi River and the docks of New Orleans, was in effect an acknowledgment that Americans could not be kept out of Louisiana.[11] Spanish officials knew that they were caught on the horns of a very painful dilemma: Promote the development of a vigorous population in Louisiana or the colony could not be sustained, but generate this population with subversive Americans and the colony would be undercut from within. The Spanish royal government chose to gamble, and, according to Thomas Jefferson, Spaniards who "had once seen the folly of settling Goths at the gates of Rome,"[12] began to encourage Americans to settle in Louisiana by granting them large land concessions; that is, a policy evolved between 1795 and 1797 that was intended to seduce Americans with generosity, purchasing their loyalty with free land and liberty of conscience, if not necessarily of worship.

In the long run giving Americans free run of the Mississippi River valley only accelerated "the occupation of the great Mississippi valley by men of English speech, [which] was the most momentous event in the history of the United States and one of the most momentous in the history of humanity."[13] On April 2, 1796, Trudeau wrote Carondelet from St. Louis that "during the past six weeks some American families have arrived to settle on our side of the river. Some Frenchmen have come as well. The latter are settling at St. Charles on the Missouri, while the Americans . . . are developing isolated farmsteads."[14]

De Luzières was positioned right at the vortex of these swirling demographic and political developments. From his residence he could virtually see the bobbing heads on the hordes of Americans marching westward through the greater

9. ISHS, TP, no. 153.
10. Carondelet, "Military Report," in *Louisiana under the rule of Spain, France, and the United States, 1785–1807: social, economic, and political conditions of the territory represented in the Louisiana purchase,* ed. James Alexander Robertson, 2 vols. (Cleveland: Arthur H. Clark Co., 1911), 1:297.
11. See Whitaker, *The Spanish-American Frontier,* 200–222.
12. Jefferson quoted in ibid., 103.
13. Alvord, *Illinois Country,* 414.
14. PC, Leg. 212A.

Ohio River valley. No one in Spanish Louisiana was better positioned to witness the events that were transforming the Mississippi Valley and shaping the history of the North American continent. And de Luzières was himself part of the story. He persuaded himself that he could recruit safe Americans, those who would remain loyal to the Spanish regime in Louisiana and would not sabotage his beloved system of benevolent monarchical government. His truculent words, "I continue to aver that I will live and die more attached than ever to the authority of kings and to the countries they rule,"[15] were no doubt heartfelt.

In May 1796, de Luzières sat down in his office, the view from which swept eastward across the Mississippi, extending deep into American territory, and wrote an eight-page recruiting pamphlet (see Part 2, document no. 17), *An Official Account of the Situation, Soil, Produce, &c. of that Part of Louisiana which lies between the Mouth of the Missouri and New Madrid."* De Luzières's pamphlet is a unique and altogether remarkable document, and it forcefully demonstrates that by the spring of 1796 Spanish authorities, most especially Governor Carondelet, had finally come round to the view that the best means of increasing Louisiana's population with stalwart agriculturists was to invite in the Americans from the Ohio River valley. De Luzières extolled the virtues of Spanish Illinois—healthy climate, oodles of rich, free land, no taxes whatsoever, convenient waterways for commerce and communication, and no lawyers to swindle honest settlers with their "chicanery."[16] This last point was no doubt music to the ears of many frontiersmen, including Daniel Boone and his son, Daniel Morgan Boone, for the Boones' problems with lawyers in Kentucky helped drive them westward into Spanish Illinois a few years later. Indeed, it's not much of a stretch to speculate that the Boones read and were influenced by de Luzières's pamphlet.

Religion was a major sticking point when it came to admitting Americans to Spanish Illinois, for after all, the title of the Spanish king was "His Most Catholic Majesty." This makes the precise language regarding religion employed by de Luzières—or at least the individual who translated his pamphlet—that much more significant: "In the Illinois country, as in all Louisiana, the greatest and most reasonable liberty of conscience *and action is allowed, and every one may go and come and do,* without any obstacle or contradiction, whatever is not injurious to the king's interest, or that of any one else."[17] This language

15. De Luzières to Carondelet, August 1, 1796, PC, Leg. 212A.

16. Lawyers (barristers), as opposed to notaries, were forbidden in Louisiana under both the French and Spanish regimes. Legal cases were handled administratively rather than through an adversarial process.

17. Document no. 17, printed below, Part 2. My italics. I have not been able to find de Luzières's original French version of this pamphlet, which would be interesting to compare with the English version. And the translator remains unknown.

could certainly be construed as permissive of public worship, indeed, even for permission to erect Protestant churches. This of course was never done during the colonial era in Louisiana, but, nevertheless, de Luzières's pamphlet presents the most liberal position on religious toleration ever to appear in the province before the Louisiana Purchase. Both de Luzières, and most especially Carondelet, were worried about this liberality. Carondelet warned about its dangers, and de Luzières responded that he was "perfectly well aware of all the delicacy and difficulty" attendant upon admitting Protestants to Louisiana.[18] Nevertheless, they were both willing to take the risk in order to attract those immigrants they considered essential to the colony's survival.

Manuel Gayoso de Lemos, who replaced Carondelet as governor general of Louisiana in August 1797, did not agree. Within a month after becoming governor he drafted an eighteen-point directive entitled "Instructions that the post commandants of this province must observe concerning the admittance of new colonists."[19] It's instructive briefly to compare Gayoso's directive with de Luzières's recruitment pamphlet, which was written only fifteen months earlier. De Luzières's pamphlet is all bright and positive, all liberal and encouraging; Gayoso's directive is all dour and negative, all restrictive and discouraging. Gayoso decreed that no unmarried immigrant could request a concession until he had "honorably" tilled the soil for four consecutive years, after which he might apply, with no guarantee of success (Article no. 4); no merchant could request agricultural land, for as a town dweller he had, by definition, no need for such land (Article no. 11). This was an absurd provision in a place like Ste. Genevieve, where major merchants like Louis Bolduc and Jean-Baptiste Vallé were also substantial agriculturists. Gayoso did recognize that earlier—irresponsible—administrations had permitted some Protestants to settle in Louisiana, a colony owned by His Most Catholic Majesty of Spain. These adult Protestants could remain, but their children had, *absolutely*, to be raised as good Roman Catholics. Any Protestant parent in Louisiana who refused to agree to this, "even should they be persons of high status (*beaucoup de considération*)" must forthwith leave the colony (Article no. 6). And of course all newcomers were required to be good Catholic farmers or artisans (Article no. 7).

In comparing Gayoso's outlook on religion and that of de Luzières and Carondelet, we see the difference between hard, stiff-necked Spanish Roman Catholicism and the softer, more latitudinarian version of the faith that characterized the Low Countries, homeland of both de Luzières and Carondelet—

18. De Luzières to Carondelet, September 21, 1797, PC, Leg. 214.
19. Ste. Genevieve Civil Records, Official Documents, no. 13, microfilm in Missouri Historical Society, St. Louis.

AN OFFICIAL ACCOUNT

OF THE

SITUATION, SOIL, PRODUCE, &c.

OF THAT PART OF

LOUISIANA,

WHICH LIES BETWEEN THE MOUTH OF THE MISSOURI
AND NEW MADRID, OR L'ANSE A LA GRAISE, AND
ON THE WEST SIDE OF THE MISSISSIPPI.

TOGETHER WITH AN

ABSTRACT OF THE SPANISH GOVERNMENT, &c.

I. THE underwritten, knight of the Great
Cross, of the order of his most *Christian
Majesty*, &c. living at New Bourbon, near
St. Genevieve, on the river Missisippi, in
the western district of the Illinois country
belonging to his *Catholic majesty the king of
Spain*, certify and attest to whomsoever
it may concern, that during about four
years that I have been living in the Illinois
country, I have travelled in it, and examined it, with as much attention as exactness, from the village of St. Charles on the
left bank and near the mouth of the Mis

Title page of de Luzières's recruitment pamphlet, 1796. Reproduced from the original printing done by John Bradford in Lexington, Kentucky. Courtesy of the Library of Congress.

and also of the famous sixteenth-century advocate of toleration and modera-
tion, Erasmus of Rotterdam.

In any event, de Luzières was so confident that he was arguing a good case
for Spanish Illinois, so sure that reasonable men must prefer an enlightened
monarchical regime to a government dominated by caviling lawyers that after
having his pamphlet translated into English,[20] he hand carried it to Lexington,
Kentucky, and had it printed up by John Bradford. Bradford had founded the
Kentucke Gazette in August 1787 (changed to *Kentucky* in 1789), and his press
was one of the very rare such facilities west of the Appalachian Mountains at
the time.[21] No printing press existed in Upper Louisiana until the *Missouri
Gazette* commenced publication at St. Louis in English in July 1808. When de
Luzières argued for the benefits of maintaining an enlightened monarchical
regime in the center of North America (and the Spanish regime at the time
was certainly such a regime), the French aristocrat was on the wrong side of
history, but he was honestly and passionately, even intelligently, wrong.

De Luzières's entire trip to Kentucky occupied only about six weeks, which
means he must have traveled by pirogue (rather than a bulkier, slower bateau)
and must have spent little time in Lexington.[22] We know virtually nothing
about his brief sojourn there, nothing about where he resided and nothing
about how he went about distributing his recruiting pamphlet after Bradford
had run it off his printing press. However, the pamphlet circulated widely,
even making its way eastward over the mountains into Wythe County, Virginia, where Moses Austin, future lead king of territorial Missouri, had founded
a small settlement. Austin had heard earlier of the rich lead mines in Spanish
Illinois from other sources, but he certainly did scrutinize de Luzières's pamphlet and it may well have been the deciding factor in his decision to pull up
stakes in Austinville, Virginia, and move west in December 1796. This connection would also account for Austin's visit to de Luzières's residence once
he had arrived in the Ste. Genevieve–New Bourbon area, as well as for the fact

20. It seems likely that the translator was Monsieur Gensac (or Jensac), whom de Luzières recommended several times for appointment as official translator in the Ste.
Genevieve–New Bourbon region and who appears on de Luzières's 1797 census of New
Bourbon (see Part 2, documents nos. 23 and 27). This appointment was never forthcoming, however, and Gensac does not seem to have remained for long in the region.

21. Bradford receives two entire columns in the *Dictionary of American Biography*, rev.
ed. (1964), s.v. Bradford, John; see also Thomas D. Clark, ed., *The Voice of the Frontier:
John Bradford's Notes on Kentucky* (Lexington: University Press of Kentucky, 1993), esp.
97–98.

22. He would have gone down the Mississippi River to the Ohio, up that to the Kentucky, ascended that to Frankfort, capital of Kentucky, disembarked there and proceeded
overland for thirty miles to Lexington.

that de Luzières mentioned Austin by name when he later enumerated the resources of Spanish Illinois.[23]

In 1796 de Luzières was enjoying better health than he had since arriving
in the Illinois Country, and upon returning to New Bourbon at the end of
June he was, for a change, in good humor. He wrote Tardiveau: "I'm infinitely
grateful for your fine seeds. I'm especially interested in those for artichokes
when you receive them. I can't find my note about the best way to raise aspar-
agus. I must have either sent it or given it to Monsieur Clamorgan or Cerré.[24]
When I get it back, I'll send you a copy." Whatever their bodily ills or ill for-
tunes, these native-born Frenchmen were determined to cultivate vegetables
to satisfy their discriminating palates, although it's unlikely that they had any
success raising artichokes in Upper Louisiana.

The parish of Ste. Genevieve was larger in 1796, both in geographical scope
and number of inhabitants, than the nuclear village of Ste. Genevieve, for the
parish encompassed the scattered new settlements that lay south of the village,
the most important of which were at New Bourbon, Bois Brûlé, and the Saline.
When Ste. Genevieve's priest, Paul de St. Pierre, compiled a census of his whole
parish in September 1796, he reckoned that Ste. Genevieve proper contained a
total of 772 human beings—female and male, black and white, free and slave.[25]
He also reckoned that his entire parish contained a total of 1,333 souls, and in
his tabulations for this larger entity he included several categories that did not
appear in his village census—Indians and non-Catholics.

The parish of Ste. Genevieve was therefore substantially more diverse than
the village of Ste. Genevieve, and it was even more diverse than St. Pierre's
bald census figures revealed, for the fifty-two non-Catholics residing in the
parish were by definition Americans; no Protestants existed within the traditional population of the area—Frenchmen, Canadians, Creoles, and a handful of Spaniards posted in Ste. Genevieve that made up the Spanish garrison

23. Concerning Moses Austin, see David B. Gracy II, *Moses Austin: His Life* (San Antonio: Trinity University Press, 1987), esp. 53–54. On Austin, see also James Alexander Gardner, *Lead King: Moses Austin* (St. Louis: Sunrise Publishing Co., 1980); George P. Garrison,
"A Memorandum of M. Austin's Journey from the Lead Mines in the County of Wythe in
the State of Virginia to the Lead Mines in the Province of Louisiana West of the Mississippi, 1796–1797," *American Historical Review* 5 (April 1900): 541–42. De Luzières's mention of Austin may be seen below, Part 2, document no. 29.

24. Letter of June 29, 1796, Illinois State Historical Library, Tardiveau Papers (hereafter ISHL, TP), no. 297. Clamorgan was the St. Louis merchant and notorious womanizer,
Jacques Clamorgan, and Cerré the wealthy and influential Gabriel Cerré, whose daughter
had married Auguste Chouteau in 1783.

25. University of Notre Dame Archives, IV-5-1, South Bend, Indiana. These archives
contain masses of documents—in French, Spanish and Latin—pertaining to St. Pierre
and his life in the Mississippi River valley.

there. Moreover, the parish also contained Anglo-American Roman Catholics, many of them from Kentucky, where Bardstown was the first American center of the Catholic faith west of the Appalachian Mountains. St. Pierre's 1796 census of Ste. Genevieve and environs provides a unique glimpse of the rapidly changing demographics of the region during the early 1790s. Only ten years earlier, the villages and parish of Ste. Genevieve had been, for all intents and purposes, coterminous, and quite likely contained not a single Protestant resident.

De Luzières's initiative to bring the settlers from Gallipolis to Spanish Illinois was almost a total flop; most of these French people opted to remain in the Ohio River valley, to in effect become Americans. One of the few who did move to the Spanish side of the Mississippi, although not under de Luzières's auspicies, was Antoine Saugrain. A child of the Enlightenment, Saugrain was one of those wonderfully cosmopolitan Frenchmen who could be found throughout the New World during the eighteenth century. He was a highly educated medical doctor, chemist, and mineralogist who had worked in South America during the 1780s before winding up in the Ohio River valley in the early 1790s. Saugrain finally abandoned Gallipolis, moved to St. Charles on the lower Missouri River in 1799, and then on to St. Louis in 1800. He provided medical supplies to Lewis and Clark in 1804 and remained until his death in 1820 the best-known physician in St. Louis.[26]

Ironically, de Luzières's other immigration initiative, that of persuading Americans from Kentucky to move westward across the Mississippi and become Spanish citizens, seems to have been a signal success. Striking evidence of this is seen by comparing the population of New Bourbon in late 1795 and late 1796, based on figures compiled by Lieutenant Governor Trudeau.[27] In

---

26. Concerning Saugrain, see *Wikipedia,* s.v. Antoine Saugrain; Jocelyne Moreau-Zanelli, *Gallipolis: Histoire d'un mirage américain au XVIIIe siècle* (Paris: L'Harmattan, 2000), 71–74, 75, 269, 352, 392; Hélène Fouré-Selter, *Gallipolis Ohio: Histoire de l'établissement de cinq cents François dans la vallée de l'Ohio à la fin du XVIIe siècle* (Paris: Jouve & Cie, 1939), 14–18; Frederick A. Hodes, *Beyond the Frontier: A History of St. Louis to 1821* (Tucson: Patrice Press, 2004), passim. Saugrain is mentioned as living at Gallipolis in document no. 6 in Part 2 of this volume.

Another curious case was that of Jacques Missé, who in 1832 at age eighty-six years applied in Ste. Genevieve for benefits due him as a veteran of the American Revolution.

He had served with the French expeditionary force, gone back to France, but returned to North America (Gallipolis) in 1791. After two years, he moved on to Ste. Genevieve, where he died and was buried in 1834. See affidavit in Collection 3636, Ste. Genevieve Folder 401, Western Historical Manuscripts Collection, State Historical Society of Missouri, Columbia. I am indebted to Helen V. Crist for providing me with her translation of this fascinating document.

27. Houck, ed., *Spanish Regime,* 1:324, 2:141.

1795 New Bourbon had 150 free white persons, but a year later it boasted 274 free persons, including 6 free mulattoes and 2 blacks. Further evidence, impressionistic to be sure, appeared in November 1796, when François Vallé observed from his home in Ste. Genevieve: "The number of Americans thus far settled at Ste. Genevieve and New Bourbon is very small. But for the past six months, substantial-looking folks are arriving every day to request agricultural lands for the very large number of families who wish to settle down here beginning next April."[28] Ultimately, this influx of Americans surely helped to undermine the Spanish and French colonial regimes in Louisiana, but in the short term Spanish authorities concluded that it would be in their best interests to welcome productive American agriculturists to Upper Louisiana.

28. Vallé to Carondelet, November 10, 1796, PC, Leg. 208A.

7

Civil and Military Commandant

De Luzières was handsomely rewarded for his success in recruiting American settlers for Spanish Illinois. Carondelet, before he left office as governor general of Louisiana, decided to do a final favor for his fellow countryman from Flanders, and a very large one it was indeed. Carondelet would appoint de Luzières commandant of a new administrative district in Upper Louisiana, centered at New Bourbon but including the budding settlements along the Saline and Aux Vases creeks and extending south to the Rivière de la Pomme (Apple Creek is today the southern boundary of Ste. Genevieve County). Gayoso de Lemos, Spanish governor at Natchez, was in line to replace Carondelet as governor general of Louisiana, and de Luzières broke the news first to Gayoso "that I will be rewarded for my success in promoting the immigration from Kentucky."[1] Even before his official appointment as commandant of New Bourbon de Luzières wanted to make sure that Gayoso would "not oppose this initiative" made by Carondelet only months before he left his office in New Orleans.

Carondelet drafted his official letter appointing de Luzières commandant of the New Bourbon District on June 1, 1797, and it took the usual three months for this missive to be carried upriver to Ste. Genevieve. Sunday, September 17, 1797, was the best day of de Luzières's life in the New World. After morning Mass, François Vallé, commandant of the Ste. Genevieve District and de Luzières's close friend, assembled all the residents of Ste. Genevieve

1. De Luzières to Gayoso, May 17, 1797, Papeles de Cuba, legajo 213, Archivo General de Indies, Seville (henceforth this collection will be cited simply as PC [Papeles de Cuba] followed by the legajo number).

and New Bourbon and officiated at de Luzières's official installation ceremony. Ste. Genevieve's militia company was drawn up in raggedy ranks to lend an appropriate touch of martial atmosphere to the occasion (de Luzières's official title was commandant civil et militaire),[2] and likely these citizen soldiers fired a volley from their flintlock fusils to put a stamp of finality to the ceremony. Vallé would then have hosted a dinner in his vertical-log house overlooking South Gabouri Creek—a dinner served by black slaves on a linen tablecloth adorned with French faïence, sterling silver flatware, and crystal stemware.[3] De Luzières's salary was one hundred pesos (piastres or dollars) per annum, as was François Vallé's as commandant in Ste. Genevieve.[4]

The newly formed New Bourbon District was an artificial construct—carved, without much rhyme or reason, out of the Ste. Genevieve District to its north and the Cape Girardeau District to its south. But there is no evidence that the commandants (respectively, François Vallé and Louis Lorimier) of these latter districts objected to having their territories cannibalized to serve de Luzières's interests, for he was seen as totally nonthreatening, a cooperative ally rather than a political rival. One of the curious anomalies produced in this process was that the settlements of Shawnee and Delaware Indians along the north bank of Apple Creek fell within de Luzières's district, while everyone knew that Lorimier was the designated handler of these particular tribes; indeed, Lorimier had been made commandant of the Cape Girardeau District in 1793 specifically to serve in this role. In the six-odd years of its existence, before American acquisition of Louisiana swept it away, the New Bourbon District never achieved any status as an administrative or religious center. Although de Luzières as commandant had the right (indeed, the obligation) to draft legal documents of all sorts, no *greffe* (depository for official records) was established at New Bourbon; while there was talk about building a chapel at New Bourbon as an adjunct to the parish church in Ste. Genevieve, this was never done. Documents that de Luzières drafted were deposited at the *greffe* in Ste. Genevieve, and when he and his wife attended Mass on Sundays they were obliged to traipse the several miles into Ste. Genevieve.

As soon as de Luzières was installed as commandant of New Bourbon, he set about trying to leverage that position to use it as a steppingstone for further advancement. He requested that King Carlos IV of Spain grant him the

2. De Luzières to Carondelet, September 21, 1797 (see Part 2, document no. 24).

3. François Vallé would have inherited these luxury items from his father, François *père*. See Carl J. Ekberg, *François Vallé and His World* (Columbia: University of Missouri Press, 2002), 268–69.

4. Abraham P. Nasatir, "Government Employees and Salaries in Spanish Louisiana," *Louisiana Historical Quarterly* 29 (October 1946): 154–55.

rank of captain in the regular army (as opposed to the militia), *with the appropriate compensation,* wanting the position as much for the increase in salary as the honor. Not being able to compose this request in proper Spanish, de Luzières was obliged to send it to his son Carlos de Lassus, who was then commandant in New Madrid, to get it written up in correct form. Despite his aristocratic lineage, and despite the fact that Carlos was already a breveted lieutenant colonel, de Luzières never obtained a commission in the regular Spanish army (as opposed to the militia). François Vallé and Louis Lorimier each sought the same honor and each was similarly rejected. Vallé's father, François *père,* illiterate though he was, had been granted a lieutenancy in the Spanish army, but he was a unique case, being the only man from Upper Louisiana ever to receive a regular army commission at any rank during the Spanish regime.[5]

Despite being rejected for a commission in the Spanish army, de Luzières's influence in military affairs in Upper Louisiana was extensive. His commandancy at New Bourbon made him ex officio captain of the local militia company, and he appointed his youngest son, Camille, second lieutenant. Interestingly, de Luzières selected the American Israel Dodge as first lieutenant. Israel, along with his brother John, had abandoned Kaskaskia for Spanish Illinois in the late 1780s, and Israel was the only native American ever to serve as an officer in a militia company in the region.[6] In St. Louis de Luzières's son, Carlos de Lassus, had replaced Zénon Trudeau as commandant of Upper Louisiana.[7] Under his command, in addition to the small garrison of Spanish regulars, were three militia companies at the end of the colonial era. Carlos's younger brother, Jacques-Marcellin, was captain of one of these companies, and Antoine Soulard (virtually de Luzières's adopted son, as we saw earlier) captain of another.[8] If Spanish Louisiana had been attacked by rambunctious Americans (and some western frontiersmen were persistently advocating

5. See Ekberg, *François Vallé,* 213, 217.

6. De Luzières to Carondelet, October 1, 1797, PC, Leg. 214. John Dodge died prematurely in 1795, but both his widow and his brother Israel appear on de Luzières's 1797 census of New Bourbon (see Part 2, document no. 27).

7. Governor Gayoso informed de Luzières of his son's appointment as lieutenant governor in a letter from New Orleans dated February 26, 1799 (PC, Leg. 216). In this letter Gayoso defined Upper Louisiana as everything from the post of Espérance (Campo del Esperanza), situated across the Mississippi from present-day Memphis, "to the farthest settlements heading up." For a plan of Campo del Esperanza, see Morris S. Arnold, *Colonial Arkansas, 1686–1804: A Social and Cultural History* (Fayetteville: University of Arkansas Press, 1991), 22.

8. See "Relación de los Señores Oficiales de Milicias de le Puesto de Sn Luis," 1803 in PC, Leg. 2368.

such an attack), de Luzières and his family members would have been at the forefront of the colony's defense.

As it turned out, the grandest military maneuver that de Luzières ever conducted occurred in December 1803, when he led the New Bourbon militia to New Madrid. There all the militia companies of Upper Louisiana assembled to attend the execution of a Mascouten Indian, Tewanayé, who had killed (likely with some justification) David Trotter, a purveyor of bad whiskey. This chilly occasion was intended as a show of force to the Indians who witnessed the execution by firing squad.[9]

As newly appointed commandant of the New Bourbon District, de Luzières went right to work exercising his legitimate powers. On September 27, 1797, ten days after his installation ceremony in Ste. Genevieve, de Luzières drafted what was in effect a passport for two free black men who wished to paddle a pirogue-load of apples down the Mississippi to New Orleans.[10] Apples were frequently shipped from the Illinois Country to Lower Louisiana, the climate of which did not favor apple trees, and these two black men required a passport to document the fact that they were free persons, rather than runaway slaves. It's within bounds to hope that these former slaves, having raised themselves up to become small-time entrepreneurs, got a good price for their produce when they arrived a month or so later at the docks in New Orleans.

Then, during much of the autumn of 1797, de Luzières busied himself compiling a detailed census of his district. This enumeration provides a demographic snapshot of the region's three communities—New Bourbon, the Saline, and Bois Brûlé—within the district (see below, Part 2, document no. 27). Of the three, New Bourbon had the largest population (both free and slave), although the Saline had the largest number of households. This was because many households at the Saline consisted of a small cabin inhabited by a single male. These men had come to work at the salt springs, and many of them were recently arrived Americans.[11]

Only nineteen of ninety-three households in the New Bourbon District included black slaves, although they constituted roughly 30 percent of the region's population. This was a slightly lower percentage than at neighboring Ste. Genevieve, where the slave population had been growing rapidly since the early

9. See Carl J. Ekberg, *Colonial Ste. Genevieve: An Adventure on the Mississippi Frontier* (Gerald, Mo.: Patrice Press, 1985), 122–23.

10. See Part 2, document no. 25.

11. Michael K. Trimble, Teresita Majewski, Michael J. O'Brien, and Anna L. Price, "Frontier Colonization of the Saline Creek Valley," in *French Colonial Archeology: The Illinois Country and the Western Great Lakes,* ed. John A. Walthall (Urbana: University of Illinois Press, 1991), 165–88.

1750s. Interestingly, the hardiest demographic group in de Luzières's enumeration was black slave women, based on the percentage of persons who
lived past fifty years of age. And the ratio of black children to slave women of
child-bearing age was higher than of children to women in the white population, although the ratio of males to females was similar in both black and
white adult populations. This likely indicates that fertility among the blacks
was higher than among the whites, and that infant mortality, which was high
among all groups, was no higher among blacks than whites. This in turn
suggests that the material conditions of life for slaves—food, clothing, and
shelter—were not markedly inferior to those of the free white settlers. The relative health and vigor of the slave populations within the Creole communities of
Upper Louisiana is worth noting.[12]

Carondelet had appointed de Luzières commandant of the New Bourbon
District as a reward for his success in recruiting new settlers for the region,
and as commandant he dealt in person with newcomers who came requesting land. In October 1800, John Matthews, a farmer from North Carolina,
came to New Bourbon with his wife, two children, and an assortment of animals and agricultural implements. In accordance with Governor Gayoso's
1798 directive, Matthews swore before de Luzières that he and all members of
his family were Roman Catholics, that he was legitimately married, that the
animals he claimed were his own, and that he would be loyal to His Catholic
Majesty of Spain. De Luzières accepted Matthews's oath and gave him permission to request land from Ramón de Lopéz y Angulo, chief financial officer of
Louisiana. Accordingly, Matthews requested 600 square arpents on the north
branch of the St. Francis River, some thirty miles west of New Bourbon (no
western boundary was ever set for the New Bourbon District), and, doubtless
at de Luzières's suggestion, ingratiatingly informed López y Angulo that "the
suplicant is praying unceasingly for your long life."[13] Was Matthews, in craft-
ing a request whose language was surely strange to American eyes, serious
about living and dying as a subject of His Catholic Majesty, or was he already
confident in the year 1800 that the west bank of the Mississippi River was on
the cusp of becoming part of the American republic? In any case, López y Angulo must have granted his request, for in January 1806 the U.S. Government
Land Office confirmed Matthews's title to 640 acres (roughly 743 square arpents) of land on the "waters of the St. François."[14]

12. See Ekberg, *Colonial Ste. Genevieve*, 204, 224.
13. Ste. Genevieve Civil Records (hereafter SGCR), Concessions, no. 66, microfilm in
Missouri Historical Society, St. Louis.
14. *American state papers: documents, legislative and executive, of the Congress of the United States, Public Lands* (Washington, D.C.: Gales and Seaton, 1832–1861), 3:309 (hereafter
ASP, PL).

Newly arriving Americans were important as part of de Luzières's efforts to bolster the population of Upper Louisiana, but he also facilitated land grants for the local Creoles. In these cases, the legal process was a bit different. For example, in October 1799 Joseph Chevalier Jr. approached de Luzières with a request for four hundred square arpents of land on which he proposed to develop a farmstead and raise livestock. Doing what no American could do, Chevalier predicated his request on the "antiquity of his father in this area," as well as his own personal devotion to His Catholic Majesty.[15] Adding that he wished simply to "live peacefully as a farmer," he submitted his request to de Luzières, who supported it by noting that not only was the Chevalier family a longtime and honorable part of society in Upper Louisiana but that Joseph Jr. also possessed special skills and resources as an agriculturist because that had been his occupation since "his most tender youth." De Luzières then forwarded the request to the Spanish lieutenant governor in St. Louis, Carlos de Lassus, who just happened to be de Luzières's son, and he approved it with celerity.[16]

As real estate began to pile up in de Luzières's New Bourbon District, complexities and difficulties were bound to arise. In the Bois Brûlé section of the district (i.e., along the Mississippi River down toward the Saline) de Luzières appointed a deputy, Louis Coyteux, to help deal with the problems. In the spring of 1800, de Luzières conveyed land to one Humphrey Gilson, a portion of which had apparently already been granted to one Isaac Davis. De Luzières sent a directive to his deputy down at Bois Brûlé, addressing it *and* concluding it with "Mon cher Coyteux," a French turn of phrase containing a *soupçon* of condescension that clearly delineated the hierarchical relationship between the two men; it was a phrase that de Luzières had used every day as lord of the manor back home in northern France. Coyteux was ordered to see if he could work things out amicably between the two claimants so that Gilson would stay put at Bois Brûlé and not seek an alternative concession elsewhere.[17] We don't know the result of this case, but Coyteux, who served de Luzières in a variety of capacities, and his work are significant for understanding how Spanish Illinois was governed in the late colonial period. Coyteux was an interesting and sometimes controversial fellow, and his life in Upper Louisiana is worth a brief examination as part of the larger de Luzières story.

15. The Chevalier family had been in the Illinois Country at least as early as 1750. See Natalia Maree Belting, *Kaskaskia Under the French Regime* (Urbana: University of Illinois Press, 1948; rpt. ed., Carbondale: Southern Illinois University Press, 2003), 101–2.
16. SGCR, Concessions, no. 22.
17. Ibid., no. 118.

Coyteux arrived in St. Louis from the Montreal region, where the Coyteuxs were a long-established family,[18] sometime in the late 1780s. He was educated, signed his name with an intricate flourish, was trained as a gold and silver smith, and was perhaps the most highly skilled artisan in Upper Louisiana at the end of the eighteenth century. At St. Louis in 1789 he crafted for Joseph Hortiz (José Ortiz) six sterling silver place settings for 120 piastres, repaired a set of earrings for 5 piastres, and made two plain rings for 5 piastres each.[19] Leaving St. Louis circa 1790, he migrated down the Mississippi to the Bois Brûlé area south of Ste. Genevieve, built a log cabin ("cabanne en boulins")[20] there, and became associated with Louis Lorimier, also a French Canadian and the handler par excellence of the Shawnee and Delaware Indians in the area. In April 1794, Coyteux was working on behalf of Lorimier to distribute provisions—maize, bacon, flour, tobacco, and so forth—to the local Indians.[21]

The mid-1790s were a tense time in Upper Louisiana as rumors flew about an impending American invasion of the colony, and Coyteux was one of several men arrested on suspicion of treason and shipped off to New Orleans for interrogation. But Commandant François Vallé in Ste. Genevieve mounted a spirited defense of Coyteux, writing directly to Governor Carondelet (something he rarely did) to vouch for Coyteux's integrity and loyalty.[22] Coyteux was fully exonerated and by the summer of 1795 he was back living in his log cabin at Bois Brûlé practicing his craft as a shaper of precious metals.

But Coyteux was a man of independent mind, and he had a knack for attracting attention from both civil and religious authorities. Shortly after arriving in the Ste. Genevieve area, he had taken up with one Josette Parker,[23] an immigrant to Spanish Illinois from the state of Georgia. By 1796 Coyteux and his concubine and their two children, François and Louis Jr., were all living

18. See Cyprien Tanguay, ed., *Dictionnaire généalogique des famille Canadiennes depuis la fondation de la colonie jusqu'à nos jours,* 7 vols. (Quebec: Eusèbe Senéchal, 1871–1890), 3:107–8. Coyteux was usually rendered as "Coiteux" in Canada, and that form occasionally appears in Illinois Country records.

19. See bill to Hortiz, August 24, 1789, Chouteau Collection, Box 1, Missouri Historical Society, St. Louis (henceforth MHS).

20. See SGCR, Estates, no. 73.

21. See Lorimier's journal in Louis Houck, ed., *The Spanish regime in Missouri; a collection of papers and documents relating to upper Louisiana principally within the present limits of Missouri during the dominion of Spain, from the Archives of the Indies at Seville, etc.,* translated from the original Spanish into English, 2 vols. (Chicago: R. R. Donnelley & Sons Company, 1909), 2:82.

22. Vallé to Carondelet, March 23, 1795, PC, Leg. 2371.

23. It is quite likely that Ms. Parker was the daughter or sister of Eleizer Parker who appears on de Luzières's 1797 census of New Bourbon (see Part 2, document no. 27).

under one roof at Bois Brûlé. At the time, the parish priest in Ste. Genevieve was a conscientious barefooted Carmelite from Germany, Paul von Heiligenstein, known locally as the Abbé de St. Pierre (French version of Heiligenstein).[24] St. Pierre began to badger Coyteux about his irregular relationship with Ms. Parker, perhaps especially because of the couple's two children. According to the priest's own account, he approached Coyteux in person and invited him to stop in at the rectory after Mass some Sunday for a little chat. Coyteux ignored the invitation, whereupon the solicitous St. Pierre went to his pen and dispatched an "urgent note" to Coyteux requesting that he make a special trip (about five miles) from Bois Brûlé to Ste. Genevieve to discuss the issue. Again Coyteux brazenly ignored the priest's entreaty.[25]

St. Pierre had come to America during the Revolution as a chaplain in General Rochambeau's French army. Possessing a military sense of good order, discipline, and chain-of-command, the priest went to Commandant François Vallé in Ste. Genevieve for help; the use of civil authorities to support the church on an urgent issue of public morality was entirely in keeping with the laws of Spanish Louisiana.[26] On August 8, 1796, Vallé, although Coyteux's friend, sent the reprobate an order "to expell within twenty-four hours from his household an English woman because their cohabitation is contrary to good morals and to the ordinances of His Majesty [i.e., Carlos IV of Spain]," explaining that he was issuing this order because of "repeated requests made by Monsieur de St. Pierre, curate of the parish." Coyteux buckled under the pressure brought to bear on him jointly by the religious and civil powers of Ste. Genevieve; he consented to marry Josette Parker. The Abbé de St. Pierre himself made an honest woman of Ms. Parker by turning her into Madame Coyteux in the parish church of Ste. Genevieve on September 26, 1796, and in the same document legitimized her two children.[27]

A year after Coyteux's marriage, de Luzières became commandant of the newly created New Bourbon District, within which fell Coyteux's residence at Bois Brûlé. In that same neck of the woods lived one Frederick Kester ("Custer" on de Luzières's 1797 census),[28] a salt maker by trade, an American by origin, and an Anglican in religion. Kester borrowed 201 piastres from

24. Concerning St. Pierre's career in Ste. Genevieve, see Ekberg, *Colonial Ste. Genevieve,* 403–12 and passim.
25. The basic source on the St. Pierre-Coyteux squabble is found in SGCR, Miscellaneous Papers 2, no. 50.
26. See Jack D.L. Holmes, "'Do It! Don't Do It'! Spanish Laws on Sex and Marriage," in *Louisiana's Legal Heritage,* ed. Edward F. Haas (Pensacola, Fla.: Perido Bay Press, 1983), 19–42.
27. Ste. Genevieve Parish Records, Book B, Marriages: 36.
28. See Part 2, document no. 27.

Coyteux in November 1797. He had signed a note, in de Luzières's presence, putting his personal possessions and cattle up as security, and when he did not repay the loan Coyteux was forced to go to de Luzières and seek relief. On February 4, 1798, Coyteux sent de Luzières a request to seize and sell Kester's mortgaged property so that Coyteux could recover his 201 piastres. This was a very simple process with no lawyers involved, for lawyers were prohibited in Spanish Louisiana, as they had been in French Louisiana. De Luzières, as civil authority in his district, would review the written evidence in camera and declare his solo decision. De Luzières moved swiftly, and the next day, Monday, February 5, he issued his decree: Kester was given one week to repay Coyteux or face the prospect of having his mortgaged property seized and sold at public auction. To make sure that both parties understood, de Luzières brought the two men into his office (headquarters of the New Bourbon District), situated within his residence, and had them countersign his written decision in front of two witnesses. Coyteux penned his usual graceful and elegant signature, in keeping with his profession as a highly skilled artisan; Kester wiped the cow dung off his hands and scratched out some semblance of his name, decipherable but barely so.

Kester, a rough-and-tumble American frontiersman, didn't cotton to being pushed around by the refined Frenchman who governed the New Bourbon District. He casually ignored the deadline set by de Luzières. On April 4, 1798, Coyteux again appealed to de Luzières: Kester had not paid up, he gave the impression that he never intended to, and he even mocked Coyteux about his debt. Coyteux wanted de Luzières to carry out his threat, seize and sell Kester's mortgaged property, and retrieve Coyteux's money for him. Unfortunately for us, the paper trail here goes stone cold dead. This does suggest, however, that Coyteux finally got satisfaction—if he had not, further documentation on the affair would surely have survived in Ste. Genevieve's colonial records.

Coyteux was one of the better educated francophone citizens within de Luzières's jurisdiction, and it was natural that these two men became acquaintances, even friends, although scant imformation exists about their relationship. Sometime after being named commandant at New Bourbon, de Luzières appointed Coyteux his deputy at Bois Brûlé; we saw previously that in April 1800 de Luzières asked Coyteux to settle a minor land dispute. A few months later, however, a much, much more serious case arose in the area. Widow Duff complained to de Luzières that her twelve-year-old daughter Marie had been raped by one Thomas Allen.[29] Any scholar who has studied the history of Ste. Genevieve, or for that matter of all Upper Louisiana, during the eighteenth

29. SGCR, Litigations, no. 114, dated July 14, 1800.

century is shocked when the word "raped" leaps off the page of a manuscript produced in that time and place. Ste. Geneviève had been a very close-knit nuclear village, with a commandant and a parish priest, a village in which everyone knew everyone else. Rapes, likely even of slave women, occurred very rarely, and of a pre-pubescent white girl—really quite beyond the realm of the conceivable in the traditional Creole community. De Luzières must have shaken his head in disbelief about the vicious nature of some of these American immigrants, many of whom he had helped to recruit as immigrants to Spanish Illinois.

De Luzières flew into action. Jeremiah Perelle, "commissiare de police" at the Saline, was ordered to assemble a posse of four men, "well-mounted and well-armed," track down Allen and arrest him, seize all of his possessions and place them in the custody of Louis Coyteux. Frustratingly, we don't know the outcome of this case, but this much can be said: The three principles in the case—Widow Duff, her daughter Marie, and Thomas Allen were all newcomers to the area. Furthermore, Allen seems to be just the type of person that the authorities, including de Luzières, had hoped to bar from settlement in Spanish Illinois; he owned no house (he was living with one Burns),[30] owned no land, and had no wife. Allen was apparently a young, deracinated ne'er-do-well at this point in his life. Once again, the result of this case remains unknown, although Thomas Allen evidently survived whatever charges may have been brought against him. Indeed, he apparently worked hard and prospered in the region, and in 1818 the U.S. Government granted him a 640-acre concession at Bois Brûlé.[31]

Pinckney's Treaty (officially San Lorenzo) of 1795, which opened the Mississippi River to unfettered American commerce, created special vexations for de Luzières in his role of commandant of the New Bourbon District.[32] Bad blood began to brew across the great river, between New Bourbon and Kaskaskia, in the early spring of 1799. On March 12, James Dunn,[33] sheriff of Randolph County, Northwest Territory, United States of America, crossed the

30. Very likely this was Michael Burns, who appears on de Luzières's 1797 census of Bois Brûlé (see Part 2, document no. 27) with several unmarried men living in his household.

31. See *ASP, PL,* 3:290. It is possible that this concession was to Thomas Allen Jr.

32. Whitaker, *Spanish-American Frontier,* 200–222.

33. James Dunn was the first sheriff of Randolph County (1795–1800), which was carved out of St. Clair County in 1795. After his career in law enforcement, Dunn became a builder and in 1803 constructed a jail in Kaskaskia for which he was paid $270.35 (see *Combined History of Randolph, Monroe and Perry Counties, Illinois, With Illustrations Descriptive of their Scenery and Biographical Sketches of some of their Prominent Men and Pioneers* [Philadelphia: J. L. McDonough and Co., 1883], 100, 101, 102, 122, 126, 132, 149). I am indebted to Emily Lyons of Chester, Illinois, for this information on Dunn.

Mississippi in his patrol pirogue, stomped across the plowlands of the Grand Champ, and hiked up the hill to the residence of Pierre-Charles de Lassus de Luzières, military and civil commandant of the New Bourbon District, province of Upper Louisiana, territory of His Catholic Majesty, King Carlos IV of Spain. This was the same James Dunn who had sold a black slave to de Luzières a month earlier (see Part 2, document no. 32). Dunn delivered to de Luzières a formal complaint against Joseph Barbier, a resident at the Saline, New Bourbon District.[34] The gist of the complaint was that Barbier owed eighty-eight piastres (dollars) and thirty cents to one Robert Nicolson, a resident of Kaskaskia and apparently a friend of Sheriff Dunn. Should Barbier refuse to pay up, Dunn threatened to arrest him and toss him into Kaskaskia's jail, conditions in which in 1799 would have been less than cozy. Charges and countercharges, depositions and counter-depositions flew during the summer of 1799. Finally, on October 6, 1799, de Luzières rendered his opinion: "All things considered," Nicolson's claim against Barbier appeared to be fabricated ("fausses prétentions") and Sheriff Dunn's charges against Barbier were rejected. De Luzières sent both Barbier and Dunn written notification of his decision.[35]

Dunn, according to de Luzières, responded "very indecently" to this judgment, which was surely an understated description of the kind of language current on the Mississippi frontier in the late eighteenth century. One can well imagine the scene in the tavern in Kaskaskia frequented by the English-speaking crowd on the evening of Sunday, October 6, the day that Dunn was handed de Luzières's decision. As the evening wore on, the American frontiersmen (doubtless including Dunn and Nicolson) at the bar raised their glasses of fiery corn liquor—"Damn the King of Spain to hell, Damn all European aristocrats, most especially Mister Loosiers." The Americans would have their revenge. They smelled through their cigar smoke that history was on their side, that they should not only have the right to navigate the entire length of the Mississippi River but should absolutely control one of the world's most important waterways.

Within a week's time, an opportunity arose that seemed a veritable godsend to the Americans from Kaskaskia. Barbier's pirogue loaded with freshly harvested Illinois-Country apples destined for New Orleans was spotted out on the Mississippi caught in a slack current, and the Americans pounced. What happened was recounted in a sworn deposition given by Joseph Barbier and

34. Barbier appears on de Luzières's 1797 census as a resident of the Saline section of the New Bourbon District (see Part 2, document no. 27).

35. See de Luzières's decree in PC, Leg. 216B.

his *engagé*, Jean-Marie Godineau. At 3 o'clock on the afternoon of Monday, October 14, 1799, the two men, bloodied and battered, appeared at de Luzières's residence to tell their hair-raising story. Neither of the deponents could sign his name, but each of the two official witnesses, Domitille Dehault (de Luzières's wife) and Israel Dodge, signed with flourishes, Domitille choosing to use the family's original aristocratic name, dating from before the de Lassus and de Luzières additions had been piled on. Hardly had Barbier and Godineau begun their voyage downriver, when another pirogue drew alongside and three Americans from Kaskaskia, led by none other than Sheriff Dunn, leaped aboard Barbier's vessel. The Americans, flintlock pistols ("pistolets") in hand, ordered Barbier forthwith to direct his pirogue to the American side of the river, and when he refused hand-to-hand combat with fists and paddles ensued— in a rocking-and-rolling pirogue loaded with apples, in the middle of the Mississippi River. Somehow Barbier and Godineau succeeded in fending off their assailants long enough to beach their vessel on the Spanish side of the river. They then proceeded immediately, despite bleeding wounds on their heads and upper bodies, to de Luzières's house to lodge their complaint.[36]

De Luzières handled this difficult situation as well as he could. He ordered, "On Behalf of the King," Jeremiah Perelle, his "commissaire de police" at the Saline, to gather a posse, detain Dunn and his accomplices, and help Barbier and Godineau get safely off downriver in their pirogue in the direction of New Orleans.[37] By the time that Perelle and his posse arrived on the west bank of the Mississippi, Dunn and his henchmen had paddled their pirogue back to the east bank of the river. Barbier apparently succeeded in getting his Illinois-Country apples to market in New Orleans without further mishaps, and the city's chefs could proceed with producing their savory *tartes aux pommes* for the discriminating Creole residents.

But de Luzières was bothered by the brash aggressiveness of the Americans from Kaskaskia and kept ruminating about the issue of their rights on the Mississippi River. His anxieties were compounded in early November 1799 while visiting his friend, François Vallé, commandant in neighboring Ste. Genevieve. Another visitor *chez* Vallé that day was the loud-mouthed braggart from Kaskaskia, John Rice Jones.[38] Jones informed de Luzières in no uncertain terms that General Arthur St. Clair, governor of the Northwest Territory, was

36. This legal deposition, dated October 14, 1799, may be found in PC, Leg. 216B. A slightly different account of this episode, dated November 3, 1799, may be found in a letter, apparently from de Luzières to Carlos de Lassus, in PC, Leg. 2366.

37. See declaration, October 14, 1799, PC, Leg. 216B.

38. Concerning John Rice Jones in Kaskaskia, see Alvord, *Illinois Country,* 367–68, 372, 424; Mason, ed., *Chicago and Illinois,* 230–70.

Charles (Carlos) Auguste Dehault de Lassus, second-eldest of de Luzières's children. Born in Bouchain in 1767, he served as Spanish lieutenant governor in St. Louis from 1799 to 1804 and presided over the transfer of Upper Louisiana to the United States in February 1804. Reproduced courtesy of the Missouri History Museum, St. Louis.

claiming that Pinckney's Treaty had conveyed to the United States of America the entire breadth of the Mississippi River—from its headwaters all the way downstream to Baton Rouge, bank to bank, and all islands in between.[39] This of course was not true, for the treaty conveyed to Americans only the right to navigate on the river and use the docking facilities in New Orleans. We cannot know with certainty who was misconstruing the terms of Pinckney's Treaty, St. Clair or Jones, for either man was fully capable of fabricating such intimidating bluster.

39. De Luzières to Carlos Delassus, November 8, 1799, PC, Leg. 2366.

Several months before these events occurred, de Luzières's son, Carlos Delassus, had been promoted to become lieutenant governor of Upper Louisiana.[40] De Luzières's various unsettling encounters with Americans prompted him to write to Delassus asking for clarification of the specific terms of Pinckney's Treaty. Apparently, Delassus's response eased his father's mind a bit by accurately explaining the treaty,[41] but it is nevertheless clear that the arrival in the Illinois Country of aggressive Americans, in addition to possible ambiguities in Pinckney's Treaty, much complicated de Luzières's job as commandant at New Bourbon.

40. Trudeau handed power over to Delassus on July 28, 1799 (see de Luzières to Delassus, August 7, 1799, PC, Leg. 216B).
41. I've not been able to find Delassus's letter to his father.

8

End of the Adventure

During the late 1790s, Americans living in the Northwest Territory were gazing greedily westward across the Mississippi River. They were confident that the Spanish regime on the west side of the river was living on borrowed time and that they would soon be masters of the entire Mississippi Valley. De Luzières wrote to his friend Tardiveau in July 1798 that "the famous [John Rice] Jones of Kaskaskia wants to wager 300 piastres [dollars] that within three months the American flag will be planted in the middle of New Orleans and that this entire colony will belong to the United States."[1] Jones was off by a few years in his prediction, but his braggadocio nicely captures American sentiment in the Illinois Country as the eighteenth century was winding down. It is agreeable to ponder the possibility that someone, if not the destitute de Luzières himself, was sufficiently quick witted to engage Jones in his proposed wager.

After becoming governor general in 1792, Carondelet had thrown himself into the task of turning Louisiana into a functioning, profitable, and defensible Spanish province. Indeed, the governor's early support of de Luzières's grand commercial scheme and his willingness to bolster Louisiana's population by accepting Protestant immigrants, were part and parcel of this daunting task. Pinckney's Treaty, by fully opening the Mississippi to American commerce and accepting U.S. sovereignty of the east bank of the river down as far as the 31st parallel (i.e., the present northeastern boundary of the state of Louisiana between Baton Rouge and Natchez, Mississippi), rocked Carondelet's world. He had fought American advances into the Mississipppi Valley

1. De Luzières to Tardiveau, July 16, 1798, TP, no. 360.

tooth and nail, even attempting to resurrect the harebrained plan to foment a rebellion in Kentucky, separate it from the Union and bring it into alliance with Spain. The crafty and treasonous American general, James Wilkinson, had supported such a scheme in the late 1780s, and did so once again in 1794, but by 1795 even his fevered brain deemed it utterly impractical.[2]

Pinckney's Treaty was signed in the monastery of San Lorenzo de El Escorial outside Madrid in October 1795, and by June 1796 Carondelet was candidly acknowledging that it was not in his "power any longer to restrain the eruption of the people from the western American States, who are approaching and going to establish themselves on the eastern bank of the Mississippi. . . . Five or six thousand of those ferocious men who know neither law nor subjection are those who are starting the American establishments and are attracting in their footsteps the prodigious emigration both from the Atlantic States and from Europe, which menaces the *Provincias Internas* [i.e., Louisiana and New Mexico]."[3] Carondelet characterized these American frontiersmen as "sort of determined bandits" and understood that it was rapidly becoming beyond his capacity to contain them.

When Carondelet appointed de Luzières commandant of the newly formed New Bourbon District, the governor already understood that Spanish Louisiana was doomed. But de Luzières did not, or at least did not want to admit it to himself. He soldiered stalwartly on, compiling the marvelous 1797 census of his district and making endless recommendations for improving and strengthening Spanish Illinois. De Luzières was a dyed-in-the-wool monarchist, but he was a monarchist of the enlightened variety, sincerely believing that monarchy was the best political system for organizing human society for the greater good of all. Although a traditional Roman Catholic, he never justified monarchy on religious grounds, never argued that kings derived their power and authority exclusively from God and were therefore answerable only to the Almighty. De Luzières had imbibed too much of the progressive spirit of the Enlightenment for that. He wanted monarchy to prove its value and validity by being useful, by serving the interests of human beings in the here-and-now. Concerning the role of government in human society, de Luzières's ideas were not all that far removed from those of Thomas Jefferson—they were after all of the same generation of eighteenth-century thinkers (De Luzières was five years older). Of course, the two men disagreed

2. Arthur P. Whitaker, *The Spanish-American Frontier, 1783–1795* (Boston: Houghton Mifflin Co., 1927), 191–212.

3. Carondelet to the Marqués de Branceforte, June 7, 1796, in Abraham P. Nasatir, ed., *Before Lewis and Clark: Documents Illustrating the History of the Missouri, 1785–1804*, 2 vols. (St. Louis: St. Louis Historical Documents Foundation, 1952), 2: 439–40.

radically about which type of government was best suited to serve the earthly ends of humanity that both ardently desired.

The final years before the Louisiana Purchase were not happy ones for de Luzières and his wife, Domitille-Josèphe. As a Spanish administrator, de Luzières faced the looming threat of the young, aggressive American republic pushing westward; Domitille, as a person even more isolated on the American frontier than her husband, seemed to be slowly losing her mental bearings. When Moses Austin visited the de Luzières household near New Bourbon, he described Madame de Luzières's odd behavior:

> One mile from St Genevieve Down the River is a Small Village Called New Bourbon of about 20 Houses. At this place, I was introduced to The Chevaleer Pierre Charles De Hault De Lassus, a French Nobleman Formerly of the Council of the late King of France. . . . Madame De Lassus did not appear to support the Change of Situation so well as the Chevalier. I was examining a larg Piece of painting, which was in Madame De Lassus Bed Chamber, representing a grand Festival given by the citizens of Paras, . . . on the birth of the Dauphin and a Parade of all the Nobles on the same Occasion. She came to me and putting her finger on the Picture pointing out a Coach There said . . . my situation is now strangly Chang'd.[4]

There is something slightly chilling about Madame de Luzières's understatement that her situation was "strangly Chang'd" from what it had been in France. The flight from the French Revolution—which had taken the de Luzières family from Valenciennes to Le Havre to Philadelphia to Pittsburgh and finally to New Bourbon—had perhaps induced a culture shock of such force as to render madame a touch daft. As Austin's curiosity in her painting demonstrates, the canvas that had been lugged across the Atlantic Ocean and halfway across North America was a strange apparition on the trans-Mississippi frontier. One may certainly sympathize with Madame de Luzières's plight: she had left behind perhaps the most refined civilization that human beings have ever contrived to create on this earth to endure the rudeness of the American frontier.[5] Madame perhaps kept body and soul

4. George P. Garrison, "A Memorandum of M. Austin's Journey from the Lead Mines in the County of Wythe in the State of Virginia to the Lead Mines in the Province of Louisiana West of the Mississippi, 1796–1797," *American Historical Review* 5 (April 1900): 541–42.

5. This point is brought home in the catalog to a recent exhibit at the National Gallery of Art in Washington, D.C.—*Renaissance to Revolution: French Drawings from the National Gallery of Art, 1500–1800*, ed. Margaret Morgan Grasselli (Washington, D.C.: National Gallery of Art, 2009).

together by fixing her attention on that precious relic of a lost lifestyle in pre-Revolutionary France.

Nevertheless, some bright, even glittering, events did enliven the lives of Madame and Monsieur de Luzières in late colonial Louisiana. In the spring of 1796, the de Luzières's third-born child, Jacques-Marcellin Ceran de Hault de St. Vrain, married in St. Louis Marie-Félicité, daughter of the local merchant, Louis Dubreuil.[6] This marriage, on Monday, May 2, of a genuine French aristocratic family with one of a wealthy bourgeois was a type of family alliance totally in keeping with European traditions: the bride brought the money into the union, the bridegroom the distinguished name. De Luzières and Domitille traveled by *bateau* upriver from Ste. Genevieve and spent two weeks in St. Louis during their son's wedding festivities, which were the highlight of the social season in St. Louis in the spring of 1796.[7] A son from this successful marriage, Ceran St. Vrain (1802–1870), became a legend, a larger-than-life figure, in the far-western fur trade during the nineteenth century, creating, in partnership with William Bent, the famous trading house of Bent, St. Vrain and Company.[8]

Le tout St. Louis came to the St. Vrain-Dubreuil marriage, and no less a personage than Lieutenant Governor Zénon Trudeau witnessed it, as did Antoine P. Soulard. Soulard had served in the French royal navy alongside Jacques-Marcellin de St. Vrain and had descended the Ohio River from Pittsburgh in Madame de Luzières's party during the winter of 1793–1794. After arriving in Upper Louisiana, Soulard was sponsored by de Luzières, who viewed him as an adopted son.[9] Soulard himself had recently married Julie Cerré (daughter of the wealthy merchant, Gabriel Cerré), linking him by marriage with Auguste Chouteau, who had married Julie's older sister, Marie-Thérèse, in 1786. Soulard, a man with a French naval officer's *savoir faire*, ascended with amazing

6. St. Louis Old Cathedral Parish Records, Marriages (microfilm at the Lindbergh Branch of the St. Louis County Library).

7. See de Luzières to Carondelet, May 2, 1796, Papeles de Cuba, legajo 212A, Archivo General de Indies, Seville (henceforth this collection will be cited simply as PC [Papeles de Cuba] followed by the legajo number). Notice that de Luzières wrote this letter on the very day of his son's marriage. Collot remarked (Georges-Henri-Victor Collot, *A Journey in North America, containing a survey of the countries watered by the Mississippi, Ohio, Missouri, and other affluing rivers,* Christian Bay, ed., 3 vols. [Florence: O. Lange, 1924] 1:254) in 1795 that "all conveyances are made by water" between Ste. Genevieve and St. Louis, for no passable roadway existed between these two nerve centers of Spanish Illinois at the time.

8. See Stephen G. Hyslop, *Bound for Santa Fe: The Road to New Mexico and the American Conquest, 1806–1848* (Norman: University of Oklahoma Press, 2002), 391–98; David Lavender, *Bent's Fort* (Lincoln: University of Nebraska Press, 1972).

9. See Part 2, documents nos. 6 and 9.

speed and agility into the upper stratum of St. Louis society. His naval training meant that he was well versed in geometry and trigonometry, and Governor Carondelet soon appointed him surveyor general of Upper Louisiana, a
position he retained as an American citizen after the Louisiana Purchase.[10]

A second happy de Luzières marriage occurred in August 1802 in Ste. Genevieve, when the de Luzières's youngest child, Camille de Lassus de Luzières,
married Mathilde Villars, as high ranking a young lady as could be found on
the Mississippi frontier. She was the daughter of Don Louis Dubreuil Villars,
first Spanish commandant in Ste. Genevieve (1770–1776), and Marie-Louise
Vallé, daughter of François Vallé I and sister of François II, the latter serving
as commandant in Ste. Genevieve at the time of this marriage.

The witnesses to this marriage offer an interesting eclectic mix of the pow-
er elite in Ste. Genevieve at the time—some were native-born French (de
Luzières himself, his son Jacques-Marcellin, and Augustin-Charles Frémon
Delaurière), some were Creoles (i.e., born in the Illinois Country) of French-
Canadian ancestry (François Vallé, Jean-Baptiste Vallé, and Jean-Baptiste
Pratte), but two (John Price and Dr. Walter Fenwick) were recently arrived
Americans, who were gradually integrating themselves into the traditional
francophone community.[11] Price would later build the first brick structure
(which still stands) in Ste. Genevieve on the northeast corner of Market and
Third Streets, and Fenwick would be killed nine years later in an infamous
duel on Moreau's Island in the Mississippi River.[12] One of the bridegroom's
brothers (Jacques-Marcellin) came down from St. Louis for the wedding, but
the oldest and most powerful (by far), Lieutenant Governor Carlos Delassus,
did not, for his signature does not grace the marriage record. Perhaps family
tensions generated by de Luzières's deep indebtedness to Delassus (described
below) accounted for his absence.

Camille, who had descended the Ohio River with his mother during the
winter of 1793–1794, was the only one of the de Luzières children still residing at home with his parents in New Bourbon during the first years of the
nineteenth century. In addition to helping with the family's agricultural enterprises, Camille served as second lieutenant in the New Bourbon militia,

10. See Margot Liberty, Lee Irwin, and W. Raymond Wood, "The Missouri River Basin
on the 1795 Soulard Map: A Cartographic Landmark," *Great Plains Quarterly* 16, no. 3
(1996): 183–98.

11. Ste. Genevieve Paris Records (hereafter SGPR), Book B, Marriages, p. 88, microfilm
St. Louis Country Library, Lindbergh Branch.

12. In 1799 Jacques Maxwell, parish priest in Ste. Genevieve, tried, with help from de
Luzières and François Vallé, to get Fenwick an official appointment "in his double professions of doctor and surgeon" (see letter dated March 26, 1799 in PC, Leg. 2366), but there
is no evidence that they succeeded.

and as interim commandant of the New Bourbon District when his aging father was indisposed. Camille's judgments in several minor civil cases may be found in the Ste. Genevieve Civil Records.[13]

During the year after Camille's wedding, events in Upper Louisiana moved with a breathtaking rush. On March 6, 1803, Indiana territorial governor William Henry Harrison wrote from Grouseland, his home in Vincennes on the Wabash River, to Lieutenant Governor Carlos Delassus that the cession of Louisiana to France had been definitively concluded.[14] This news would have arrived on Delassus's desk in St. Louis within a week (George Rogers Clark had first blazed the overland trail between Kaskaskia and Vincennes in 1778), in mid-March 1803, which was two and one-half years after the secret Treaty of San Ildefonso had been signed by which Spain ceded Louisiana to France. The freshest political news from the Atlantic world always arrived in the region via Pittsburgh and the Ohio River, for it wasn't until May that Delassus received from New Orleans a copy of the Spanish royal order ceding Louisiana to Napoleon.[15]

A few months later, on August 2, 1803, Harrison wrote again, this time informing Delassus that France's cession of Louisiana to the United States seemed to be a done deal. This meant that de Luzières and his wife—born as subjects of the French Bourbon monarchy and having become subjects of the Spanish Borbón monarchy—learned in the spring of 1803 that they had become citizens of Napoleonic France, and then within a matter of months that they were soon to become citizens of the United States of America. These geopolitical revolutions, orchestrated in European capitals, would have mortified Monsieur and Madame de Luzières to the very bottom of their hearts, for the two political regimes they detested most in the entire world were Revolutionary France and republican United States of America.

As the grand commercial scheme that de Luzières, Audrain, and Tardiveau had envisioned was collapsing, de Luzières retreated into a more traditionally aristocratic enterprise—the pursuit of vast landed estates. His close friend, Lieutenant Governor Zénon Trudeau, was complaisantly willing to cooperate. De Luzières began with an extravagant request, asking Trudeau for a square league (7,056 arpents or roughly 6,000 acres) in the lead mining district a

13. See, for examples, Ste. Genevieve Civil Records, Litigations, nos. 13 and 69, microfilm at Missouri Historical Society, St. Louis.

14. Letter in Box 2, Delassus–St. Vrain Collection, Missouri Historical Society St. Louis (henceforth MHS).

15. De Luzières to Delassus, May 23, 1803, PC, Leg. 218, acknowledging the news sent from St. Louis to New Bourbon on May 18. François Vallé posted a translated copy of the order in Ste. Genevieve during the first week of June 1803 (Vallé to Delassus, June 5, 1803, PC, Leg. 217), and very likely de Luzières did the same thing in New Bourbon.

day's ride west of New Bourbon. De Luzières's petition laid out an ambitious plan for mining that included bringing his eldest son, Pierre-Joseph Delassus, from Holland to Upper Louisiana to help with the project. Trudeau granted de Luzières the square league requested on "a branch of the river St. François [today's St. Francis]," but Pierre-Joseph never crossed the Atlantic, the mining plans never came to fruition, and the U.S. Land Office commissioners eventually disallowed the grant.[16]

Trudeau conveyed additional large concessions to de Luzières—1,000 square arpents along Establishment Creek north of Ste. Genevieve and 810 arpents in the Ste. Genevieve District. Interestingly, the latter claim was based on the argument that de Luzières had built a cabin on the land in which a free black woman was living.[17] Then there was an additional grant of 500 arpents on the headwaters of Establishment Creek,[18] and 100 arpents along the Rivière de la Saline (Saline Creek) for the purpose of developing a maple sugar camp.[19] De Luzières evinced great hope in the future of the maple sugar industry in Upper Louisiana.[20] Once Carlos Delassus became lieutenant governor of Upper Louisiana, even Madame Domitille-Josèphe de Luzières got into the land-grab action. On September 17, 1799, her son granted her—shamelessly, one might note—4,000 arpents of land along the St. Francis River.[21] All of these far-flung concessions made in the twilight of the Spanish regime in Louisiana were surveyed by de Luzières's very dear friend, Antoine Soulard, and the U.S. Land Office eventually rejected them all.

But de Luzières's eager reach in pursuit of land stretched further afield— much further. In 1799 he petitioned the U.S. Congress to grant him 4,000 acres in the Northwest Territory near the mouth of the Illinois River.[22] He justified this request on the grounds that the Congress had already conveyed some compensatory concessions to other persons who had, like de Luzières,

16. See *American state papers: documents, legislative and executive, of the Congress of the United States, Public Lands* (Washington, D.C.: Gales and Seaton, 1832–1861), 3:584, 599–601. Hereafter *ASP, PL*.

17. *ASP, PL*, 2:467.

18. See survey dated March 15, 1800, in Amoureux Collection, MHS, St. Louis.

19. *ASP, PL*, 2:472. In the hope of making this concession secure, de Luzières went to his friend Jean-Baptiste Vallé and on the very same day that Vallé became the first American commandant of the Ste. Genevieve District (May 10, 1804) had him confirm the concession that Trudeau had initially made (see Ste. Genevieve Civil Records [hereafter SGCR], Concessions, no. 25, microfilm at Missouri Historical Society, St. Louis); to no avail, U.S. land commissioners rejected the claim in 1810.

20. See his commentaries appended to the 1797 New Bourbon census, reproduced below, document no. 29.

21. *ASP, PL*, 2:467.

22. See Part 2, document no. 33, "Memorial to U.S. Congress."

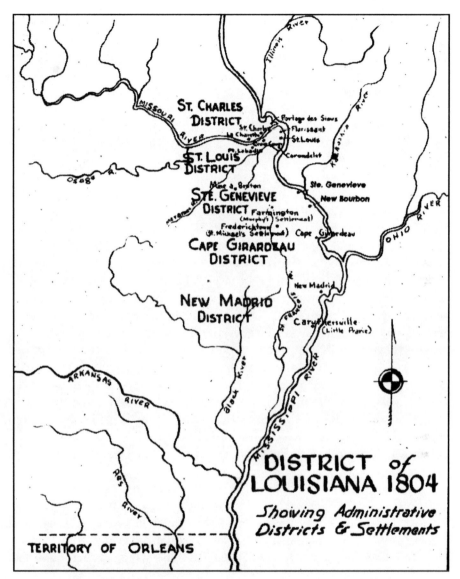

District of Louisiana (Upper Louisiana) in 1804. Notice the settlement at New Bourbon, although the New Bourbon administrative district was suppressed soon after the Louisiana Purchase. Adapted from Frederic A. Culmer, *History of Missouri for High School Students.*

been defrauded by the Scioto Company. De Luzières even went to the trouble to ask his old acquaintance, General Arthur St. Clair, governor of the Northwest Territory, to support his petition. St. Clair responded, in perfectly serviceable French, that he had no clout in the federal government but attempted to mollify de Luzières with a charming postscript: "I love the French very much. Is not the proof in the way I massacre their language?"[23] Assuming that the petition made it safely cross-country to Philadelphia, no evidence exists that Congress even considered providing satisfaction for de Luzières, who, after all, was a foreign national at the time.

On October 1, 1803, the marqués Sebastián Nicolás de Casa Calvo, last governor general of Spanish Louisiana, sent a dispatch to Lieutenant Governor Carlos Delassus detailing the retrocession of the province to France and then its cession to the United States. This letter arrived in St. Louis the middle of February 1804, and Delassus sent copies to his father along with a cover letter dated February 20. This packet of letters and dispatches did not reach de Luzières in New Bourbon until February 27, for such were the vagaries of the post in Upper Louisiana at the time.[24] Of course (as previously noted), these dramatic political occurrences had been known in the region since as early as August 1803. When de Luzières received Delassus's correspondence at the end of February 1804, the American Captain Amos Stoddard had just passed through Ste. Genevieve on his way upriver to St. Louis, and the father took it upon himself to inform the son that Stoddard had been commissioned by the Napoleon's prefect in New Orleans, Pierre-Clément Laussat, to receive Louisiana on behalf of the French government before then accepting it from France on behalf of the U.S. Government. By the time that Delassus received his father's letter from New Bourbon he had already met Stoddard face to face in St. Louis.

It goes virtually without saying that all this passing around of an enormous land mass, of undetermined extent but roughly the size of the United States as it existed at the time, was done by a handful of men in knee britches without the approval of, or even the knowledge of, the many men and women, black, red, and white, free and slave who happened to be living out their quotidian lives in the vast territory.

---

23. See de Luzières to St. Clair (May 28, 1799) and St. Clair's response from Cincinnati (March 4, 1800) in William Henry Smith, ed., *The St. Clair papers; the life and public services of Arthur St. Clair, soldier of the Revolutionary War, president of the Continental Congress, and Governor of the North-Western Territory, with his correspondence and other papers* (Cincinnati: Robert Clarke and Co., 1882), 2:491–94.

24. De Luzières to Delassus, February 27, 1804, Box 3, Delassus–St. Vrain Collection, MHS.

Stoddard finally appeared in St. Louis on February 24, and on Thursday, March 8, 1804, Delassus ordered his scribe, Joseph Hortiz, to post a public manuscript notice (since no printing press existed in St. Louis at the time.) written in French that on the morrow between 11:00 A.M. and 12:00 noon Stoddard would receive Upper Louisiana on behalf of the French republic.[25] Curiously, Hortiz did not bother to mention the fact that Stoddard would, the very next day, receive the province on behalf of the United States. Stoddard observed tears in the eyes of St. Louis's citizens as the American flag was raised over their frontier city. The American captain did not wish to acknowledge it, but these were surely tears of regret and sadness at losing a benign monarchical regime, not of delight and joy at acquiring an American republican government.[26]

At Stoddard's request, Delassus drafted for him brief descriptions of the most prominent men in Upper Louisiana at the time. Delassus went on at some length about the virtues of Antoine Soulard, Louis Lorimier, Pierre Chouteau, and Delassus's younger brothers, Jacques-Marcellin and Camille. But his description of his father was conspicuously brief: "Entirely devoted to public affairs. He has earned the approval of the captain general of Havana. He is my father. I can recommend him only with the zeal of a citizen servant."[27]

A month later, as if to confirm his son's appraisal of him as a man "devoted to public affairs" (which of course de Luzières never saw), de Luzières wrote that he felt compelled to draft a detailed inventory of all the official documents that had been deposited in the archives of the New Bourbon District during his tenure as commandant. He would do three copies, one for himself, one for Delassus, and one for Stoddard, for despite the fact that de Luzières was heartbroken about the coming of American sovereignty to the west bank of the Mississippi River he wished to see an orderly transition, he continued his devotion to public affairs. He bit his lower lip and concluded the letter to his son with a terse understatement: "It is not without pain and regret that I understand that this letter will be my last official correspondence with you. I will nevertheless continue to pray to God that he maintain you in his holy and worthy keeping."[28]

25. See ms. notice in ibid.

26. See William E. Foley, *The Genesis of Missouri: From Wilderness Outpost to Statehood* (Columbia: University of Missouri Press, 1989), 138–39.

27. Document dated March 6, 1804, Box 3, Delassus–St. Vrain Collection, MHS. See letter from Captain General Luis de Las Casas to de Luzières (May 20, 1794, printed in *ASP, PL,* 3:600) in which Las Casas praises de Luzières for his work in helping to prepare Spanish Illinois for an anticipated American invasion during the winter of 1793–1794.

28. Letter in Box 3, Delassus–St. Vrain Collection, MHS. None of the three inventories that de Luzières compiled in April 1804 seems to have survived, and at some point many

When de Luzières wrote this letter on April 10, 1804, the New Bourbon District, *his* district, had already been extinguished, for on March 10 Stoddard had named Jean-Baptiste Vallé commandant of the Ste. Genevieve District of Upper Louisiana, and this new American district included all of what had been with de Luzières's jurisdiction. The New Bourbon District had always been an administrative anomaly, indeed a bit of a geopolitical absurdity. Carondelet had created it as a favor for a friend, simply to serve the vanity and political ambitions of his Flemish countryman, de Luzières. De Luzières as commandant of the district for seven years never had a substantial influence on the administration of Spanish Louisiana. His largest direct contribution to the history of North America was his successful effort to recruit Americans to migrate to Upper Louisiana during the decade preceding the Louisiana Purchase. Nevertheless, something heroic inheres in his valiant efforts to maintain a terrestrial universe, against the tides of history, in keeping with what he deemed the celestial powers wanted on this earth. Moreover, during his tenure as commandant he generated a treasure trove of source documents pertaining to Upper Louisiana in late colonial times. A sampling of these illuminating writings, never before published and including his detailed 1797 census of New Bourbon, are presented in translation in the second half of this volume.

As the macrocosm of world events chagrined de Luzières during the last years of his life, so also did the microcosm of his personal finances. He had fled France a wealthy man, but his travels and troubles in the New World had bled him white. His various schemes for agriculture, commerce, and mining had not panned out, and he spent the last years of his life in embarrassing financial straits, becoming hopelessly dependent upon the largesse of his son, Lieutenant Governor Delassus. In 1800 de Luzières was forced to beg Delassus to pay off his debt of some 204 piastres to François Moreau, a wealthy merchant in Ste. Genevieve.[29] But this was only a small fragment of de Luzières's indebtedness. As soon as Delassus arrived in Upper Louisiana in 1796 to take command at New Madrid, his father had become heavily indebted to him, and this indebtedness only increased after Delassus moved up to become lieutenant governor at St. Louis in 1799.

In October 1801, Delassus sat down at his desk in St. Louis and sorted out all the receipts for payments he had made on his father's behalf to virtually every member of the power elite in the region—in Ste. Genevieve, in New Bourbon, in St. Louis, and in Kaskaskia—between July 1796 and Septem-

---

of the documents from the New Bourbon archives were integrated into the Ste. Genevieve Civil Records, where they may yet be found.

29. See letter dated August 23, 1800, in Box 2, Delassus–St. Vrain Collection, MHS.

ber 1801. De Luzières was incomparably the biggest debtor in Upper Louisiana, and Delassus's tidy tabulation of his father's debts runs more than eight manuscript pages in small script.[30] Included among the products that kept the de Luzières's household running in rather lavish style are lots and lots of imported fabrics: woolen, cotton, silk—from England, Ireland, France, Flanders, Russia, China (Nanking).[31] Lots and lots of alcoholic beverages: wine, whiskey, beer, rum, tafia (crude variety of rum), peach brandy. Some local products appear, such as six buffalo robes purchased from Auguste Chouteau, whose men were bringing them into St. Louis from up the Missouri River. Delicacies included olives, olive oil, coffee, tea, sugar, fruit preserves (from Havana), chocolate, mustard, cheese, and ham. Ham may well have been a local product, but the price of the cheeses (two piastres a piece) suggests that they were imported. De Luzières consumption of European produce in New Bourbon while running wildly in debt is reminiscent of Thomas Jefferson drinking fine French wines at Monticello while his plantation went to hell in a handbasket.

According to de Luzières's own account (his 1797 census of New Bourbon) his household included eight black slaves, and he bought another slave in 1799 (see Part 2, document no. 32). But he also hired labor to help out with domestic chores, including two free black women. Delassus paid Catin (diminutive of Catherine) eighty piastres over a five-year period, and Zabet (diminutive of Elisabeth) twenty. It's impossible to determine the rates at which these wages were calculated, but in any case eighty piastres was a good deal of money in that time and place. De Luzières also paid out twenty piastres to "Monsieur Pratt's old black maid." "Pratt" was evidently the wealthy merchant of Ste. Genevieve, Jean-Baptiste Pratte, and the maid in question was his slave. Nevertheless, the twenty piastres in wages seem to have been paid to her directly, and not to Pratte as rent for his slave. This is one of several sources that suggest slaves could, and did, earn their own money on their own free time in the Illinois Country.[32]

The listing of de Luzières's hired help includes a final curious entry designating ten piastres for "Madame Louison, midwife." During the five-year period 1796–1801, no woman within the extended de Luzières family living in New Bourbon was bearing children, which must mean that this midwife had been hired to facilitate the birth of Agnès, a black slave child born in February

30. SGCR, Land Transactions (Mortgages), no. 52.

31. When fabrics are identified as from "Russie" and "Nankin" (Nanking) it's possible that these fabrics were woven (in England or France) in the Russian or Chinese style rather than having in fact come from those exotic faraway locations.

32. See the case of Jasmin in Carl J. Ekberg, *François Vallé and His World* (Columbia: University of Missouri Press, 2002), 170, 176, 184–86, and Part 2, document no. 25.

1800 and baptized in April.[33] Agnès survived infancy (only one-in-three children, black or white, did in that society), became an American (although a slave) with the Louisiana Purchase, and was eventually bought at auction sale by Camille Delassus from his father's estate in 1807 for $215.00.[34]

In any event, Delassus compiled the account of his father's indebtedness to him in St. Louis on October 17, 1801, signed it, and hand carried it down to Ste. Genevieve two weeks later.[35] Delassus obviously deemed this an urgent trip, for we just saw that he had not even bothered to come down to Ste. Genevieve for the wedding of his younger brother Camille. The total amount of bills paid by Delassus on behalf of his parents was a very substantial 7,425 piastres over a five-year period. The de Luzières family had demonstrated ever since setting foot in North America in 1790 a prodigious talent for burning through large sums of money to maintain a lifestyle somewhat in keeping with what they had enjoyed back home in Flanders—the "douceur de vivre" that, according to Charles-Maurice de Talleyrand, the famous diplomat and voluptuary, characterized life in eighteenth-century France for members of the upper classes.

On November 3, de Luzières examined the account and countersigned it, and then he and his wife agreed to mortgage "all of their possessions, moveables and unmoveables, those present and those to come, of whatever nature they may be" to provide security for their debt. In early February 1804, Delassus again journeyed to Ste. Genevieve to deal with his parents' indebtedness. This time the amount was a whopping 16,300 piastres, including some unresolved debts going back ten years to the time that de Luzières had been in business with Pierre Audrain and Bartholémé Tardiveau.[36] Although bankrupt, Monsieur and Madame de Lassus de Luzières were permitted to live out the remaining two years of their lives in the relative comfort of their residence near New Bourbon.

After the death of de Luzières and his wife in 1806, Marie-Philippe Leduc, Carlos Delassus's former secretary from St. Louis, helped cope with the mess of his estate.[37] In New Bourbon on June 21, 1807, he officiated at an auction sale of cattle and black slaves. A total of nine slaves were sold at this sale, of which Camille bought four.[38] In keeping with the French Black Code, first introduced

33. SGPR, Baptisms 1786–1820, p. 125.

34. See document dated June 21, 1807, in Box 3, Delassus–St. Vrain Collection, MHS.

35. SGCR, Land Transactions (Mortgages), no. 52.

36. See legal document dated February 9, 1804, in Box 3, Delassus–St. Vrain Collection, MHS.

37. Robert R. Archibald, "Honor and Family: The Career of Lt. Gov. Carlos de Hault de Lassus," *Gateway Heritage* 12 (Spring 1992): 38–40.

38. Auction sale, June 21, 1807, Box 3, Delassus–St. Vrain Collection, MHS.

to Louisiana in 1724, no young child was separated from its mother.[39] For Jupiter, Camille paid $10.00, which price reveals that he bought the slave, who had become infirm and unable to work, only to care for him in his old age. A decade earlier, Camille and Jupiter had worked together shoulder-to-shoulder, one a French aristocrat and the other a black slave, plowing the fields of the de Luzières plantation. Jupiter seems to have lived until 1811, when he was buried in the consecrated ground of Ste. Genevieve's now-historic cemetery.[40] Proceeds from this sale, 1,761 piastres, hardly put a dent in de Luzières's debts, however. Carlos Delassus retired from the Spanish army in 1811 and spent much of the last three decades of his life (he died in New Orleans in 1843) working to pay off family debts and restore the family's good name and honor.[41]

Leduc also helped distribute some personal effects that remained in the family. "Skirts, corsets, and linens" were conveyed in equal shares to Camille's wife, Mathilde Villars, and to the wife of Camille's older brother Jacques-Marcellin, Marie-Félicité Dubreuil. Leduc sequestered de Luzières's most precious and intimate personal effects—a large cross, a small cross, the medal for the Order of St. Michel, a gold watch, four snuff boxes, and a medal bearing Louis XVI's portrait—and had them sent to Carlos Delassus, head of the family, who was at that time serving in New Orleans. It's not clear what happened to de Luzières's library, "consisting of close to 600 volumes after 78 were sold to pay [debts] to Monsieur [Jean-Baptiste?] Bequette."[42] However, it's worth noting that this library was certainly the largest ever assembled in Upper Louisiana during the colonial era. When the founder of St. Louis, Pierre Liguest Laclède, died in 1778, he left a library of two hundred volumes, which Auguste Chouteau purchased from Laclède's estate and enlarged to more than six hundred volumes by the time of his death—but that occurred in 1829.[43] We don't know the titles in de Luzières's library, other than an *Encyclopédie*, but most, if not all, of his books had accompanied him across the Atlantic Ocean from France, along with his high-tech millstones and his daughter's harp.

In February 1804 Captain Stoddard passed through New Bourbon and noted that it consisted of some thirty-five houses.[44] Stoddard likely underestimated

39. See Article XLIII in *Code Noir. The Colonial Slave Laws of French Mid-America*, trans. Grady Kilman, with Carl J. Ekberg, Pierre Lebeau, and William Potter (Naperville: Center for French Colonial Studies, 2004), 44–45.

40. See SGPR, Burials 1787–1837, p. 92.

41. Archibald, "Honor and Family," 32–41.

42. Leduc to Delassus, February 18, 1807, Box 3, Delassus–St. Vrain Collection, MHS.

43. William E. Foley and C. David Rice, *The First Chouteaus, River Barons of Early St. Louis* (Urbana: University of Illinois Press, 1983), 24.

44. Amos Stoddard, *Sketches, historical and descriptive, of Louisiana* (Philadelphia: Mathew Carey, 1812), 216.

a bit, for de Luzières's 1797 enumeration of New Bourbon proper (see Document no. 27 below) lists thirty-eight households. In any case, all the houses have now disappeared, and the village's former site is dominated by a local commercial company, Loida Agricultural Services. One may stand there in the midst of farm equipment and fertilizer tanks and gaze—eastward across the Mississippi River toward the site of old Kaskaskia, and southward to the hilltop several hundred yards distant where de Luzières's residence stood at the end of the colonial era.

The landscape in the area has changed little since his day (including the huge swath of plowlands stretching from the foot of the hills to the Mississippi), but the hilltop is barren (except for the remains of a decaying pig sty). De Luzières's residence has also long since disappeared, although the abandoned structure at the foot of the hill near U.S. Highway 61 may contain oak logs scavenged decades ago from de Luzières's house.[45] The unpaved service road leading down the hillside was likely created by de Luzières to provide access from his residence to the Grand Champ, and beyond to the west bank of the Mississippi River. This road is the only visible artifact dating from the eighteenth century, although a treasure trove of material culture doubtless lies beneath the ground surface of the area.

The casual observer detects nothing in this engaging scene to suggest that a French nobleman in culottes and with powdered hair once held court here as Spanish commandant of the New Bourbon District, and it is hard to imagine an aristocratic family living there in more or less lavish style. But that's the way it was on the Mississippi frontier during the 1790s when Pierre-Charles de Hault de Lassus de St. Vrain de Luzières and his family enjoyed from their house "the full scope of this seductive view," in the words of their compatriot and fellow expatriot, Nicolas de Finiels.[46]

De Luzières last two years on earth were not made more pleasant by the fact that he had become a U.S. citizen, for he was inflexibly opposed to the American republican regime that had acquired Louisiana. As he witnessed the throngs of Americans pushing into the Mississippi Valley, he had observed to Governor Carondelet, "I nevertheless aver that I intend to live and die more devoted than ever to royal authority and monarchical government."[47] Antoine

45. The file in the Historic American Buildings Survey (Library of Congress) on the de Luzières residence incorrectly identifies this existing structure, located below the hills, as the de Luzières residence. But the de Luzières house is no longer standing, and the misleading HABS report should be either totally rewritten or expunged from the files.

46. *An Account of Upper Louisiana,* ed. Carl J. Ekberg and William E. Foley and trans. Carl J. Ekberg (Columbia: University of Missouri Press, 1989), 46–47.

47. Below, Part 2, document no. 18.

De Luzières's burial record, Ste. Genevieve, 1806. The location of his grave in the historic cemetery in Ste. Genevieve is unknown. Reproduced courtesy of the St. Louis Archdiocesan Archives, Shrewsbury, Missouri.

Burial Record of Pierre-Charles Delassus de Luzières

December 21 [1806] has been buried in the cemetery of Ste. Genevieve the body of Pierre-Charles Delassus de Luzières, former civil and military commandant of New Bourbon. He was a native of France and was sixty-seven [in fact, sixty-eight] years old. In witness thereof, I have signed.

Soulard, who de Luzières had sponsored when he arrived in Upper Louisiana in 1794, was more flexible and opportunistic. He wrote to the U.S. land commissioners in 1806 that his "fidelity to support the Constitution of the United States" was one of his "constant Principles and my invariable rule of action."[48] Just as well that de Luzières never read those words of his former protégé, for he surely would have considered them a betrayal of their once common loyalty to the Bourbon monarchies of France and Spain.

It was no small life that de Luzières had lived on two continents. But he was interred without fanfare in a now-forgotten grave on December 21, 1806, the darkest day of the year, in the graveyard (now the Historic Cemetery) in Ste. Genevieve, for New Bourbon, never having been a parish, never had a proper burial ground. Jacques Maxwell, the Dublin-born priest serving as curate in Ste. Genevieve, dryly inscribed in the burial record that de Luzières was the former civil and military commandant of New Bourbon, that he was a native of France, and that he was sixty-seven years old. Maxwell's error in noting de Luzières's age (he was in fact sixty-eight) is emblematic of how quickly de Luzières was brushed aside with the coming of American government to Upper

48. Soulard to Land Commissioners, May 2, 1806, *The Territorial Papers of the United States,* Vol. 13, *The Territory of Louisiana-Missouri, 1803–1806,* comp. and ed. Clarence E. Carter (Washington, D.C.: U.S. Government Printing Office, 1913), 534. I am indebted to Anne Woodhouse of the Missouri Historical Society for providing me with this document.

Louisiana. His job had vanished and his status vastly diminished—for he was no longer a district commandant under the Spanish monarchy, and the U.S. Constitution specifically prohibited the existence of a hereditary aristocracy on American soil. Within a matter of years his grave, and that of his wife, were as long forgot as any loyalty to the Bourbon king of Spain, whom de Luzières had served to the very best of his considerable abilities.

Part II

Source Documents

||||||||||||||||||||||||||||||||||||||||||||||||||||||||||||||||||||||||||||||||||||||||||||

Most of the letters and documents presented below were written by de Lu-zières between 1793 and 1804, during which entire time he lived in the Mississippi River valley; a handful were written by other persons but pertain directly to de Luzières, his dreams, his plans, and his activities. De Luzières's correspondence emanated overwhelmingly from his residence at New Bourbon in Spanish Il-linois, although he wrote a scattering of letters from other locales in the Mis-sissippi Valley—New Orleans, St. Louis, and New Madrid. I selected documents that are illustrative of de Luzières's life and work on the Mississippi frontier, and, more important, those that illuminate the larger geopolitical and cul-tural scene in the region at a critical time period, when the Spanish regime in Louisiana was crumbling and Americans were in droves pushing up to the Mississippi River from the east. I translated all documents from French origi-nals, except de Luzières's recruitment pamphlet (document no. 17), which he had translated into English before having it printed and distributed in Lex-ington, Kentucky. The documents appear in chronological order.

No. 1

De Luzières had been in New Orleans for several weeks when he addressed this letter to Governor Carondelet. He sketches out plans for bringing his family to the Mississippi Valley from Pittsburgh, as well as the French immigrants recently settled at Gallipolis on the upper Ohio River. His proposals for stimulating development in Upper Louisiana were fleshed out in his next letter (see below). De Luzières got back to the Illinois Country from New Orleans in August 1793 and immediately set to work overseeing construction of his residence at New Bourbon. His family finally arrived there safely from Pittsburgh in February 1794. François Vallé was first citizen of Ste. Genevieve and soon to become commandant. Israel Dodge had immigrated from the east side of the Mississippi and was one of the foremost citizens of New Bourbon. Bartholomé Tardiveau was de Luzières's business partner.

De Lassus de Luzières to Carondelet
Papeles de Cuba, legajo 214, Archivo General de Indies, Seville (henceforth this collection will be cited simply as PC [Papeles de Cuba] followed by the legajo number) New Orleans, April 30, 1793

Monsieur le Baron:

The spot where I'm proposing to build my residence, and where verily the principal families of farmers from Gallipolis will also settle, will be called New Bourbon. This is part of a concession originally granted to Monsieur François Vallé of Ste. Genevieve, who in turn ceded it to Sieur [Israel] Dodge, who in turn ceded half of it to Monsieur [Bartholémé] Tardiveau, who in turn ceded it to me as a gift. I beg Your Excellency to approve and accept the primitive transmissions of title for this concession.

On this portion of farmsteads, already granted by the government, I intend to introduce the productive method of agriculture employed in the Chatellerie de Bouchain, province of French Hainault, our former and common homeland [*patrie*] But independently of this I wish to work with Your Excellency to seek out mines for lead and other minerals in the Illinois. I wish to employ practical and advantageous methods to exploit them as is done in Germany and Savoy. I beg Your Excellency to authorize Monsieur Zénon Trudeau, commandant [i.e., lieutenant governor] of the Illinois, . . . to grant to me the land where I will find the said mines, together with surrounding land sufficient to permit their exploitation, always provided that it has not been previously granted to others.

I've brought with me to America Monsieur Derbigny, my son-in-law, his wife and their child, as well as my two youngest sons [Jacques-Marcellin-Léon and Philippe-François-Camille], all of whom will surely come to join me next autumn along with my wife and our people [*nos gens*] numbering six. I therefore would hope that Your Excellency will certainly authorize Monsieur Zénon Trudeau to grant each to my son-in-law and my son a plantation at the place in the Illinois that they will select, and of an extent proportional to the agriculture and settlements that they plan to develop there.

Monsieur le Baron,

Your humble and very obedient servant,

De Hault de Lassus

No. 2

Many of de Luzières's proposals to Governor Carondelet during the spring of 1793 would be reiterated in his comments on the 1797 census of New Bourbon, revealing that his proposed reforms were advancing very slowly—if at all. De Luzières's impassioned plea for an all-out war against the Osage Indians seems curiously grandiose and reveals a newcomer's relative ignorance of, and naivete about, Indian affairs in Upper Louisiana. In addition to the fact that such a war was not an objective practicality, the Chouteau brothers in St. Louis, who had intimate trading relations with the Osages and likely had children by Osage women, would never have countenanced a war à l'outrance against this tribe.[1]

De Luzières to Monsieur le Baron [de Carondelet]   PC, Leg. 214
New Orleans, May 1, 1793

Monsieur le Baron:

For fear of abusing Your Excellency's goodwill and kindness with excessive correspondence concerning the Illinois, I will assemble here all the remaining topics pertaining to the prosperity of this fascinating colony. These are based either on the wishes and tasks of the principal habitants [of Illinois] or on the detailed observations that I myself have made while conducting an exact survey of the various districts of this colony.

1. See Gilbert C. Din and A. P. Nasatir, *The Imperial Osages: Spanish-Indian Diplomacy in the Mississippi Valley* (Norman: University of Oklahoma Press, 1983), passim; also William E. Foley and C. David Rice, *The First Chouteaus: River Barons of Early St. Louis* (Urbana: University of Illinois Press, 1983), 45–59; Frederick A. Hodes, *Beyond the Frontier: A History of St. Louis to 1821* (Tucson: Patrice Press, 2004), 252–55; Tanis C. Thorne, *The Many Hands of My Relations: French and Indians on the Lower Missouri* (Columbia: University of Missouri Press, 1996), 91–97.

1. Surgeon-Doctor for Ste. Genevieve and New Bourbon

I reported verbally to Your Excellency that there is no surgeon or doctor at Ste. Genevieve, and that during my short visit to that region I myself witnessed several accidents that became nastily aggravated because of the absolute lack of this precious aid for humanity. Your Excellency therefore agreed to my proposition to accept Sieur Le Moine, presently residing at Gallipolis, as Surgeon-Doctor and grant him a salary of 15 piastres per month. He will establish his residence at New Bourbon, a neighboring place to Ste. Genevieve, and will care for the sick and wounded of both places. I've taken advantage of Monsieur Audrain's departure [for the Ohio River valley] to inform the said Sieur Le Moine of his appointment and the salary associated with it, and to urge him to get on with his relocation. It only remains for me to ask Your Excellency to be kind enough to send me his brevet, or other documents, to validate his appointment so that I can convey it to him when I arrive at Ste. Genevieve, where he will doubtless have already arrived.

[Carondelet's marginal note: This article is granted and the brevet for surgeon of the new settlements is granted to Monsieur Le Moine with the salary of 15 piastres.]

2. Midwife

Ste. Genevieve has only one, old midwife. Independently of the general interest that I always have in mind for the greatest good for this colony, I have in this case a personal interest, because of my recently married daughter, to make sure about the abilities of this midwife. The result of intelligence that I have gathered concerning her is that a majority of the habitants do not have great confidence in her. Moreover, she is very old and continues to live in the old town of Ste. Genevieve with four or five of the remaining residents. She is little inclined to agree with the majority of folks who are much put out with and inconvenienced by the very frequent flooding of the river. They decided several years ago to relocate their residences to two new areas. One of these, which is the most populous, is on the Petite Côtes [Little Hills] and it retains the name, "Ste. Genevieve." The other, which is less populated, is on the Grandes Côtes [Big Hills] and henceforth will be called New Bourbon. Because of this situation [i.e., the absence of a good midwife], so critical for humanity and so adverse for the increase of the population, I believe that Your Excellency will approve that I am proposing the means to remedy this inconvenience to prevent such disastrous consequences. Therefore, I am honored to recommend that he accept the person named Dame La Caisse, presently living at Gallipolis, as midwife for Ste.

Genevieve and New Bourbon and to grant her a modest salary of 6 or 7 piastres per month. I can assure Your Excellency that the said Dame La Caisse is very well educated and possesses uncommon theoretical knowledge. She has practiced with happy success and has earned accolades from educated folks, as well as gaining the confidence of the general populace of Gallipolis.

[Carondelet's marginal note: There are some problems with this article that at present cannot be resolved.]

3. Transfer of the church, the commandery, and the records from
   Ste. Genevieve, and construction of a new church

Your excellency has seen in the preceding article the reasons why the habitants of Ste. Genevieve have established two new communities on the hills. The little map herewith attached will permit him to gain an overview of this locality and district, as well as the locations of the old town of Ste. Genevieve, the new town, and New Bourbon. The new town of Ste. Genevieve, situated on the little hills, contains the largest number, as well as the most substantial, of the colony's habitants. It is therefore only right that it be unified within its boundaries and that the principal and parish church is being transferred there, along with the rectory, the commandery and the records office. It is equally just that the adjunct chapel, which the curé [i.e., the Abbé de St. Pierre] agrees to serve, should be located at New Bourbon on the big hills, where there are already about 40 residences. The said curé and habitants of the said Ste. Genevieve have already petitioned the government, requesting that it authorize and order this transfer but also asking that the building of the new church be underwritten by His Majesty.

One might well object that this last request is contrary to the usual practice, according to which the government ordinarily helps to finance only the first church in any particular locality. But to quash this objection it suffices to observe to Your Excellency that in this case there is no question of building or repairing an old church, decaying or falling into ruins, but rather it's a matter of transferring a church, constructing it anew, and enlarging it with a major effort. This is the same effort required by the unfortunate habitants, who at great expense had to change their residences; there they endured very considerable losses of goods and animals and suffered very serious illnesses caused by flooding of the river. They have exhausted the remainder of their resources building their new residences, which are still for the most part only provisional cabins. These circumstances quite demonstrate their inability to pay for the building of a new church and to give them hope that the government will deign to do so.

If, despite this just plea, overriding circumstances prevent Your Excellency from underwriting the entire expense of transferring and constructing the said church, the habitants hope with confidence that, considering their losses and their unhappy situation, Your Majesty will at least consider providing assistance as follows: 1. The modest sum of 300 piastres in cash to defray part of the costs of labor. 2. Nine hundred pounds of iron and 600 pounds of nails of different sizes. 3. Six cases of window glass. These items, plus the 300 piastres, would be divided on the basis of two-thirds for the principal church at Ste. Genevieve and one-third for the adjunct chapel at New Bourbon. Finally, a church bell is necessary that would be large enough to announce divine services, as well as giving alarm in case of emergencies or fires.

[Carondelet's marginal note: This article is agreed to, and orders will be dispatched with His Majesty's nomination of Don (Pierre) Didier as curé of the new settlements.]

4. Fences for the fields, and pasturing for the cattle

In the Illinois there is a major inconvenience that is very prejudicial to the progress of agriculture and that is an effective obstacle to the long-term prosperity of this colony. This relates to the fences for the fields that are cultivated. These fences are only put in good order and maintained from April 1 until the harvest. From the time of the harvest until April 1 the fields remain open and accessible to livestock, especially the large herds of swine. As a consequence of this practice it is impossible to cultivate winter wheat and other winter grains, and there are no managed meadows for pasturage. The simplest and cheapest means of remedying this abuse would be to maintain the fencing in good order for the entire year. This method would cost much less than the current, abusive practice of having to rebuild them almost from scratch each year in the month of April. Because the fields are open and accessible to livestock from the harvest until April 1, and the livestock are not tended to as they are in Europe, the fences are broken and destroyed, not to mention that the habitants tear them down and carry them away for firewood.

Another inconvenience that is equally very prejudicial to agriculture is the general release during the entire year of the livestock into the woods and vast prairies that are abundant in this colony. The result of this unfortunate practice is threefold: 1. The livestock, abandoned to themselves, necessarily cause incalculable damage to gardens and other enclosures that they break into and then go on their way. 2. There is a very great loss of livestock which wander off and become the prey of Indians. 3. Finally, we are deprived of milk, butter, and cheese; I know in the Illinois several colonists who own at least thirty cows and are nevertheless deprived of these resources. These disorders could be advantageously prevented if, as is done in Europe, common pastures were created, either in the woods or in the large prairies, situated both high and low, that lie near this post. There livestock could graze while tended by a guardian who would take them out each morning and bring them back in each evening. In this way, the cows could be profitably milked twice each day, as is done in our Flanders.

If the government has any problem with issuing edicts to implement these prudent recommendations, it would surely be desirable for Your Excellency at least to make them known to the commandant of the colony so that he could instruct the habitants, exhorting them to implement them, to put them into practice. For my part, I would with pleasure cooperate in every way that I possibly can.

[Carondelet's marginal note: The commandant will be ordered to assemble the habitants, and if the largest number, as well as the most consequential, agree with these recommendations they will be enacted.]

5. Military commandants and garrisons in all the posts

Since the private discussions that Your Excellency permitted me to hold with him, it has occurred to me that he was very much persuaded of the necessity of establishing military commandants in all the posts. They would have no financial or commercial connections with the habitants, but would exhibit the talents, the deft touch, and the firmness necessary to fulfill their important responsibilities. Your Excellency has also appeared to be equally persuaded of the utility of establishing a shared garrison in the posts [i.e., Ste. Genevieve and New Bourbon] of this colony that would be large enough to be respected. This garrison would also spread some hard currency, the circulation of which by stimulating economic activity and promoting good habits would effectively contribute to the general well-being of the habitants. I can only join my hopes with his [Your Excellency's] so that this colony will soon enjoy a redoubled effect of Your Excellency's patronage.

[Carondelet's marginal note: This article has been sent to the court for consultation.]

6. War against the Osages and praise for the Shawnees

An account his been sent to Your Excellency about the excesses committed and vexations caused by the Osage tribe in the various outposts of the Illinois and Louisiana, where theft of horses and other livestock continues, indeed increases. This causes incalculable damage to agriculture and to commerce. Your Excellency still hesitates to take effective measures so that the war, already declared, against this tribe can be pursued with the strength and the zeal necessary either to persuade them to conclude an enduring peace or to destroy them totally. Monsieur Lorimier is worthy in many ways of the confidence with which Your Excellency honors him. I've discussed this serious subject with him because it would be convenient to assemble under the authority of the military commandants all the friendly Indians (whom we would supply and furnish with munitions), the young militiamen, the hunters, and others at the stockaded forts at the various posts exposed to the Osage incursions—such as St. Louis, Ste. Genevieve, New Madrid, Arkansas, and Natchitoches. They would be ordered to rendezvous at a given time in a designated place. This would be planned at the season when the Osage maize plantings were far enough along so that they could not be reseeded. From the rendezvous point the assembled force would advance with some light canons on the Osage village, attack it with vigor, and destroy it along with the maize fields. Monsieur Lorimier also thinks that during this expedition it would be prudent to gather all the habitants left behind in all the posts, along with the women and children, and place them either in forts or in the sturdiest houses. There, in case of an Indian attack, they could be protected and defended by the post garrisons, as well as the habitants left behind that are able to bear arms.

[Carondelet's marginal note: The commandant of the Illinois (Lieutenant Governor Trudeau) is ordered to mount a general and concentrated expedition against the Osage village in coordination with New Madrid, Monsieur Lorimier, and the commandants of Natchitoches and Arkansas. A sum of money will be authorized for this project.]

I'm taking this occasion to place before Your Excellency an article, which I have also articulated to Monsieur Lorimier, that has an essential bearing on the war against the Osages. This concerns the brave tribe of Shawnees. Since this tribe crossed into the territory of His Catholic Majesty [i.e., King of Spain], it has conducted itself perfectly well, in all possible situations and with no exceptions. Nonetheless, the chief of this tribe has never received from the government any testimony showing its satisfaction, and this has bothered him and hurt his feelings. Monsieur Lorimier believes that this omission can be more than rectified if Your Excellency would deign to send to this chief an official letter expressing Your Excellency's satisfaction with the manner in which this tribe has always comported itself; and furthermore expressing his total confidence in this tribe's zeal and attachment to the royal service. He should also send a decorative object and some usual small present.

[Carondelet's marginal note: Monsieur de Lassus will carry a large medal, an official letter, and a present for the chief of the Shawnees.]

7. Monsieur Zénon Trudeau

The final topic for me to discuss with Your Excellency, which profoundly concerns the welfare of the entire [Spanish] Illinois, relates to Monsieur Zénon Trudeau, its present commandant. Habitants of all classes consider his appointment a harbinger of good news for the administration of this government. It is the first benefit coming from Your Excellency's protection and bodes well for the general prosperity of the colony. This officer, far from dashing our hopes, has affirmed them, and to some extent realized those depending on his position; moreover, he is also universally loved and respected. I myself have witnessed during the two-and-a-half months that I spent in that region [Spanish Illinois] the zeal, the grace, the justice, and the firmness with which, according to circumstances, he carried out the complex responsibilities of his position. Monsieur Tardiveau and I are obliged to offer to Your Excellency on this occasion homage on behalf of the entire colony. . . . I cannot dispense observing to Your Excellency that this officer [Trudeau] regulates all the commerce and trade and hunting licenses in the Missouri. This should generate some income for him, but it has been rendered null by the war with the Osages. . . . The means to improve his situation, which Your Excellency will surely find equitable and just, would be to provide him with the same annual salary as the commandant at New Madrid, who has far fewer needs. . . . I would be very happy if in returning to Illinois to settle down there I would be authorized to inform that brave and excellent commandant of your satisfaction with his service and your intention to improve his salary.

[Carondelet's marginal note: Destruction of the Osages will greatly revivify commerce and trade. As a consequence, Monsieur Trudeau, whom I will gladly maintain as commandant of his post while he continues to function as he does at this time, will see his income increase, which present circumstances prevent me from doing.]

I am with the very profound respect, Monsieur le Baron,
Your very humble and very obedient servant,
de Hault de Lassus

No. 3

Henri Peyroux de la Coundrenière's two dispatches of November 14, 1793, constituted his last-ditch effort to thwart de Luzières's plan to have the locus of a new settlement, New Bourbon, situated on the hills just south of Ste. Genevieve, where de Luzières was in the midst of building a large residence. Notice that Peyroux avoids attacking de Luzières personally, but confines his arguments for locating New Bourbon at the Saline, where Peyroux owned large tracts of real estate, to geographical and political considerations. Lieutenant Governor Zénon Trudeau soon removed Peyroux as commandant of Ste. Genevieve, with the connivance of de Luzières and François Vallé (whom Trudeau named to replace Peyroux as commandant), and of course Peyroux lost the argument over the location of New Bourbon.[2] Peyroux's suggestion that the government should subsidize mixed white-Indian marriages is especially important coming from a man who owned an Indian slave. Moreover, Peyroux's language on this issue is significant (mariage des blancs et indiens) *for his use of* indiens *rather than* sauvages *and for the fact that he uses gender-neutral terms (not* indiennes*), his choice of words suggesting that at least in principle he countenanced marriages between Indian men and white women.*

Henri Peyroux de la Coudrenière to Carondelet   PC, Leg. 207B
November 14, 1793

Monsieur:

I am certainly delighted that Your Lordship has decided to accord his protection to the new settlement called New Bourbon. And it is with the greatest satisfaction that I will obey his orders to lend all my efforts to contribute to its success. Monsieur de Luzières is still ill. His house is completed, and when he has moved in he will come and spend several days with me as he has promised. There, relieved of the persons who surround him, we can at our ease discuss the means to promote this new settlement.

When Monsieur de Luzières arrived here last year, he saw only the environs of the old village and some new residences in the hills. The site of New Ste. Genevieve displeased him, with good reason, and he decided to establish his residence at a little hamlet that is only sixty arpents [roughly two miles] distant. Because this hamlet is very high up the view it affords is charming. But a fine view is not sufficient for establishing a great settlement. This hamlet is so badly situated that 100 families could never subsist there. There are in the area only two or three little springs from which flow a tiny stream of water that gets lost within a couple of hundred feet from the source. The high elevation of the place makes digging wells difficult. A little stream flows about 20 arpents [roughly three-quarters of a mile] distant but this is dry half the year, and as I write not a drip of water flows in it. Besides this hamlet is very far from the Mississippi, and to reach it one must travel 50 arpents [roughly 1.8

---

2. Trudeau and Vallé were friends and maintained a back-channel correspondence between St. Louis and Ste. Genevieve during the 1790s (see Box 1, François Vallé Collection, Missouri Historical Society [hereafter MHS], St. Louis).

miles] of plowlands and marshes on a poor road that has the disadvantage of being closed off at both ends by gates. Thus is the situation of the place today called New Bourbon. The importance of this name and the large perspective of Your Lordship require me to provide him with a faithful portrait of the situation of this new settlement.

There is another place more happily situated that would better merit this name. This is the small village of the Saline, which is only about 100 arpents distant. This small village is located on the bank of the Mississippi between two rather considerable streams, one named the Rivière aux Vases and the other Rivière de la Saline. This place is extremely fertile and rich in fish [*poissonneux*]. Stone for lime and other building materials are found there, as well as stones suitable for making millstones. More than 20,000 families could be settled on the banks of the two streams, and more than 100 watermills could be built capable of milling all year long. Immediately above the Rivière de la Saline is the point of Bois Brûlé, which forms on the Mississippi a prairie five leagues long and one wide that is covered with woods of all sorts. Behind this prairie is a slightly elevated area half covered with grass and half with fine trees. This contains about 100 square leagues, drained by small streams, of which not a single arpent cannot be cultivated advantageously. Thus New Bourbon, being placed at the Saline, would soon find itself the center of the finest settlement of the Illinois and with time would become a large city. I'm planning to draft a map of the region this winter [1793–1794] and will send it to Your Lordship.

The importance of this place persuaded me five years ago to inform Monsieur [Esteban] de Miró [governor general of Louisiana, 1783–1791] about it and to ask him permission to transfer there the troops, the commandery, the royal effects, and the records center [greffe]. Monsieur de Miró granted permission with certain conditions. This transfer has been postponed because the [old] village of Ste. Genevieve was at that time still a considerable place that required protection until the habitants had established new settlements up in the hills. But today things have very much changed: the old village contains only seven or eight houses, and it would be time to effect this transfer if Your Lordship wishes to permit it.

I have the honor of being very respectfully Monsieur the very humble and very obedient servant of Your Lordship.

   Henri Peyroux

PS: I have had the honor of discussing with Your Lordship in a letter of last July 12 the possibility of creating a new company of militia in this district. If he would desire it, this new militia company could be attached to New Bourbon.

Henri Peyroux de la Coudrenière to Carondelet   PC, Leg. 207B
November 14, 1793

Monsieur:

My desire to contribute to the success of the important settlement of New Bourbon impelled me to place before the eyes of Your Lordship the means that I believe to be the most appropriate to achieve that end.

1. Establish this new town at the Saline, where sure and convenient river ports exist for pirogues and bateaux. This place has the additional advantage of being located almost directly across the Mississippi from the mouth of the Kaskaskia River, on which are located American settlements.

2. Create at New Bourbon an independent parish separated from that of Ste. Genevieve by the Rivière aux Vases. These two neighborning parishes could be served by the same curé until such time as the population is large enough to require two.

3. Have two bridges constructed, one over the Rivière aux Vases and the other over the Rivière de la Saline. Establish several saw and flour mills, and procure an advantageous outlet for planks and beams of black walnut and cedar, with which the region abounds.

4. Provide the necessary security and tranquility for the region with respect to the Indians, encouraging marriages between whites and Indians with free gifts. This is the surest and most humane means to succeed in civilizing and taming the Indians.

5. Place a company of cavalry, or other armed forces, at New Bourbon.

6. Make this place independent of St. Louis. Without this independence, New Bourbon will always be buffeted by intrigues, interferences, and personal interests. If Ste. Genevieve had been made independent twenty years ago, its district would be vastly more populated than it is.

7. Place the northern boundary of New Bourbon at Joachim Creek and the southern boundary at the bayou closest to the mouth of the Ohio River. It was Colonel [George] Morgan who asked the district of New Madrid be extended northward up to Cape St. Cosme, from which has resulted many inconveniences. The Illinois Country has always begun at the mouth of the Belle Rivière [Ohio], and the district of New Madrid could be indemnified to the south down as far as the St. Francis River.

8. Give to the commandant of New Bourbon the same powers as the one in St. Louis, for conceding lands and for other issues. It would also be convenient that civil acts and publications be done in the French language up to the time that the Spanish language becomes more widespread in this region.

9. Provide the commandant with gifts for the Indians in the neighborhood, such as the Loups [i.e., Delawares], Shawnees, Peorias and Kaskaskias. Pro-

vide him with 500 piastres per year for his lodging and that of the troops, and also provide rations of foodstuffs per day to compensate for expenses he will be obliged to make entertaining foreigners and local notables.

I have the honor of being with respect for Your Lordship, Monsieur,

Your very humble and obedient servant,

Henri Peyroux

No. 4

Frederick Jackson Turner included this curious document (in the original French) when he compiled and edited the correspondence of Edmond-Charles Genêt, French minister to the United States.[3] Genêt wrote it, apparently in the autumn of 1793, in his usual breathless and ungrammatical style, and sent it to Charles de Pauw, one of his agents in the Ohio River valley, for distribution. But the harangue struck the Lexington, Kentucky, printer John Bradford as so bizarre and inflammatory that he refused to print it.[4] Had it been printed and distributed, it is hard to imagine that its wild revolutionary rhetoric would have had much effect on any of the French Creoles residing in the Mississippi Valley. Genêt's harangue must be compared with the more soberly reasoned recruiting pamphlet written by de Luzières in the spring of 1796, which was printed by John Bradford in Lexington, Kentucky (see below, document no. 17).

The Free French to their Brothers in Louisiana

The moment has arrived when despotism must disappear from the earth. France is now free, a constitutional republic, after having informed men of their rights and having won signal victories over her numerous enemies. Not content with successes for herself alone, France proclaims to all peoples that she is prepared to offer strong support to those who wish to follow her virtuous example.

Frenchmen of Louisiana you still love your former country; your attachment to her is innate in your hearts. The French nation knows your feelings. She is indignant to see you as victims of her former tyrants [i.e., the Bourbon dynasty] and she has the power to avenge you. A perjured king, lying

3. *Annual Report of the American Historical Association for the Year 1903* (Washington, D.C.: U.S. Government Printing Office, 1904), 2:265–69.

4. See Bradford's rejection letter to de Pauw, dated December 19, 1793, in ibid., 1:1023–24. See also Frederick Jackson Turner's classic essay on the Clark-Genêt affair, "The Origin of Genêt's Projected Attack on Louisiana and the Floridas," *American Historical Review* 3 (July 1898): 650–71.

ministers, base and arrogant courtiers grown fat on the sweat and blood of the people, who've paid the price of the excesses. The French people, fed up with the outrages and irritated at the injustices they'd endured, rose up against their oppressors, who disappeared like dust in a gust of wind.

Profit from this important lesson, Frenchmen of Louisiana, your hour has finally arrived. It's time that you cease being slaves of a government to which you have been shamefully sold. It's time that you cease being driven like cattle by men who are necessarily your enemies, by men from whom a single word could deprive you of all you hold dearest, your liberty and your possessions.

Spanish despotism has surpassed all others in viciousness and stupidity. This regime, which has made the name Spanish execrable on the entire American continent, has it not stained all of its steps with barbarism? Has it not ordered, or at least permitted, the massacre of 20 million persons under the guise of hypocritical religion? Has it not in order to satisfy its insatiable greed depopulated, impoverished, and degraded entire countries? It has crushed you, and continues ceaselessly, to crush you with persecutions.

And what has been the fruit of so many crimes? The nullity, the dishonor, the misery of Spain in Europe; the brutalization, slavery, and death of an infinite number of American inhabitants.

When Indians wish to harvest fruit, they cut down the tree. That's the way of despotism.

In fact, tyranny doesn't care about the fate of nations, everything is sacrificed to passing pleasures, everything must bend to its will.

Frenchmen of Louisiana the injustices you've endured have only too surely persuaded you of these truths. Your pains have doubtlessly engraved on your souls a profound desire for honorable revenge.

Compare your situation with that of your friends and neighbors, the liberated Americans. See the province of Kentucky, deprived of markets and unjustly burdened with obstacles to its commerce—which, nevertheless (thanks to its free government alone), continues to grow rapidly and already foretells a prosperity that makes the Spanish regime tremble.

Consider these last words, for they are the secret of all despotic regimes; they conceal their abominable intentions. Human beings were born to love one another, to be unified, to be happy. And this would happen if kings, those who claim to be God's image on earth, did not seek to divide them and thwart their happiness.

Kentucky's population has grown up in several years. Your colony, which is better situated but which lacks liberty, is slipping every day.

Free Americans, after having spent some time cultivating their lands and increasing their production, are ensured of peaceably enjoying the fruits of their labor and initiatives. All that you possess is dependent upon the whims of Viceroys [governors general of Louisiana], who are almost always greedy, unjust, and vindictive.

These are the evils that can be forestalled with resolution, courage, and energy. In a flash you could change your destiny. Misfortune to you if you miss this opportunity, for henceforth the name Frenchman will be despised by all kings and their accomplices. This will make your chains that much the heavier and make you vulnerable to unheard of troubles.

You quiver with indignation; you want to deserve the title of glorious free men. But the fear of failing, the fear of not receiving support undermines your zeal. Know this well that your French brothers, who have successfully attacked the Spanish government in Europe, will soon appear on your coasts with naval forces, and that the republicans out West are ready to descend the Ohio and Mississippi rivers accompanied by a large number of French republicans to come to your aid under the banners of France and of Liberty. All of this guarantees you total success. So demonstrate residents of Louisiana, prove that despotism has not paralyzed you, that you maintain in your hearts French courage and audacity, that you are worthy of being free and independent, for we wish you to join not our empire but that of liberty. Become your own masters. You can adopt a republican constitution, and supported by France (insofar as your weakness prevents you from defending yourselves) you can freely unite with her and with your neighbors in the United States; you can cement with the two republics an alliance, based upon the most liberal principles, in which all of our political and commercial interests would be joined. Your fatherland would derive the greatest benefits from this happy revolution, and your glory would be equal to the happiness that you and your children will enjoy. No weakness! No pusillanimity! Only boldness and resolution! Then things will roll [*ça ira*].

Audaces Fortuna juvat (Fortune smiles on audacity)

No. 5

For about six months, from the autumn of 1793 to the spring of 1794, Spanish Illinois experienced genuine panic about an invasion that would supposedly be led by George Rogers Clark and financed by Edmond-Charles Genét, French minister to the United States. The danger of such an attack was vastly exaggerated and, of course, it never materialized. But de Luzières was particularly worried because at this very time his family was on its way down the Ohio River and would have to pass George Rogers Clark's establishment near Louisville. Astonishingly, this letter informs us that de Luzières had actually brought millstones (which had a reputation for excellence) with him from France. In mid-nineteenth century, Charles de Pauw's grandson, Washington C. DePauw, was a major benefactor of DePauw University in Greencastle, Indiana.

De Hault de Lassus de Luzières to Carondelet   PC, Leg. 207B
December 26, 1793

Monsieur le Baron:

Messieurs [Louis] Vandenbendum and [Pierre] Ménard learned from General [George Rogers] Clark and other folks at the Falls [of the Ohio, i.e., Louisville] that this general has decided to stop and seize all riverboats, barges, and pirogues that descend the Ohio carrying flour, foodstuffs, and other materials destined for Louisiana. He's even said that he's impatiently awaiting the boats coming down loaded with flour and biscuit, millstones, and milling equipment. Therefore, Monsieur le Baron, the 3,000 barrels of flour, the biscuit, the beautiful millstones from France, the iron fittings, the sifting devices, and other equipment required for our mill at New Madrid that Monsieur Tardiveau is working on (which is en route along with my poor and unfortunate family) surely have been or will be stopped and seized along with all of our possessions. . . .

The army in question [i.e., Clark's] is composed of American vagabonds and some French renegades. Messieurs Despot [Charles de Pauw], La Chaise, and [André] Michaux[5] are the principal officers. This rogue Despot has tried to engage some of [Pierre] Ménard's men and equipment. He is offering one piastre per day, part of the booty, and 1,000 acres of land to be selected on the Spanish side [of the Mississippi]. This same rogue has suggested the most scurrilous schemes to Monsieur Portell [Spanish commandant at New Madrid]. Because he [de Pauw] wishes to send a boat to New Orleans, doubtless to forewarn his wife, Ménard has told Monsieur Portell to seize it as it passes. Here then is the strategy of this army of villains: They will divide into two groups. The first, and the strongest, commanded by Clark will proceed to New Madrid, and then successively downriver to every outpost all the way to New Orleans, where four to six frigates will arrive by sea. The second corps will proceed to Vincennes on the Wabash to increase its strength, and then go on to seize St. Louis and the other posts of the Illinois. . . .

---

5. Michaux was a botanist and political agent who had met Edmond Genêt before heading west out to the Ohio River valley. On his interesting sojourn in North America, see *Dictionary of Canadian Biography,* s.v. "André Michaux," by J. F. M. Hoeniger. See also See Michaux's "Journal," in *Early Western Travels, 1748–1846* (Cleveland: A. H. Clark Co., 1904), vol. 3.

I pray you to present our respectful homage to Madame la Baronne and to Mademoiselle Philippe [the Carondelets' daughter]. My health continues to languish. I leave it to you to decide whether all these events and the attending deep anxieties will contribute to my recovery.

I am, with very great respect, Monsieur le Baron,
Your humble and obedient servant,
De Hault de Lassus

No. 6

An anonymous and barely literate person wrote this account of a daunting descent of the entire length of the Ohio River, from Pittsburgh to the Mississippi. More than a dozen French persons (excluding crew members), all of whom seem to have been refugees of some sort from the French Revolution, made up the boating party: Madame de Luzières (her husband was busy arranging to get their new house built at New Bourbon), two of their unmarried sons, Jacques-Marcellin-Léon and Philippe-François-Camille, their daughter, Jeanne-Félicité-Odile, Jeanne's husband, Pierre Derbigny, future governor of the state of Louisiana, Cruzel de St. Martial, "former doctor to the king," Antoine Soulard, former French naval officer who would acquire renown as a surveyor in Upper Louisiana, Albert, who seems to have been a domestic of the de Luzières family, three nuns of the Order of St. Clare, along with several of their domestics, and, finally, the unknown author of the account. Almost miraculously, the trip was safely accomplished, no serious mishaps and no loss of life, and Derbigny brought news to Spanish Illinois that the bizarre Genêt-Clark plan to invade Spanish Louisiana was coming to naught. This account may be compared with other, more or less contemporaneous, accounts by Frenchmen.[6]

Descent of Ohio River,
December 11, 1793—February 14, 1794

The Monongahela River is very navigable for 100 miles upstream, and the Allegheny River is navigable for 300 and some odd miles. These two rivers converge at Pittsburgh and form the Ohio River, which is navigable for its entirety.

6. See Georges-Henri-Victor Collot, A *Journey in North America, containing a survey of the countries watered by the Mississippi, Ohio, Missouri, and other affluing rivers,* ed. Christian Bay, 3 vols. (Florence: O. Lange, 1924), 1: chaps. 4–14; François-Marie Perrin du Lac, *Voyage dans les deux Louisianes* (Lyon: Bruysset aîneì et Buynand, 1805), chaps. 18, 19, 20.

We left Pittsburgh on December 11 [1793] at 5:00 p.m. in the barge of Monsieur and Madame de Luzières, Derbigny and his entire family, and three nuns who are also going to the Illinois. The current was very swift. By 10:00 p.m. we had passed by Milltown Island, three miles from Pittsburgh, despite the fact that we had two bateaux attached to the barge. These were a Kentucky bateau that carried the three nuns, . . . and a Mississippi bateau belonging to Doctor [Cruzel de] St. Martial. In the Indian country [i.e., the right bank of the Ohio River] there were no farmsteads, only some huts placed at regular intervals. These are small forts for American hunters that are called block-houses [bloqueau]. In these American hunters find refuge after the hunt, for fear of Indians. The other side of the river is the American side. . . .

The youngest son of de Luzières [Philippe-François-Camille], Albert, and I went ashore to get some milk for breakfast, after having sent several times for some without getting any. We finally found some on the American side of the river about seven [?] a.m. at three sols per moque.

Toward noon came on board our bateau three American riflemen [*riffle-ment*], that is hunters who are paid by the United States to make war on the Indians. They recounted to us what had happened to them about three weeks ago when they were 100 miles up the Muskingum River and six miles inland from its bank. At night they posted a guard while seven of them slept. Indians came and attacked them. They killed the guard, attacked the others and killed three, including a brother of one of the young men who were visiting us. The Indians swept in with tomahawks. Five [Americans] saved themselves. They're from Anda, twenty miles from Marietta. . . .

All night long frightful slabs of ice swept by, and we were in constant fear that they would crush the *bateaux*. This ice came out of the Muskingum River, which continues to be navigable. At 4:00 a.m. Dr. St. Martial was on guard duty and he gave a false alarm, claiming that a pirogue [*canot*] was coming alongside of us. We jumped to our firearms and ran to look, but we saw nothing. . . . He had mistaken the ice, which was floating down as a huge slab, for an Indian pirogue. I was always fearful of what might happen to the ladies, especially for Madame Derbigny who was very pregnant. The last false alarm had frightened her a great deal. . . .

The 17th [of December] Monsieur [Jacques-Marcellin-Léon] de St. Vrain went out to hunt with Albert. Monsieur Derbigny and Dr. St. Martial went out two hours later. They all came back at night having seen nothing.

The 18th two gentlemen from Marietta came and told Monsieur Derbigny that returning hunters had seen a large party of Indians twenty miles away. This put us on our guard. We prepared our firearms and gave an order to head for shore in case of an attack. . . .

Toward 10 a.m. [December 21] we jumped out onto an ice raft . . . and tried to push off. Finally we succeeded in getting out into the river because there was enough water. Toward 11 a.m. we broke free and got going among slabs of ice half-a-foot thick that filled the river. Avoiding getting crushed a hundred times, we arrived at Belpray [Belpre, Ohio today] on the Indian bank of the river. . . . Belpray is a very pretty spot, nice plain where there are three villages, all three well protected with palisades. There are four pavillons in each village, all protected with palisades to keep out the Indians. In the evening all the families retreat into the fort. From the three villages three men go out to scout for Indians and return to alert the families when Indians are in the area. . . .

At 10 a.m. [December 24] we arrived at Gallipolis. We had much trouble landing because of the ice along the shore. . . . Monsieur Derbigny was pressed to have fresh bread made for our trip and to take care of some other business. . . .

[December 25] Monsieur and Madame Derbigny, St. Martial and Soulard went to dine at the commandant's. . . . The commandant at Gallipolis is a very knowledgeable officer, and excellent officer who was a captain in the Queen's Regiment before the French Revolution. He is a very pleasant officer and was one of the first to come here as part of the Scioto Company.[7] He finally settled at Gallipolis, where he became commandant of the militia with a salary of $32.00 per month. . . .

Madame de Luzières and messieurs St. Martial and Soulard lodged with Monsieur Mantel. The nuns, Madame and Monsieur Derbigny, St. Vrain, and Camille took the boats into a creek to protect them from the ice. . . . The ladies spent a peaceful night, even though they were not protected from Indians. The night of [December] 28–29 Madame Derbigny was terribly frightened when during the night a nocturnal bird came and snatched a chicken. She awaken her husband and told him that Indians were about. Monsieur Derbigny woke us and told us that he feared she would have a miscarriage; we were always fearful on her account. . . .

January 1, 1794, in the morning the residents of Gallipolis built a bonfire to celebrate the coming of the New Year. . . .

The 5th in the morning the day appeared very fine. . . . I dressed myself and went to see Gallipolis, which I not yet done because of my illness. First I visited Monsieur Mantel, and then I went to see the ladies who were lodged with

7. This was François-Anaclet le Dossu d'Hébécourt, one of a dozen or so French aristocrats, including de Luzières, who were involved in the Scioto fiasco (see Jocelyne Moreau-Zanelli, *Gallipolis: Histoire d'un mirage américan au XVIIe, siècle* [Paris: L'Harmattan, 2000], 152, 267, 268, 287, 293, 362, 392).

Madame Vandenbendem. Then I went to see Monsieur Sogrun [Saugrain], Monsieur Debecourt [d'Hébécourt], and Monsieur Petit. I dined with the ladies and passed the evening with Madame de Luzières, who remained alone with Madame Vandenbemden.[8] I went back on board at 11 p.m. . . .

We left [January 6] about 3 p.m. with a Mississippi boat that had been loaded with flour, whiskey [qouisqui], cider, and apples. On leaving Gallipolis, we fired off all of our guns. . . . Early in the morning [January 7] we went hunting. We saw many turkeys but they were at a distance and we didn't manage to kill any. In the evening we returned to the hunt along with an American hunter. Arriving on shore we saw many turkeys. We killed many, each of the five of us killing one. The American hunter killed one and wounded several.

The 16th at 12:00 in the morning, seeing that the ice was increasing and become thicker, he [Derbigny] went into Louisville both to gather intelligence and to find lodgings for the ladies. The morning of the 18th we sent Albert and Bastien to break up the ice so that we could take the boats into the creek at Louisville. The 19th . . . Monsieur [Michel] Lacassagne came to visit us and to invite all of us to dine at his place. . . . We spent the afternoon with his ladies and several gentlemen and took tea. Madame Derbigny sang a very pretty song; if it had not been for her timidity she would have sung even better. Monsieur Derbigny then sang some tunes from Marseilles, and Monsieur Lacassagne also then sang. . . . [9]

Louisville is very well situated on the American side of the river. There are very pretty houses, well-built, all located on a beautiful street and all aligned

8. Antoine F. Saugrain moved on to become a well-known medical doctor in St. Louis. Concerning his astonishing career in North America, see H. Fouré Selter, ed., *L'Odyssée Américaine d'une famille française: le docteur Antoine Saugrain* (Baltimore: Johns Hopkins University Press, 1936); Moreau-Zanelli, *Galllipolis*, 71–74, 75, 269, 352, 392; Hodes, *Beyond the Frontier*, 231, 232, 314, 333, 336, 414, 425, 428, 469, 509, 523, 525, 537. Petit was very likely A. G. Petit d'Arçon, another medical doctor caught up in the Scioto affair (Moreau-Zanelli, *Gallipolis*, 434).

Madame Vandenbemden was the wife of Louis B. Vandenbemden, a Flemish engineer who moved to Spanish Illinois and was involved in a number of engineering projects there during the decade preceding the Louisiana Purchase (see Abraham P. Nasatir, *Spanish War Vessels on the Mississippi* [New Haven, Conn.: Yale University Press, 1966] 96, 225, 293–94, 335, 340; Houck, ed., *The Spanish Regime in Missouri; a collection of papers and documents relating to upper Louisiana principally within the present limits of Missouri during the dominion of Spain, from the Archives of the Indies at Seville, etc., translated from the original Spanish into English*, 2 vols. [Chicago: R. R. Donnelley & Sons, 1909], 2:127, 131, 137, 226, 393, 398; Finiels, *Account of Upper Louisiana*, 3, 4, 60–61).

9. Michel Lacassagne was an *émigré* French merchant who built one of the finer houses in early Louisville. He was peripherally involved in the Wilkinson conspiracy, which advocated secession of Kentucky from the federal union (see Whitaker, *Spanish-American Frontier*, 191, 194, 212).

just like in Philadelphia. . . .

The 25th . . . we passed the falls, starting with the barge. . . . The morning of the 26th . . . Monsieur St. Martial's bateau arrived where the barge was, . . . and then we went to fetch the nuns who were in Louisville. We took the small bateau down through the little falls and met up with the barge.

The 31st we learned that a company of Americans was stationed at the mouth of the Cumberland River and that the Spanish government [of Louisiana] had put ten or twelve Indian tribes—Delawares, Chickasaws, Cherokees, and others—along the [lower] Ohio; and furthermore, that Monsieur [Louis] Lorimier [commandant at Cape Giraradeau] was at the mouth of the Mississippi [i.e., Ohio] with his Indians . . . and that he had orders to protect us. . . .

February 1 at 1:00 a.m. we passed the Wabash River on the Indian side. . . . The Wabash is a very fine river, very navigable. The post of Vincennes is located 150 miles upstream. . . . Toward 10 a.m. we passed the salt spring on the Indian bank of the river, and at about 2 p.m. we were at the Grand Cavern. . . .

About 11:00 a.m. [February 2] we passed the mouth of the Cherokee [Tennessee?] River. On the American side of the river there was an island in front of the mouth. We passed to the right of this island, from which we had forty-five miles to go to the mouth of the Ohio. We continued on our route and stopped about 6:00 p.m. for fear of arriving at the mouth before we wanted to, at 3:00 or 4:00 a.m. . . .

About 7:00 a.m. [February 3] we saw a large bateau along with three pirogues that were going down to the Mississippi. . . . It was an American who was descending to L'Anse à Graisse [New Madrid] with an Indian of Monsieur Lorimier. They came on board, and we gave them a slug of whiskey. . . . Monsieur St. Martial's bateau, with me aboard, proceeded across the Mississippi. I had left Madame de Luzières's boat and boarded that of Monsieur St. Martial because he was descending to L'Anse de la Graisse, which was my own destination. Madame de Luzières's boats [i.e., hers and that of the nuns] were heading upriver to the Illinois Country. . . .

No. 7

This letter is the first indication that the much-dreaded Franco-American invasion of Spanish Louisiana was collapsing, which was a huge relief to Lieutenant Governor Trudeau in St. Louis. The Osage threat also soon disappeared, thanks perhaps to the efforts of the Chouteau brothers. Trudeau also explains in this letter why he was relieving Peyroux of his command in Ste. Genevieve, simultaneously revealing that de Luzières had swung decidedly into the political orbit of the Vallé family. François Vallé replaced Peyoux as commandant in Ste. Genevieve, although Peyroux was exonerated and eventually returned to Upper Louisiana in 1799 as commandant at New Madrid.[10]

Trudeau to Carondelet   PC, Leg. 209
St. Louis, January 28, 1794

Dear General:

At this moment it appears that Clark's famous expedition has been entirely abandoned. The last news I've received claims that this has been done by the very men he had engaged. Lack of money has provoked all sorts of disagreements among these officers. The famous treasurer [André] Michaux has not been able to pull things together, and de Pauw is said to be destitute. I'm awaiting the men that I've had posted at Vincennes and the Falls [of the Ohio, i.e., Louisville] to get further information. . . . [11]

The Big Osages, outraged that we did not send them any traders last year [1793], have returned from their winter hunt very disposed to make war against us. I, having fears about Clark's expedition, decided to send two small pirogues of reliable men to pacify them with diplomacy [*les contenir avec douceur*]. These men found 350 Osages preparing to march against our small settlements. The rumor among them was that when one group was ready to go they absolutely must strike. They've decided that only 150 men would be required to hit the Peorias, Shawnees, and Abenakis. I've been warned about this so as to get these tribes protected, as well as taking the necessary precautions so that we ourselves don't get humiliated. Despite this, they [the Osages] have killed a habitant on the road between Ste. Genevieve and the [lead] mine; they've stolen the Peoria's horses . . . and come into the village at night. . . . Some shots from fusils and a small canon drove them off. The next morning they were tracked but not found. No doubt their chiefs will disapprove of this conduct. I'll have more news in several days, having sent Monsieur Pierre Chouteau to them to seek out those who promised to go to New Orleans to meet with you. . . .

Monsieur de Lassus [de Luzières] continues to languish. I believe that his very difficult situation contributes not a little to the morass of gloom that

10. A curious footnote to the Peyroux story is that he had met Thomas Jefferson when he was in Philadelphia in 1792, and that ten years later Jefferson sent him a letter, dated July 3, 1803, which was carried west by Meriwether Lewis. In it, Jefferson demonstrated his woeful ignorance of the territory he had just purchased by addressing Peyroux as Commandant of Upper Louisiana presiding at St. Louis and Ste. Genevieve (contemporary copy of letter in PC, Leg. 2368).

11. Concerning Michaux and de Pauw, see Turner, *American Historical Review* 3 (July 1898): 650–71.

undermines him and carries him toward the grave. He is presently reunited with his entire respectable family, but with no servants or amenities he lacks the most essential things of life. His children plow the earth as though they had always done it; the women are the servants of the house, obliged to do everything in the household. Please believe that I am doing all that is possible to improve their existence, but have little fortune myself. Moreover, I must take great pains not to offend their sensibilities, which are extreme. I only tell you this because I know that you are interested in your virtuous compatriots who in truth merit a happier fate, to which you have perhaps the means to contribute. All the young folks are very well educated and certainly deserve something better than being simple plowmen, which they are obliged to be to have some bread that they are not yet assured of harvesting. . . .

I've been obliged to remove Monsieur [Henri] Peyroux from his command at Ste. Genevieve. His conduct has made me think that he did not return from America [i.e., Philadephia] without having some knowledge of the project [Clark's proposed invasion] that threatens us. What I have the honor of telling you officially is the exact truth. Monsieur de Lassus, extraordinarily loyal to our government, has studied and examined this official's conduct up close. Long before the invasion project was heralded, he got in touch with me and informed me that he believed Peyroux to be suspect. Day after day, de Lassus became increasingly suspicious and warned me. I concluded that the best solution would be to send Peyroux to New Madrid under the pretext of having him secure the fort there. I forewarned Monsieur Portell [Spanish commandant at New Madrid] to get rid of him by finding a pretext to send him on down to you. I did not wish to take more forceful action for fear that I may be mistaken. This issue will soon get cleared up, perhaps in his favor, which is what I wish for his sake.

Monsieur de Lassus has been much weakened by his long and serious illness, by his various afflictions, and by his deep concerns about the fate of his family, which has been here a long time now. Nonetheless, he is determined to contribute in every way with the greatest zeal to save the colony [Upper Louisiana], despite the fact that he is threatened every day from the other shore [of the Mississippi]. This is especially true since it's become known of his successful efforts to persuade the Indians and enlist them for a war against our enemies. These threats, far from discouraging him, energized him to the degree that he is resolved to endure any fate rather than abandon us. If a man like him has any need for a recommendation from someone like me, I would rush to render homage to the truth in telling you, my general, that if all the residents of the Illinois thought and behaved as he does our enemies would discover here resistance that unfortunately I cannot promise or even hope for.

Because, if there are some reliable men among us, there are also a large number whom I have reason to fear. . . .

I have the honor of being, with the deepest and most respectful loyalty, my general,

> Your humble and obedient servant,
> Zénon Trudeau

No. 8

Lorimier delivered this harangue at the height of the panic among Spanish officials that George Rogers Clark, with financing provided by Edmond Genêt, French minister to the United States, was going to invade Upper Louisiana. This occasion gave Lorimier the chance to demonstrate his importance as leader and manager of the various Indian tribes in the region and assured his appointment as commandant in Cape Girardeau. Lorimier himself was likely prepared to fight to the death against Clark, who had sacked his outpost in the Ohio country during the American Revolution. Ironically, Lorimier's two métis sons was later appointed to West Point by President Thomas Jefferson. Because several of these tribes spoke mutually unintelligible languages, presumably Lorimier delivered this harangue in French.

Louis Lorimier   PC, Leg. 210
Cape Girardeau, February 8, 1794

Harangue given to six tribes gathered at Cape Girardeau, which was ordered by [Lieutenant Governor] Zénon Trudeau on behalf of the governor general [Carondelet] of Louisiana. The tribes were: the Abenakis [Delawares], Shawnees, Piankashaws, Miamis, Peorias, and Ottawas.

My children:

I'm talking to you today on behalf of your father, the grand chief [i.e., Governor General Carondelet] of Louisiana. I'm doing this to make you remember with what generosity of soul he took you in his arms when you arrived on his lands. He received you as a good father, and his generosity extended to giving you land for farming and hunting so that you could support your wives and children. He invited you to live in accord with all the other tribes, maintaining you in tranquility while you pursued your paths with unity. He encouraged you to improve your lands so that their produce would permit you to live in abundance.

Until now, my children, I have observed with satisfaction that you have kept your word to live in peace. But right now this peace is being threatened by men who are guided only by selfishness rather than by true chiefs. These are wicked Frenchmen and Americans who reject all notions of humanity and whose comprehension has been totally stifled.

These wicked men we are describing, my children, have they not already driven you out of your previous lands? Should they not be satisfied having done that without pursuing you into your present lands, which you have requested from your father and who gladly granted them because he regards you as his own children?

My children, your father was delighted to welcome you and to provide you with a refuge so that your wives and children could live in peace, as I have already said. Therefore, since it is apparent today that plans are afoot to disrupt that tranquility, is it not up to you to demonstrate that you have an obligation to him for having saved you from the straights you were in and having welcomed you here with open arms?

Do not listen, my children, to the evil birds who flutter about your ears, who attempt to charm you with their songs, lure you into a trap, and prevent you from doing the right thing. Listen only to your father, who speaks to you sincerely and who wishes you happiness.

What will your father the grand chief, who has given you these lands, say, my children, if they are taken from you by these wicked men. He will say that he had children whom he cherished, but that they lacked courage, that they gave up these lands, while he was thinking that he had given them to his children who would make every effort to hold on to them.

Therefore, my children, each of you can watch and observe the maneuvers and initiatives of our enemies, who are putting every effort into disturbing your tranquility. As soon as I receive any information about this, I will communicate it to you. I will take every precaution necessary to protect you against their attack, and to safe guard us one and all. I invite you to take courage and I urge all the chiefs to be vigilant and attentive to harangue their young men to remain wide awake for fear of surprise.

Take courage, my children, for the master of life who recognizes the justice of your cause will provide us with sufficient forces to repel those who wish to deprive us of our possessions.

Cape Girardeau, February 8, 1794

No. 9

The grandiose plan that de Luzières—together with his business associates, Bartholomé Tardiveau, Pierre Audrain, and Louis Vandenbendum—conceived to persuade the French settlers at Gallipolis on the Ohio River to move en masse to the New Bourbon area got tangled up with the wild rumors about a proposed Franco-American invasion of Spanish Louisiana. Messieurs Auguste la Chaise and Charles de Pauw were supposedly working with George Rogers Clark on this venture, which never came to pass (see above, chap. 5). This letter reveals, for the first time, the close relationship between de Luzières and Antoine Soulard, who went on to fame as surveyor general of Upper Louisiana under both the Spanish and U.S. governments and after whom the famous Soulard Market in St. Louis is named. The fort that he helped engineer was in fact built at Ste. Genevieve on a hill overlooking South Gabouri Creek, although no use was ever made of it.

De Luzières to Carondelet   PC, Leg. 208A
New Bourbon, April 6, 1794

Monsieur le Baron:

Regarding the residents of Gallipolis, I've already informed you, Monsieur le Baron, that the pressing entreaties of messieurs [Auguste] la Chaise[12] and Despot [Charles de Pauw], who where there and spent some time trying to persuade them [the residents of Gallipolis] to follow them and join in their perfidious plans, have met with no success. Indeed, some of these emigrants have already availed themselves of the opportunity to move either to New Madrid or to the Illinois. But the largest number are waiting for help from the government [i.e., Carondelet] before they move to this colony. As soon as the rumors about an invasion and pillage of this colony have definitely ceased, and as soon as they learn that this region is tranquil, they will not hesitate to come and settle here. Monsieur Vandenbendem, one of our associates, has recently assured me that this opinion was virtually universal among the residents of Gallipolis at the time he left there to come here with this family. . . .

I've already discussed with you, Monsieur le Baron, the difficulties that significantly afflict and slow down the execution of our enterprise. What I informed you of was based only upon my observations of what was transpiring under my own eyes, in addition to what the correspondence of my associates informed me regarding the state of our affairs. Monsieur Tardiveau is at the center of the operation and he is situated advantageously to take in all aspects of it. Therefore it is in his correspondence that must be discovered the whole picture. The tableau that he has laid out for me is nothing less than encouraging. On our side there is surely no lack of energy, activity, and sacrifice. But there is a mass of things [force de choses] on the other side of the scale that weigh against all our efforts. I believe, Monsieur le Baron, that there is no bet-

12. Concerning la Chaise and de Pauw, see ibid., 650–71.

ter way to inform you of our situation than to confide in you utterly by sending an extract from one of Tardiveau's last letters. . . .

I informed you some time ago that one of my sons served in the French navy in the department of Brest [in Brittany] but was detached to Martinique. Not wishing to recognize the French republic, he fled that colony with one of his comrades, Monsieur Soullart [Soulard], son of the former commandant of the port of Rochefort. Both came to join up with my family here in America. The latter [Soulard] has the keenest desire to get into the [Spanish] service either in the colonies or in Spain. He therefore asked me to pass on to you the attached memorandum. I can guarantee you, Monsieur le Baron, of the honesty, the solid principles, the ability, and the experience of this officer who rejected the brevet of promotion that the National Assembly sent to him on Martinique. He is now directing the work on the fort being built at Ste. Genevieve, the plans for which were drawn up by Monsieur Vandenbendum. You may perhaps have occasion at this moment to employ him as an auxiliary officer, perhaps on the galleys or perhaps elsewhere, while awaiting the decision of the [royal] court on his memorandum, in case you decided to forward it. Finally, Monsieur le Baron, I would regard any assistance that you may render to Monsieur Soullart as rendered to my own child. As for my son, his comrade, although he may be animated with the same desire [to get into the Spanish service], he is foregoing it for the moment in order to help out my youngest son and my son-in-law at our perfect settlement here. As soon as this job gets done, I will surely return to your generosity on his behalf.

I beg you to accept and offer to your ladies the homage of my entire family, and never doubt the infinite respect that I have for you, Monsieur le Baron,

Your very humble and obedient servant,
De Hault de Lassus

PS: My dear daughter just gave birth very happily to a big boy, thanks to the care of Dame La Caisse, former midwife at Gallipolis, with whom she [the daughter] has been very content. As for my health, it is more difficult and debilitating than ever.

No. 10

Jean-Baptiste Sarpy was a major trader operating out of St. Louis and New Orleans with whom de Luzières had close relations. Antoine Soulard had arrived in Spanish Illinois with de Luzières, helped design the fort built at Ste. Genevieve during the spring of 1794, and would soon become Surveyor General of Upper Louisiana. Louis Vandenbendum was a Flemish engineer who also worked on the fort at Ste. Genevieve and was de Luzières's sometime business associate. De Luzières's son to whom he refers in this letter was Charles (Carlos) Auguste Delassus who was soon to become commandant at New Madrid (1796–1799) and went on to serve as lieutenant governor of Upper Louisiana (1799–1804). The grand plan to transplant en masse the French settlers at Gallipolis to Spanish Illinois collapsed, although a few did in fact make the move. De Luzières was often involved in local Indian diplomacy, and when he became commandant of the New Bourbon District in 1797 many of Shawnees, Delawares, Miamis, and Ottawas in the region resided within this district.

De Luzières to Carondelet   PC, Leg. 209
New Bourbon, September 17, 1794

Monsieur le Baron:

I'm rushing to take advantage of Monsieur Sarpy's departure for New Orleans to renew our memories and our friendship. I believe that Monsieur Soulard, who is still in St. Louis but has been doing better recently, is preparing to descend to New Madrid and then to New Orleans. Six ill folks remain in my household, and my poor wife's condition continues to cause me much anxiety. I've just learned from a courier from New Madrid that Monsieur Vandenbendum is in a very bad way and has just lost his only son. His poor wife is inconsolable about this. My biggest regret is that we are so burdened with illnesses no one from here can go down and console these good friends. . . .

Please be more persuaded than ever that in all circumstances I continue to evince my zeal for the service of the king, my new master [Carlos IV], and for the good of my new fatherland. . . . My son's letter has given me the greatest pleasure, for it not only contained news about him but also about my family in Hainault, of which I had been deprived for nearly two years. Furthermore, it informed me that the distinction and success with which he has served during the last campaign of the army of Roussillon have earned him the rank of Lieutenant Colonel. Regarding the wish he has expressed to you, Monsieur le Baron, to be transferred to the fixed regiment of Louisiana, I beg you to consider a bit the issue of his love for me [*son amour paternal*]. . . .

I've discovered, as have many others, that it's difficult to accomplish any thing good. You know better than anyone, Monsieur le Baron, with what perseverance and zeal I solicited the assistance, which you've seen fit to grant, to facilitate the transfer of the French emigrants settled on the Ohio [at Gallipolis]. And well, when my family stopped off at Gallipolis [December 24, 1793–January 6, 1794] they learned that there were ill-intentioned men there who were spreading the rumor that everyone should mistrust my initiatives to persuade them to come and settle in this colony [New Bourbon].

I have friends in Philadelphia and Baltimore to whom I will write via the Falls of the Ohio [Louisville], begging them to seek out a good European surgeon. And in case he finds the salary that you've suggested acceptable, have him leave immediately via the Ohio River for New Madrid. I can alert Monsieur Portel [Spanish commandant at New Madrid], and he can send him on down to you. . . .

September 20, 1794

Monsieur Lorimier proposed that we should meet with Monsieur Vallé at his house [in New Ste. Genevieve] to hold a council with the Shawnees, along with a few Miamis and Ottawas. We did this, and we assured them [the Indians] that you were positively persuaded that they should all continue to live at Cape Girardeau and environs, since they themselves had selected that place to settle. Moreover, from that location close to the mouth of La Belle [the Ohio] River and centrally located between New Madrid and Ste. Genevieve, they could be easily assembled in case of emergency. . . .

My daughter is very appreciative of the trouble taken by Mademoiselle Carondelet to get her some thread from London. She begs you to accept her compliments and thanks, joined with our respects to your ladies.

> Your very humble and obedient servant,
> de Hault de Lassus

PS: Mademoiselle Vallé begs Mademoiselle Carondelet to accept a sample of work done by the Abenaki Indians. Monsieur Sarpy will be carrying it down to bring to you.[13]

No. 11

This letter was written during the height of the malaria season, when mortality was highest in Spanish Illinois. De Luzières knew that stagnant waters were in some way responsible for the fevers, which were especially severe for unseasoned newcomers to the region, but of course he was totally ignorant of the vector for the malaria parasite, the Anopheles species of mosquito. Peruvian bark, also known as Jesuit bark, is the historical name of a specific remedy for malaria (because the bark contains quinine), so named because it was obtained from the bark of several species of the genus Cinchona, of the order Rubiaceae. These species are indigenous to the Western Andes of South America

---

13. Objects of Indian craftsmanship were popular in New Orleans, and likely some items were exported to Europe. For more on this see below, document no. 16.

and were first described by Jesuit priests doing missionary work in Peru. Carlos Auguste de Lassus was soon to arrive in Louisiana and be named commandant of New Madrid, much to his father's delight. De Luzières was hoping against hope that Shawnee Indians would destroy General Anthony Wayne's army as they had General Arthur St. Clair's three years earlier. His hopes were shattered when he received definite news of Wayne's decisive victory at Fallen Timbers, August 20, 1794.

De Luzières to Carondelet   PC, Leg. 209
New Bourbon, October 17, 1794

At the next opportunity, I will have the honor of sending you the plans of the habitants of Ste. Genevieve and New Bourbon addressed to His Majesty. They wish to obtain assistance for the project that they are considering undertaking by themselves. This would protect the Pointe Basse, where our best tillable fields are located, from the flooding of the river, and would also drain the stagnant waters that lie along the base of the hills where New Bourbon is located. Every year these waters cause serious illnesses, which are rampant right now.

My wife continues to be very ill and weak. Fever has again attacked Monsieur and Madame Derbigny, and for the fifth time my youngest son and my principal trusted engagé. This is because we don't have any Kina [quinquina or Peruvian bark] despite all these setbacks. Please believe, Monsieur le Baron, they are not destroying our courage, and we're full of confidence in your kindness, facing all this with strength and resolution. . . .

I'm trusting to attach to this dispatch a letter for my son [Carlos de Hault de Lassus], who is serving in Spain. I'm making the same observations to him that you yourself have proposed concerning his desire, expressed to you, that he might be posted to the fixed regiment of Louisiana. He's a good, solid military man, very receptive to my advice, and he will happily adhere to our observations. . . .

The news from St. Louis was that the Indians defeated part of General [Anthony] Wayne's army, and that they succeeded in surrounding it so that it cannot be reinforced with men, rations, or ammunition. But the most recent news coming out of Kaskaskia and Vincennes contradicts this, claiming that this general, after having completely defeated the Indians, has created a chain of outposts, one every six leagues [about seventeen miles], from his headquarters all the way to the mouth of the Wabash. This assures his communications with Kentucky, from where he just received 2,000 reinforcements that will prevent any alliance between eastern and western Indian groups. Since all the news we've received until now from Kaskaskia and Vincennes has proven false, there's room to hope that this will be as well. . . .

Poor Monsieur [Antoine] Soulard has fallen ill once again at St. Louis, and more seriously than ever. He informs me that he is afflicted with six degrees of the most violent fever, and without the care and aid of Monsieur and Madame Zénon Trudeau he would have succumbed.

I have the honor of being, with the keenest gratitude and infinite respect, Monsieur le Baron,

> Your very humble and very obedient servant,
> de Hault de Lassus

No. 12

Bartholomé Tardiveau was de Luzières's partner in attempting to bring colonists from Gallipolis on the Ohio River to the Illinois Country and in attempting to build grist and saw mills at New Madrid. These ventures failed, but Tardiveau and de Luzières remained friends and correspondents until the former's death at New Madrid in 1801. Mercury was used on into the early twentieth century both in pill form and as a topical salve for combating syphilis. It likely had some value in this regard, but also had calamitous side effects.

Tardiveau to Carondelet at New Orleans   PC, Leg. 210
November 27, 1794

Monsieur le Baron:

A cruel treatment has deprived me for a long time of the honor of presenting my respects to you. An incompetent surgeon, my neighbor, undertook a radical cure for the boils that were tormenting me. He continuously and persistently recommended the use of certain pills, which he assured me were entirely harmless and which would not at all interfere with my concentration upon business affairs. The vicious effects of these pills, which were loaded with mercury (without which je m'en defiâsse), has been to plunge me into all the horrors of a sovereign remedy intended to be punishment for my debauchery as well as an antidote for its consequences. I'm only just starting to recover from this miserable condition, and I'm obliged to remain in my room for some further time as a precaution. However, my business affairs are suffering as a consequence of my paralysis, to which I have been condemned for more than five weeks. Not being able to have the honor of conducting a face-to-face discussion with you, permit me, Monsieur le Baron, to present herein several issues.

> Signed Bartholémé Tardiveau

No. 13

Pierre Derbigny did not remain long at New Madrid, and he would soon settle in New Orleans with his wife, Jeanne-Félicité-Odile, de Luzières's only daughter. De Luzières was very close to the Vallé brothers, François and Jean-Baptiste, of Ste. Genevieve. The house that Jean-Baptiste had built in Ste. Genevieve in 1792 still stands at the corner of Main and Market Streets. Within a year de Luzières's second eldest son, Charles-Auguste (Carlos) Delassus, would become Spanish commandant of New Madrid, and he was promoted to lieutenant governor in St. Louis in 1799.

De Luzières to le Baron Carondelet   PC, Leg. 211
New Bourbon, June 9, 1795

Monsieur le Baron:

My son-in-law [Derbigny] cannot express his delight and satisfaction with the civilities that you've heaped upon him. He was especially surprised in getting off the boat at New Madrid to have Monsieur [Thomas] Portell tell him that you had notified him (by way of Bolduc's boat that had overtaken and passed his [Derbigny's] on the river) of your intention to appoint him interpreter of English at New Madrid. I cannot find, Monsieur le Baron, words to express my feelings of gratitude at this news.

Of all the pains I have endured up to this point, none has been so painful as the separation of my dear daughter [Jeanne-Félicité-Odile], who just left with her husband [Derbigny] and her children to go and live at New Madrid in order to help with the development of gristmills. But in circumstances where not only our private concerns but more importantly those of the government are involved, be persuaded, Monsieur le Baron, that there is no personal sacrifice I would not resign myself to. . . .

The reimbursement of the 2,500 piastres advanced by the government to facilitate the immigration of the French people from the Ohio [i.e., Gallipolis], I also feel that my request to be indemnified for some of the expenses of bringing my family here, as well as the others that came with, may be premature but that once the reimbursement has been effected that you will ask the intendant to consider my just requests in this regard. . . .

I recommend to your particular kindness Monsieur Jean-Baptiste Vallé, captain of the militia of this post [i.e., New Bourbon], who is carrying this dispatch. He is the brother of our worthy and brave commandant [of the Ste. Genevieve District]. Moreover, this relative, Monsieur Jean-Baptiste Vallé, is an excellent subject and very good officer, totally devoted to the government and having the personal qualities that by themselves strongly recommend him. . . .

I'm impatient to hear that your son has arrived safely and in good health at New Orleans. I'm also anxious too soon learn about the arrival of my son [Lieutenant Colonel Carlos de Hault de Lassus] in the capital. I'm hoping that as soon as circumstances permit that you will grant him a leave so that he can come and pass some time with us. My wife joins her urgent entreaties to mine to obtain this gift of your kindness toward us. . . .

Monsieur le Baron, your very humble and obedient servant,
de Hault de Lassus

No. 14

As lieutenant governor at Natchez, Manuel Gayoso de Lemos had traveled by gunboat up the Mississippi to Spanish Illinois during the autumn of 1795, visiting both St. Louis and Ste. Genevieve.[14] Aware that Gayoso was a rising personnage in Spanish officialdom (he became governor general of Louisiana in 1797), de Luzières was intent on cultivating his favor. The letter was written during the height of malarial fevers in the region, and de Luzières's family seems to have been particularly vulnerable. De Luzières's sarcasm and contempt for Americans is palpable in paragraph three, and this attitude persisted until his death in 1806. His eldest son, Carlos de Lassus, would within a year become Spanish commandant at New Madrid.

De Luzières to Gayoso de Lemos   PC, Leg. 212A
New Bourbon, November 20, 1795

Monsieur and very amiable governor:

I cannot find a better occasion to recollect your visit than to take advantage of the trip of Monsieur [Pierre] Derbigny, my son-in-law, who is descending to New Orleans. I'm confident that you will extend the same kindnesses to him that you did to me during my visit with you.

My son-in-law will give you the details of the frightful illnesses that my family and all my people have been experiencing between last April and now. My two sons [Philippe-François-Camille and Jacques-Marcellin-Léon] still suffer fevers of three degrees. I think you will agree, my dear monsieur, that we have all paid our tribute to this colony.

All is quiet regarding the Indians and our dear neighbors. And according to the reports from our children in Kentucky and Illinois, it appears that no hostile actions are contemplated against this colony.

14. Gayoso's account of this trip may be found in Nasatir, ed., *Spanish War Vessels,* 291–341.

I'm sending you some seeds from our best melons, and when my son-in-law comes back upriver I beg you to give him some seeds from your best artichokes.

I've had the satisfaction of receiving news from my son [Carlos de Hault de Lassus] who is a second lieutenant in the Walloon guards in Spain. He's sent a detailed account of his last campaign in the army of Rousillon, and has had the satisfaction of obtaining the brevet of Lieutenant Colonel. . . .

Please convey my respects to your ladies, and never doubt my eternal feelings of gratitude and loyalty toward you.

Monsieur and very amiable governor, your tres humble and very obedient servant,

> de Lassus de Luzières

No. 15

Gayoso had visited de Luzières at New Bourbon on November 14, and de Luzières wished to cultivate his favor.[15] De Lemos, Spanish lieutenant governor at Natchez, had traveled up the Mississippi River to St. Louis and Ste. Genevieve during the summer and autumn of 1795, and had visited de Luzières at New Bourbon. Despite his disavowal of possessing any ambition, de Luzières was lusting for an official appointment, which finally came when Governor General Carondelet appointed him commandant of the new district of New Bourbon in 1797. De Luzières's correspondence is rare in mentioning fishing in the Illinois Country, but apparently a great deal was done. Pierre Derbigny, husband of de Luzières's daughter, Jeanne-Félicité-Odile, was never content in the Illinois Country and eventually moved to New Orleans, where a long time later (1828) he was elected Governor of Louisiana.

De Lassus to Gayoso de Lemos   PC, Leg. 212A
December 3, 1795
New Bourbon

Monsieur and very gracious governor,

After one has passed several such agreeable days with you, it is certainly difficult to accustom oneself to being deprived of this continued pleasure. . . .

I hope to learn on the next occasion [i.e., the arrival of the next courier] that you have arrived safely and in good health at New Madrid. My children, who were out fishing, have just rejoined me. They were eager to tell me about all of the kindnesses you showered on them when you passed by their encampment.[16] In this regard, I beg you to accept my deepest thanks. . . .

15. See Gayoso's account in ibid., 310.

Although in my position I possess no ambition, I would nevertheless wish that when you present your report to the government [i.e., to Governor General Carondelet] about the Illinois Country, and when you deal with the topic of agriculture, you would mention me. I mean this relative to its progress, especially during the last two years, which is a result of my good advice and the good example I have set. This may be seen regarding the best methods of cultivation, in choosing the best lands for the different types of production, and the progress that I believe will develop as a consequence. . . .

I'm requesting that you may continue your kindnesses toward my son-in-law [Pierre Derbigny] and his family. When you see them, I beg you to scold them for their long silence in our regard. . . .

Please accept the affection of my wife, together with the homage of my children. And never doubt the faithful sentiments and respectful attachment with which I have the honor of being, monsieur and very respectful governor,

Your humble and very obedient and affectionate servant,
de Lassus de Luzières

No. 16

The sources about the subject are scarce, but a substantial commerce in Indian handiwork apparently existed in the Mississippi River valley during the late eighteenth century. Lorimier seems to have been managing a substantial cottage industry in Indian crafts, no doubt using his close contacts with the Shawnee and Delaware tribes.

In 1802 Pierre Provenchère, merchant of St. Louis, sent 335 pairs of moccasins to New Orleans, where his agent, Berthe Grima, sold them for 28 piastres and 22 reales (about $28.50). See Grima's account with Provenchère for the year 1804 in the Grima family papers, Tulane University Archives, New Orleans.

Lorimier to Carondelet   PC, Leg. 208A
Cape Girardeau, December 22, 1795

I'm not sending down any [*souliers*] moccasins for you and Monsieur Cruzat, not having any ready to go. But I'll get some loaded on the next vessel going down.

Your very humble and very obedient servant,
Don Louis Lorimier
Louis Largeau

16. Gayoso anchored his galiot near the bank of the Mississippi at Cape St. Cosme, downriver from New Bourbon, and invited de Luzières's sons on board for refreshments (see ibid., 311).

No. 17

De Luzières wrote this recruiting pamphlet in the spring of 1796 and hand-carried it to Lexington, Kentucky, to be printed and distributed by John Bradford, who had founded the Kentucke [sic] Gazette *in 1787.[17] No printing press existed in Upper Louisiana until the* Missouri Gazette *was established at St. Louis in 1808, and in any case de Luzières for recruitment purposes wanted the pamphlet distributed in Kentucky. Likely the English translation was done by "Monsieur Gensack,"[18] who lived in New Bourbon at the time and whom de Luzières was promoting for the position of official translator in the region. François Vallé, who countersigned this document, was commandant of the region, including New Bourbon, in 1796, but thanks in part to the success of the pamphlet de Luzières was appointed commandant of the newly created New Bourbon District in 1797. The rare book room at the Library of Congress has an original copy, a facsimile of which was printed by the University of Kentucky Library Associates in 1956. The idiosyncratic syntax, spellings, and punctuation have been left as in the original.*

AN OFFICIAL ACCOUNT

OF THE

SITUATION, SOIL, PRODUCE, &c.

OF THAT PART OF

LOUISIANA,

WHICH LIES BETWEEN THE MOUTH OF THE MISSOURI
AND NEW MADRID, OR L'ANSE A LA GRAISE, AND
ON THE WEST SIDE OF THE MISSISSIPPI.

TOGETHER WITH AN
ABSTRACT OF THE SPANISH GOVERNMENT, &c.

I, the underwritten, knight of the Great Cross [of St. Michel], of the order of his most *Christian Majesty* [Louis XVI], &c. living at New Bourbon, near *St. Genevieve,* on the river Mississippi, in the western district of the Illinois Country belonging to his *Catholic majesty the king of Spain* [Carlos IV], certify and attest to whomever it may concern, that during about four years that I have been living in the Illinois coun-

---

17. See Thomas D. Clark, ed., *The Voice of the Frontier: John Bradford's Notes on Kentucky* (Lexington: University Press of Kentucky, 1993), 97–98.
18. See below, documents nos. 23 and 27.

try, I have traveled in it, and examined it, with as much attention as exactness, from the village of St. Charles on the left bank and near the mouth of the Missouri, to New Madrid, formerly known as *l'Anse a la Graisse,* and that in all this extent of more than a hundred leagues in length, there is an immensity of very rich and fertile land, proper for all sorts of culture.

That I have verified with my own eyes and in person, that wheat, rye, barley, oats, Indian corn, cotton, tobacco, hemp, flax, Irish and sweet potatoes, and all sorts of pulse and vegetables are raised there with the greatest success.

That there is in the same country, an uncommon quantity of natural pasturage and meadows, and that the artificial ones which cultivated there succeed perfectly.

That fruit trees, such as apples, pears, peaches, apricots, cherries, plumbs, &c. grow as perfect as quick.

That the climate is very healthy, the seasons very regular, the summers & winters moderate, and the falls of so long and agreeable duration, that they often last till the fifteenth of January.

That there is no country better calculated to raise stock of all kinds that the Illinois, on account of the great abundance of range, both in the prairies and woods, and of the shortness of the winters.

That the woods are well stocked with timber, such as red, white and green oak, walnuts of all kinds, sycamores, plantanes, aspen, poplar, ash, elm, mulberry, cedar, pine, and sugar maple; these last are so abundant, that a sufficient quantity of sugar and molasses may be extracted from them to answer the consumption of the colony.

That there is in this whole district, a great number of creeks and springs fit to have sorts of mills erected thereon.

That there are several salt springs, from the waters of which excellent and handsome white salt is extracted without much difficulty; the best, and for the present the one that is most worked, and has four kettles going, is at about a league from New Bourbon.

That finally, there is in this country a great quantity of iron, lead and copper ores, and of stone coal; lead ore in particular, is so very abundant, that where they work it, they are generally at no other pains than to pick it up on the surface of the ground; this is about a day's journey from St. Genevieve.

That all the inhabitants of this district, are permitted without distinction, to make salt and work the mines, in such extent of ground as may be allotted them upon their own choice.

That there is also in the same country, a great number of very handsome quarries of building stone, most of which are calcarious.

That it is notorious that in the Illinois country, as is the case in all Louisiana, government grants *gratis* and without any expenses whatever (even without any office charges for titles and patents) as much land as chose to settle there can cultivate, use and desire, proportionably to the strength of their families, their circumstances, their trade or profession, and in such place as they may choose.

That it is equally notorious that in the Illinois country, that there is no kind of tax or levy, either upon the inhabitants, their cattle or their lands, and that the name of government is known there only by the favors it bestows, and the public advantages it procures.

That this country is so far blessed, as to be exempt from chicanery & lawyers.[19] Most of the law-suits (which are scarce) are decided upon and terminated, either amicably, or before the commandants of the garrisons, who unite in their persons the civil and military authorities; or else by arbitration, and always without any expense.

That before the end of six months, there will be at the principal garrisons of the Illinois country, such as St. Louis, St. Genevieve, New Bourbon and New Madrid strongly built water mills, for the double purpose of grinding and sawing, which is already accomplished in the first mentioned place, and in a state of great forwardness in the three others.

That this country is possessed of the most commodious & quick means of exporting her produce to certain and advantageous markets, as well as by the easy navigation of the Mississippi, as by the preference she is assured of on the part of government in favor of the growth of its soil.

That the fur trade is very flourishing in this country, and that from the constant endeavors of government to ameliorate it, there is no doubt but it will rise to a still greater importance.

That the Indian nations, all friendly to Spain, not only contribute to the success of the fur trade, but also to the subsistence of the inhabitants for three fourths of the year, by furnishing meat, tallow & oil in abundance to the garrisons and villages.

That the rivers and creeks abound with excellent fish, such as Catfish, *Achigans* [Bass], Sturgeons, Pike, Carp, Buffaloe, Oatugas [chain pickerel],[20] Eel, &c. which are easy to be caught, and are a most precious resource.

That in the Illinois country, as in all Louisiana, the greatest and most reasonable liberty conscience and action is allowed, and that every one may go and come and do, without any obstacle or contradiction, whatever is not injurious to the king's interest, or that of any one else.

That is it evident that the laborers, mechanics, carpenters, joiners, masons, smiths, coopers, cordwainers, tanners, shoe makers, weavers, turners, distillers, and particularly boat builders will meet with the greatest encouragement there in their respective trades and professions.

That the laws equally simple, wise and just, regulate in a clear and precise manner the rights, property and inheritance of the inhabitants; that among the rest there is

19. Barristers, as opposed to notaries, were forbidden in both French and Spanish Louisiana.

20. Carl Masthay of St. Louis tracked this word down and found it to be derived from Abenaki (Loup or Delaware) watagwa, which makes sense given that de Luzières had close contact with those Indians at the time he wrote.

a very interesting one, permitting all free persons of legal age, not only to dispose of their property by will, but also to name such executors as they please and in whom they can place their confidence, to execute without any judiciary expenses their last will after their decease; and that where a person dies intestate and leaves behind a wife and children, the estate is divided in two equal parts by valuation, of which the survivor gets one part and the children the other, at equal shares, unless the parents have by their marriage articles derogated from this legal disposition.[21]

In witness of all which, I have delivered this my certificate, sealed with my coat of arms, at New Bourbon in the Illinois country, the seventeenth of May, one thousand, seven hundred and ninety-six.

(SIGNED)

DELASSUS DELUZIERES

Don Francis Valle, Captain of the Militia, civil and military commandant of the garrisons of St. Genevieve and New Bourbon in the Illinois country.

We the commandant above mentioned do certify that the above signature is truly that of Mr. Delassus. We moreover attest that the facts enumerated and certified in the above certificate are really sincere and true. In witness thereof we have to these presents set our signature and ordinary seal, at St. Genevieve in the Illinois country, the eighteenth of May, one thousand, seven hundred and ninety-six.

(SIGNED)

FRANCIS VALLE

No. 18

De Luzières's ringing endorsement of monarchical government in this document reflects his growing anxiety about the ever-increasing power and influence of Americans in the Mississippi River valley. The second paragraph refers explicitly to Jay's Treaty (November 19, 1794), by which Great Britain agreed finally to relinquish the Northwest military and fur-trading outposts, and to the Treaty of San Lorenzo (Pinckney's Treaty, October 27, 1795), which established the boundary of Spanish West Florida at the 31st parallel and gave American merchants free navigation on the Mississippi River and the right to deposit their goods in New Orleans.

21. Here de Luzières briefly explains the mixture of French and Spanish legal traditions that obtained in late-colonial Louisiana. Concerning inheritance practices, French customary law (Coutume de Paris) emphasized the marriage contract and equal distribution of property, whereas Spanish law leaned toward the use of written wills and more individual choice. See Hans Baade, "Marriage Contracts in French and Spanish Louisiana: A Study in 'Notarial Jurisprudence,'" *Tulane Law Review* 53 (December 1978): esp. 44–50.

De Luzières to Carondelet   PC, Leg. 212A
New Bourbon, August 1, 1796

Monsieur le Baron:

I will abstain from discussing the present political situation. Although I agree with your brother that the most precious gift we can hope to have is patience and resignation, I nevertheless aver that I intend to live and die more devoted then ever to royal authority and monarchical government.

Apparently the English are at this moment in the midst of turning over to the Americans the posts of Detroit and Michilimackinac. Rumors at Kaskaskia have it that the treaty that has been made between Spain and the United States of America concerning the freedom of navigation on the Mississippi is broken and will not be effected.

Our wheat harvests are over. They've been excellent in both quantity and quality, and the maize is looking good. We sowed at least twice as much [apparently maize] as last year, and if no problems arise between now and the harvests they will be the largest that this post has ever seen.

I am with the most profound respect, Monsieur le Baron, your very humble and very obedient servant,

Dehault De Lassus

No. 19

When de Luzières wrote this letter, he and his wife were visiting their son, Charles (Carlos) de Lassus, who had just assumed command of New Madrid. Georges-Henri-Victor Collot (1750–1805) was a French agent who had been sent to the Mississippi Valley by Pierre-Auguste Adet, French minister to the United States. Collot's account of his travels was eventually published as A journey in North America, containing a survey of the countries watered by the Mississippi, Ohio, Missouri, and other affluing rivers; with exact observations on the course and soundings of these rivers; and on the towns, villages, hamlets and farms of that part of the new-world; followed by philosophical, political, military and commercial remarks and by a projected line of frontiers and general limits, illustrated by 36 maps, plans, views and divers cuts *(Paris: A. Bertrand, 1826). His often-reproduced map of Upper Louisiana, with a detailed inset of St. Louis, was based on cartographic work done by his aide-de-camp, Charles Warin, a trained military engineer, and was engraved in Paris by Pierre-François Tardieu.*[22]

22. Warin was attacked by a drunken Chickasaw Indian with a war club near Arkansas Post and died a few weeks later in New Orleans (see Collot, *Journey in North America*, 2:26–27).

De Luzières to Carondelet   PC, Leg. 212A
New Madrid, September 19, 1796

Monsieur le Baron

My wife and I have been at this post since the 15th of this month. It's been painful to discover that my dear son [Carlos de Lassus] did not find any occasion to get this packet sent to you. . . . I'm seizing this one to get it sent on down to you. The courier is Sieur Collot, a French general and former governor of Guadaloupe, where the English imprisoned him. . . .

I've been delighted with the progress of our work on the mills; the sawmill is ready to go. Monsieur Collot, whom I knew well at Paris and in France, has visited the project site here with me. He was astonished to find this in this desert, in this remote end of the world, a project of this importance and so solidly constructed.

Pray give our respects to all members of your family, and I am with respectful loyalty,

De Lassus [de Luzières]

No. 20

De Luzières was still visiting his son in New Madrid when he wrote this letter. The letter provides a rare glimpse into one of the stranger episodes in the history of late colonial St. Louis. Modeled in a vague manner after the famous Jacobin Club in revolutionary Paris, this association of Sans Culottes in St. Louis advocated replacing the royal Spanish regime with a French republican government. Like revolutionaries in Paris, these provincial counterparts sought to mix revolutionary politics with public festivities. De Luzières's prose virtually drips with his utter disgust for anything that smacked of republican politics. France did, of course, nominally reacquire Louisiana in the third Treaty of San Ildefonso in 1800.

De Luzières to Carondelet   PC, Leg. 212B
New Madrid, October 17, 1796

Monsieur le Baron:

I've already reported to you the rumors circulating in the Illinois Country concerning the impending cession of Louisiana to France. And since then my son, [Carlos] de Lassus, has informed you about the confidential information he's received on this subject. It remains for me today to tell you about the indecent scenes that have transpired in St. Louis on this occasion. Already an association called the "Sans Culottes" has been created. This is led by one Monsieur [Louis] Cogniart, an agent of a business man in New

Orleans named Langust. This association frequently sponsors public festivals and dances, to which folks are invited in the name of the Sans Culottes. During these entertainments frightful songs are sung, which could perusade even the most loyal subjects to revolt. . . . This association has been brazen enough on September 22 to rouse all the most important residents of the post [St. Louis], including the priest, wishing them a good year and shouting catcalls. In such circumstances, I certainly pity my friend Zénon Trudeau [lieutenant governor at St. Louis] in the critical and embarrassing situation in which he finds himself. He is necessarily caught between the desire to suppress and put a stop to such indecent disorders and the fear of damaging the good relations that prevail between Spain and France. In any case, I believe that you should definitely take prompt and effective action to stop, and if possible eradicate, these public acts of disrepect and contempt against the authority of our good government. . . .

I've learned with great pleasure that our habitants of Ste. Genevieve and New Bourbon continue to be very peaceable and tranquil, despite the efforts of some residents of St. Louis to stir them up. I have already corresponded with the brave and upright Monsieur [François] Vallé, strongly urging him to maintain good order in his post. But I will return there quickly to get together with him and make use of the faith that a majority of the good citizens have in me to get them to persevere in their good principles and to protect them from the contagion [of revolutionary ideas]. . . .

I beg you to proceed with the kind offer that you've had the goodness to make of placing my youngest son [Philippe-François-Camille de Lassus, born December 20, 1778, in Bouchain] as a cadet in one of His Majesty's regiments. If I have not been pursuing this issue it's because this young son is the only one of our children still left with us at our plantation at New Bourbon, and he is for us a most precious possession. . . .

The lands surrounding this post [New Madrid] everywhere offer superb locations for all sorts of agricultural production, and they're easy to cultivate. Its immense size could attract and sustain a very large population. . . . [23] But to attract people and get them to settle here the government must be willing to advance some foodstuffs to those who would like to come and settle. It must also provide medications appropriate for the illnesses that newly arrived folks usually suffer from shortly after they arrive.

I am with the greatest possible respect, Monsieur le Baron,

> Your very humble and obedient servant,
> de Hault de Lassus père

23. See 1797 New Madrid census in Houck, ed., *Spanish Regime*, 2:393.

No. 21

Spanish colonial administrators in Louisiana were caught on the horns of a dilemma: populate the colony or lose it to enemy attack or internal atrophy; but populate the colony with Americans and face the prospect of losing it to cultural submersion and/or political and religious subversion. De Luzières and Governor Carondelet, despite their reservations, adopted a more or less liberal position, agreeing that Americans of all religious persuasions should be admitted providing they were politically safe. And the twelve months following Vallé's letter given here witnessed a marked increase in American immigration. The results may be seen in the 1797 New Bourbon census, which includes persons from some of the most radical Protestant groups.

François Vallé to Carondelet   PC, Leg. 212A
Ste. Genevieve, November 10, 1796

I've received your lordship's official letter dated July 1 of this present year. This orders me to admit to this jurisdiction [i.e., Ste. Genevieve and environs] only Americans that may be categorized as good workers and solid [*honnette*] men, and to shun and drive off all manner of vagabonds. It further specifies that a 500-piastre fine shall be levied upon me if, contrary to your orders, I permit bad characters to move in. I hope, Monsieur, that after my vigilance and the cares that I have taken to ensure that your goals are met, I will merit your continued confidence.

The number of Americans thus far settled at Ste. Genevieve and New Bourbon is very small. But for the past six months, solid looking persons are arriving every day to request agricultural lands for the very large number of families who wish to settle down here beginning next April. At first only the men would come to produce foodstuffs, without which they would threaten the area with famine as well as exposing themselves to it. Given the large number of families to which agricultural lands have already been promised, plus those that I know positively will come to request them, I have asked Monsieur Trudeau, your commandant, to advise me concerning the quantity that the government wishes to admit in each. He responded that, not having received yet any precise orders about this subject (which meant that he would have to consult with you), and that expecting to receive your response at the earliest next spring, I could in the meantime make a selection from among the Americans who will be arriving each month. I should admit the Catholics and the well-to-do folks, especially those owning black slaves, and exclude all others while awaiting your orders. I will adhere to this. The increase in the population and the increasing diversity of folks [*le mélange de nations*] means that maintaining good order is more difficult. A region where folks live separately on remote plantations obliges me to tell you of my need to have a dozen good soldiers, young men capable of moving about expeditiously to where they may be required for the purpose of maintaining good order. Experience has taught me, Monsieur, that a single armed soldier [*une simple bayonnette*] in one of our outposts always gets more respect than an entire detachment of militia. Militiamen are always indulgent with one another, not wishing to make any enemies. An official drummer would be yet more essential. Our commander in chief [Lieutenant Governor Zénon Trudeau in St. Louis] knows this very well, but he has always postponed asking you while awaiting happier times.

May God be your holy guardian.

Ste. Genevieve of the Illinois, 10 November 1796

Signed François Vallé

No. 22

Although plagued with upper respiratory problems, in addition to his nagging malaria, de Luzières assiduously maintained his correspondence. Everyone in the Illinois Country, including slaves, shared seeds during the spring planting season. It was part of the communitarian ethos of the region. Madame Cerré was the wife of the famous trader, Gabriel Cérré, whose daughter, Marie-Thérèse, married Auguste Chouteau in 1786. Audrain had never detested America and Americans the way de Luzières did, and he was happy to "join 'em rather than fight 'em" when his interests dictated it. Moses Austin, the famous lead-mine entrepreneur, would eventually pay a visit on the de Luzières family at their residence in New Bourbon.[24]

De Luzières to Tardiveau
Illinois State Historical Library, Tardiveau Papers, no. 335
New Bourbon, February 2, 1797

24. Concerning Audrain's life in America, see Warren J. Wolfe, "The First American Citizen of Detroit: Pierre Audrain, 1725–1820," in *Detroit in Perspective* (Winter 1981): 45–47. See *La vie aux Illinois au XVIIIe siècle: souvenirs inédits de Marie-Anne Cerré*, ed. Marthe Faribault-Beauregard and trans. Michel Thibault (Montreal: Société de recherche historique, 1987); concerning Moses Austin, see David B. Gracy II, *Moses Austin: His Life* (San Antonio: Trinity University Press, 1987), esp. 53–54. On Austin, see also James Alexander Gardner, *Lead King: Moses Austin* (St. Louis: Sunrise Publishing Co., 1980); George P. Garrison, "A Memorandum of M. Austin's Journey from the Lead Mines in the County of Wythe in the State of Virginia to the Lead Mines in the Province of Louisiana West of the Mississippi, 1796–1797," *American Historical Review* 5 (April 1900): 541–42.

I learn, my respectable friend, with much pain that you are again incommoded with your health. . . . I myself for the past fifteen days have felt poorly. This is consuming me and bothers me to the point that everything annoys and displeases me. On top of this, right now I'm laid low with a bad cold, and I'm passing sleepless night coughing. I'm just hoping that the coming of the "belle saison" will cure all these ills. I'll try to get some seeds sent to you via [Pierre] Derbigny's barge. I'm expecting some from Madame [Marie-Anne] Cerré in St. Louis that I'll gladly share with you. . . .

It's reported from Vincennes that our former associate, Audrain, has been named clerk in Detroit. More than ever, masses of Americans wish to settle on our side [of the Mississippi]. Among those recently arrived is one named Monsieur Austin, owner of lead mines in Virginia, who comes highly recommended by the Spanish consul in Kentucky. He has the plans, the means, and the knowledge to establish a large manufactory of lead, in bars, balls, shot, and so forth. It's said with certainty that there are an infinite number of barges and boats on the Ohio loaded with families destined to arrive in Upper Louisiana.

> Your very humble and affectionate servant,
> De Luzières

No. 23

De Luzières begins this letter by describing what became one of the worst Mississippi floods of the late colonial period, that of 1797, which pushed New Bourbon and Ste. Genevieve to the brink of famine during the winter of 1797–1798. Joseph Fenwick and his son, Dr. Walter Fenwick, were two of the prize immigrants that de Luzières's recruitment efforts brought to Spanish Illinois during the 1790s. The doctor, who married Julie Vallé, was tragically killed in a duel on Moreau's Island in 1811. Monsieur Gensac (his first name remains unknown) was a valuable but brief addition to New Bourbon's population. He appears on de Luzières's 1797 enumeration but then drops out of sight. It is interesting to see that de Luzières was keeping close tabs on the United States Congress, which he knew might well play a role in the eventual fate of Louisiana.

De Luzières to Carondelet   PC, Leg. 212A
New Bourbon, June 12, 1797

Monsieur le Baron:

Our plaine basse [i.e., the Pointe Basse] has utterly disappeared, and the surface is but one vast sea. . . . I can assure you that our crops are entirely lost, and that we will have no means to subsist or to sow our fields with spring wheat next year. . . .

Having no doubt that you will take this matter under serious consideration and that you will take the necessary steps to provide the upper colony [Upper Louisiana] with subsistence and to prevent the dreadful consequences of a famine, . . . I'll hazard here some thoughts about what local, and least expensive, resources may be utilized to that end. . . .

Monsieur [Joseph] Fenwick, along with the numerous and well-to-do Catholic families that he brought with him from Kentucky, having carefully reexamined the area where he had hoped to settle down near New Bourbon, . . . has decided to look at other places. He found one very advantageously situated on the [Mississippi] river between Cap d'Ail and the Rivière à la Glaise. . . .

It is absolutely indispensable to appoint some interpreters of the English language at both St. Louis and Ste. Genevieve. I'm presuming to recommend that for the latter post you appoint Monsieur Gensac, a French émigré from St. Domingue, who already performs this function when he is asked to do so. I can assure you, Monsieur le Baron, that you could not make a better choice. This young man is very trustworthy, well brought up, and very talented. Everyone who knows him takes a very lively interest in his future, and I would myself share in his gratitude should you deign to appoint him.[25]

Absolutely nothing new from our neighbors [i.e., the Americans], who seem to be very tranquil. We're impatience to hear the results of what the Congress, which convened this past May 15th, decided relative to affairs with France.

I am with very respectful devotion, Monsieur le Baron, your very humble and very obedient servant.

Dehault De Lassus

No. 24

De Luzières had known since May 1797 that he was to be appointed commandant of the newly created New Bourbon District, which was a departing gift from his friend, Governor Carondelet, who was about to leave office. This letter is his official response to Carondelet once the appointment had become official. His in-

25. Several times de Luzières recommended that Gensac be made official interpreter at New Bourbon, and he appears as a single male on de Luzières's 1797 census of New Bourbon (see below, document no. 27). But Gensac was never appointed and he did not remain long in Upper Louisiana.

stallation ceremony, which must have occurred in front of the parish church in Ste. Genevieve immediately following mass, was surely one of the highlights of de Luzières's life. He would soon set to work on his masterpiece, the comprehensive census of the New Bourbon District, including his extensive commentary on the region.

De Luzières to Carondelet   PC, Leg. 214
New Bourbon, September 21, 1797

Monsieur le Baron:

I receive with both joy and gratitude the dispatch attached to your official letter of June 1st by which you appoint me civil and military commandant of New Bourbon and its dependencies. I was installed and recognized in that position on Sunday the 17th of this month by Monsieur François Vallé, commandant of Ste. Genevieve, pursuant to your orders, in the presence of the militia and residents of Ste. Genevieve and New Bourbon, who assembled for the occasion. And, pursuant to what you prescribed in the said dispatch to establish a boundary separating the new post from the commanderie of Ste. Genevieve, I will proceed immediately with this task in conjunction with the said Monsieur Vallé. We will be advantageously assisted with this task by Sieur [Thomas] Madden, a well-to-do, honest, educated surveyor, who owns many slaves. I decided three months ago to get him settled on a farmstead close to New Bourbon, and I persuaded Monsieur [Antoine] Soulard to take him as an assistant surveyor for the districts of Ste. Genevieve and New Bourbon....

Concerning the boundary between New Bourbon and Cape Girardeau, ... I'd like it to extend down to the Rivière à la Glaise. I've discussed this with Monsieur [Louis] Lorimier, ... who approves of this boundary....

My district contains the majority of the Indians who are settled here—the Shawnees, the Abenakis, the Miamis, and so forth. They come to me frequently asking for bread and flour, which is impossible to refuse them, for I am one of those whom they call their father....

I'm asking again that at the first opportunity you have sent up to me a flag displaying His Majesty's coat-of-arms, so that it will be known that New Bourbon is an official command post.

God keep you in his holy guard, Delassus de Luzières

No. 25

This rare document does not make it clear whether the two free blacks were functioning as entrepreneurs in this situation, or whether they themselves were engagés employed by a third party not mentioned. Neptune and Jasmin would

have carried a copy of the document with them down the Mississippi to New Or-
leans as evidence that they were not fugitive slaves. François Jasmin had been a
Vallé family slave who purchased his freedom, and he appears as head of a large
household on both the 1787 and 1791 Spanish censuses of Ste. Genevieve. This
was one of de Luzières's first official acts as the newly appointed civil and military
commandant of the New Bourbon District.

Passport for Neptune and Jasmin   PC, Leg. 214
New Bourbon, September 27, 1797

The free blacks named Neptune and Jasmin, residing respectively at Ste. Genevieve and New Bourbon, have permission to proceed to New Orleans with two pirogues [canots] loaded with apples, which will be manned by two or three other engagés. Inscribed by us, commandant of the said New Bourbon, September 27, 1797.[26]

de Lassus de Luzières

No. 26

As newly appointed commandant of the New Bourbon District, de Luzières was eager to establish a military presence at his new post. His choice of militia officers is interesting and revealing. Israel Dodge, an American but a Roman Catholic, could represent the large number of new American immigrants to the district; Camille Delassus's appointment was a classic piece of traditional Old Regime nepotism; Tonnellier was an educated Parisian, who had served as sometime school master in Ste. Genevieve; and Gabriel La Chance came from a well-known local family of French-Canadian background. These familial backgrounds of these officers therefore represented most of the diversity contained in New Bourbon's populace—French, French-Canadian-Creole, and American.

26. Concerning Jasmin's life, first as a slave and then as a free man, see Carl J. Ekberg, *François Vallé and His World,* (Columbia: University of Missouri Press, 2002), 170, 176, 184–86. Apples were shipped frequently from the Illinois Country to the New Orleans area, where the climate is not suitable for apple cultivation. Louis Bolduc's financial agent in New Orleans, Berthe Grima, wrote him on January 27, 1800: "I thank you for the apples you sent me, not one of which was any good. I am nonetheless grateful to you." See Bolduc's financial account with Grima in the Grima family papers, Tulane University Archives. And on March 26, 1799, de Luzières wrote André Lopéz, secretary to Governor General Gayoso de Lemos, that come autumn he could expect to receive some "excellent apples" from de Luzières and François Vallé. See de Luzières to Lopéz, PC, Leg. 216B.

De Luzières to Carondelet   PC, Leg. 214
New Bourbon, October 1, 1797

Monsieur le Baron:

In accordance with your orders that I recommend persons whom I judge appropriate to command the company of militia in my post of New Bourbon, ... I am proposing the following subjects:

Monsieur Israel Dodge as first lieutenant of the said company. In addition to the fact that he has already served with zeal and distinction with the mounted troops in Ste. Genevieve's militia, he is a very vigorous and forthright man in whom I have the greatest confidence. Moreover, he is a large property owner, being one of the principal and notable habitants of New Bourbon. He built a flour mill here eighteen months ago, which is very useful to the public, and he has a family and several slaves.

Monsieur Camille Delassus, my youngest son, as second lieutenant of the militia. Since you have already promised and assured this for him, I can only repeat here what I have already said about him—that he had achieved the rank of reserve sub-lieutenant in the Esterházy Regiment of [French] hussars by the time I emigrated from France in 1790; that he has served here since his arrival with much zeal as a volontaire in the militia, and that he is very vigorous and intelligent.

Monsieur Louis Tonnellier as sub-lieutenant in the said militia company. He is an excellent subject, well-educated, well-born, and a former sergeant in the Ste. Genevieve militia. He has served as a public scribe with intelligence and honesty for a long time, and I'm using him to draft public documents at my post. He's the son-in-law of Monsieur [André] Deguire, a very respectable habitant of this post and former lieutenant in the militia, who resigned because of very old age. He requests that in compensation for his long and faithful service his son-in-law be appointed sub-lieutenant.

The New Bourbon District has enough men able to bear arms, not only for a complete company of regular militia but also for a brigade of 20 to 25 mounted militiamen. Such brave and well-mounted troops are necessary in this region. They are first and frequently used, both for investigating disorders committed by the Indians and for pursuing them. I propose Monsieur Gabriel La Chance to command this brigade of militia cavalry with a commission of second lieutenant. He is also an excellent subject, who has led the company of mounted militia at Ste. Genevieve. He is one of the principal and notable habitants of New Bourbon, very well-to-do and owning many slaves.

I'm proposing these various subjects for officers' positions with all the more confidence for having confirmed my choices with Monsieur Zénon Trudeau, lieutenant governor and commandant of the upper colony [of Louisiana], as well as with Monsieur François Vallé, commandant at Ste. Genevieve, of which the present post of New Bourbon was once a part. . . .

   God protect you in good health. New Bourbon of the Illinois,
     Delassus de Luzières

No. 27

De Luzières's 1797 census of the New Bourbon District, of which Governor Carondelet had just appointed de Luzières commandant, is a remarkable document in several respects: It is one of the rare censuses from colonial Spanish Illinois to be enumerated family-by-family, and it is the only such census to give place of origin and religious denomination for each head-of-family. The census also reveals New Bourbon to have been a rapidly growing community, boasting 355 free, white citizens in 1797 as opposed to 266 a year earlier.[27] Perhaps most significantly it reveals the ethnic and religious mix of an important region of Upper Louisiana as American immigration to Spanish Illinois was starting in earnest. The two Baptists enumerated are likely the first of that denomination to move to the west side of the Mississippi. Many of these Americans put down deep roots in what became Missouri Territory, and their future success may be seen in the concessions they eventually received from the United States Government (American State Papers, Public Lands). Of the many letters and documents de Luzières wrote while he resided at New Bourbon during the waning years of the Spanish colonial regime in Louisiana, the 1797 census, with the associated commentary, is his masterpiece. It is, by itself, an important enough historical document to give de Luzières a small slice of immortality.

Western Part of Illinois
Post and District of New Bourbon

Census of the population of the post and district of New Bourbon, followed by observations on the characteristics and qualities of the traditional, and the new, white residents, as well as on the colored people, both Indians and slaves. This includes commentary on their industry, their commerce, and their agriculture, as well as remarks on the means to markedly increase the prosperity of this interesting colony. The abuses that exist are criticized, and information

---

27. Houck, ed., *Spanish Regime*, 2:141. For whatever reasons, the 1796 enumeration of New Bourbon includes six free mulattoes and two free blacks, whereas de Luzières's 1797 enumeration includes only two free blacks, both women.

provided about the military forces of this post. Finally, recommendations are made about what is indispensable in order to put this post in an advantageous defensive posture.

White Residents and Their Slaves at Post of New Bourbon

Monsieur Pierre-Charles Dehault Delassus et de Luzières*[28]
  French
  Catholic
  Captain and commandant of this post
  White males in household
        to age 14: 0
        14 to 50: 1
        over 50: 3
  White females in household
        to age 14: 2
        14 to 50: 1
        over 50: 0
  Mulatto slaves: 0
  Male black slaves
        to age 14: 2
        14 to 50: 1
        over 50: 1
  Female black slaves
        to age 14: 2
        14 to 50: 2
        over 50: 0
  Total members in household: 15

André Deguire[29]
  Creole
  Catholic
  Farmer
  Whites males in household
        to age 14: 0
        14 to 50: 5
        over 50: 2

28. Those with an asterisk attached are listed on "Patriotic Donations and Loans made by the Residents of Upper Louisiana to aid Spain in the War, 1799." Printed in Houck, ed., *Spanish Regime*, 2:292–96, Houck's annotations are often helpful but not always reliable.
29. Concerning the large and important Deguire family, see Carl J. Ekberg, *Colonial Ste. Genevieve: An Adventure on the Mississippi Frontier* (Gerald, Mo.: Patrice Press, 1985), passim. This was likely André II, who was married to Marguerite Gouvereau.

White females in household
     to age 14: 0
     14 to 50: 2
     over 50: 0
Male mulatto slaves: 0
Female mulatto slaves
     to age 14: 1
     14 to 50: 1
     over 50: 0
Male black slaves
     to age 14: 0
     14 to 50: 1
     over 50: 1
Female black slaves
     to age 14: 0
     14 to 50: 0
     over 50: 1
Total members in household: 14

Israel Dodge*[30]
    American
    Catholic
    Farmer
    White males in household
         to age 14: 3
         14 to 50: 2
         over 50: 0
    White females in household
         to age 14: 0
         14 to 50: 1
         over 50: 0
    Male mulatto slaves
         to age 14: 0
         14 to 50: 1
         over 50: 0
    Female mulatto slaves
         to age 14: 0

30. Israel and his brother John were born in Connecticut and had come to the Mississippi Valley during the American Revolution. The Dodge brothers then moved across the Mississippi to Spanish Illinois circa 1787, becoming some of the first, and most important, Americans to do so. Israel's son, Henry (who appears on this census as one of the three young males in his household) went on to become the first territorial governor of Wisconsin. Concerning Israel's relationship with de Luzières, see above, documents nos. 1 and 26.

14 to 50: 1
over 50: 0
Male black slaves
    to age 14: 2
    14 to 50: 1
    over 50: 0
Female black slaves
    to age 14: 2
    14 to 50: 1
    over 50: 0
Total members in household: 14

Widow John Dodge[31]
    American
    Protestant
    Farmer
    White males in household
        to age 14: 1
        14 to 50: 1
        over 50: 0
    White females in household
        to age 14: 2
        14 to 50: 2
        over 50: 0
    Male black slaves
        to age 14: 0
        14 to 50: 1
        over 50: 0
    Female black slaves
        to age 14: 0
        14 to 50: 1
        over 50: 0
    Total members in household: 8

Job Wistoryr (Westover)[32]
    American
    Protestant

31. This was Anne Keen, widow of John Dodge, who had died young in April 1795 (see SGPR, Burials Bk. 2:27). Concerning John Dodge's tumultuous life in and around Kaskaskia during the 1780s, see Clarence Walworth Alvord, *The Illinois Country, 1673–1818* (Springfield: Illinois Centennial Commission, 1920), 352–53, 362–68.
32. Job was a carpenter and millwright born in Massachusetts in 1773, died in Washington County, Missouri, 1838. Granted 340 arpents at Rivières aux Vases, *ASP, PL* 3:300.

Farmer
White males in household
      to age 14: 0
      14 to 50: 1
      over 50: 0
Total members in household: 1

Joseph Fenwick[33]
  American
  Catholic
  Farmer
  White males in household
      to age 14: 3
      14 to 50: 4
      over 50: 0
  White females in household
      to age 14: 0
      14 to 50: 1
      over 50: 0
  Male black slaves
      to age 14: 8
      14 to 50: 2
      over 50: 0
  Female black slaves
      to age 14: 2
      14 to 50: 3
      over 50:
  Total members in household: 23

George Hamilton[34]
  American
  Catholic
  Farmer
  White males in household
      to age 14: 0

33. The Fenwicks were an Irish Roman Catholic family that came to Spanish Illinois from Maryland via Kentucky. Joseph's son, Walter, was a medical doctor who settled at Ste. Genevieve, married into the Vallé family, and was killed in a duel in 1811. Joseph was a favorite of de Luzières and was granted a lot in the New Bourbon common field (see *ASP, PL,* 3:285).

34. From Kentucky, settled in Spanish Illinois in 1797 and was married into the important Fenwick family (see Louis Houck, *A History of Missouri from the Earliest Explorations and Settlements until the Admission of the State into the Union,* 3 vols. [Chicago, R. R. Donnelley & Sons, 1908], 1:385).

14 to 50: 1
over 50: 0
White females in household
    to age 14: 0
    14 to 50: 1
    over 50: 0
Male black slaves
    to age 14: 0
    14 to 50: 1
    over 50: 0
Total members in household: 3

Nicolas Caillot *dit* Lachance[35]
    French
    Catholic
    Carpenter
    White males in household
        to age 14: 1
        14 to 50: 1
        over 50: 1
    White females in household
        to age 14: 0
        14 to 50: 0
        over 50: 0
    Male black slaves
        to age 14: 1
        14 to 50: 1
        over 50: 0
    Female black slaves
        to age 14: 0
        14 to 50: 2
        over 50: 0
    Total members in household: 7

Jean-Baptiste Lachance
    Creole
    Catholic
    Farmer

35. Concerning the large and important Caillot *dit* Lachance family, see Ekberg, *Colonial Ste. Genevieve,* passim. These census entries on this family make it apparent that the original French-Canadian family name, Caillot, was slowly being replaced in favor of Lachance.

White males in household
>to age 14: 3
>14 to 50: 1
>over 50: 0

White females in household
>to age 14: 2
>14 to 50: 1
>over 50: 0

Total members in household: 7

François Lachance*
>Creole
>Catholic
>Farmer
>White males in household
>>to age 14: 0
>>14 to 50: 1
>>over 50: 0
>White females in household: 0
>Total members in household: 1

Antoine Lachance*
>Creole
>Catholic
>Farmer
>White males in household
>>to age 14: 0
>>14 to 50: 1
>>over 50: 0
>White females in household
>>to age 14: 1
>>14 to 50: 1
>>over 50: 0
>Female mulatto slaves
>>to age 14: 1
>>14 to 50: 0
>>over 50: 0
>Total members in household: 4

Gabriel Lachance*
>Creole
>Catholic
>Farmer

White males in household
      to age 14: 0
      14 to 50: 1
      over 50: 0
White females in household
      to age 14: 1
      14 to 50: 1
      over 50: 0
Male mulatto slaves
      to age 14: 1
      14 to 50: 2
      over 50: 0
Male black slaves
      to age 14: 5
      14 to 50: 3
      over 50: 0
Female black slaves
      to age 14: 0
      14 to 50: 3
      over 50: 2
Total members in household: 19

Joseph Lachance*
  Creole
  Catholic
  Farmer
  White males in household
      to age 14: 0
      14 to 50: 1
      over 50: 0
  White females in household
      to age 14: 0
      14 to 50: 1
      over 50: 0
  Total members in household: 2

Gabriel Nicole
  Creole
  Catholic
  Farmer
  White males in household
      to age 14: 0
      14 to 50: 1
      over 50: 0

Total members in household: 1
Widow Thibault[36]
    Creole
    Catholic
    Farmer
    White females in household
        to age 14: 0
        14 to 50: 0
        over 50: 1
    Total members in household: 1

Thomas Madden*[37]
    Irish
    Anglican
    Surveyor and Farmer
    White males in household
        to age 14: 3
        14 to 50: 1
        over 50: 0
    White females in household
        to age 14: 3
        14 to 50: 1
        over 50: 0
    Male mulatto slaves: 0
    Female mulatto slaves: 0
    Male black slaves
        to age 14: 1
        14 to 50: 2
        over 50: 0
    Female black slaves
        to age 14: 3
        14 to 50: 1
        over 50: 1
    Total members in household: 15

Paul Deguire*[38]
    Creole

36. Concerning this woman, see Ekberg, *François Vallé*, 77. She is mistakenly listed as a male in the census ms.

37. Madden became well known as the assistant of Antoine Soulard, who was surveyor general for Upper Louisiana under both Spanish and American regimes. He also operated a distillery close to New Bourbon (see Houck, *History of Missouri*, 2:258).

38. Son of André Deguire and Marguerite Gouvereau, married to Marianne Caillot *dit* Lachance, the daughter of Nicolas Lachance and Marianne Girard.

Catholic
Farmer
White males in household
     to age 14: 3
     14 to 50: 1
     over 50: 0
White females in household
     to age 14: 0
     14 to 50: 1
     over 50: 0
Total members in household: 5

Louis Tonnellier*[39]
   French
   Catholic
   Farmer
   White males in household
        to age 14: 0
        14 to 50: 2
        over 50: 0
   White females in household
        to age 14: 0
        14 to 50: 1
        over 50: 0
   Total members in household: 3

Pierre Chevalier*[40]
   Creole
   Catholic
   Farmer
   White males in household
        to age 14: 1
        14 to 50: 2
        over 50: 0
   White females in household
        to age 14: 3
        14 to 50: 1
        over 50: 0

39. Tonnellier was a sometime schoolteacher in Ste. Genevieve, see Ekberg, *Colonial Ste. Genevieve,* 161, 276, 277, 281.

40. Son of André Chevalier, a storekeeper at Fort de Chartres during the French regime, he married at Ste. Genevieve Marie Deguire, the daughter of André Deguire and Marguerite Gouvereau.

Male mulatto slaves
    to age 14: 1
    14 to 50: 0
    over 50: 0
Female mulatto slaves
    to age 14: 1
    14 to 50: 0
    over 50: 0
Male black slaves
    to age 14: 1
    14 to 50: 0
    over 50: 0
Female black slaves
    to age 14: 2
    14 to 50: 1
    over 50: 0
Total members in household: 13

[Jean]-Alexis Griffard*[41]
  Canadian
  Catholic
  Salt maker
  White males in household
    to age 14: 4
    14 to 50: 2
    over 50: 0
  White females in household
    to age 14: 2
    14 to 50: 2
    over 50: 0
  Total members in household: 10

Joseph Tesserot*
  Canadian
  Catholic
  Farmer
  White males in household
    to age 14: 1
    14 to 50: 1
    over 50: 0
  White females in household
    to age 14: 0

41. See Ekberg, *François Vallé*, 80–81, 254.

14 to 50: 1
over 50: 0
Female black slaves
    to age 14: 0
    14 to 50: 2
    over 50: 0
Total members in household: 5

Etienne Govereau [or Gauvereau or Gouvereau][42]
    Creole
    Catholic
    Farmer
    White males in household
        to age 14: 0
        14 to 50: 2
        over 50: 0
    White females in household
        to age 14: 3
        14 to 50: 1
        over 50: 0
    Total members in household: 6

François Simoneau[43]
    Canadian
    Catholic
    Farmer
    White males in household
        to age 14: 3
        14 to 50: 1
        over 50: 1
    White females in household
        to age 14: 2
        14 to 50: 1
        over 50: 0
    Male black slaves
        to age 14: 1
        14 to 50: 1
        over 50: 0
    Female black slaves
        to age 14: 0

42. Ibid., 24, 32.
43. Son of Jean-Baptiste Simoneau and Marianne Vermette, he married Judith Deguire, the daughter of André Deguire and Isabel Brunet.

14 to 50: 1
over 50: 0
Total members in household: 11

Widow Bernier[44]
Canadian
Catholic
Farmer
White males in household
        to age 14: 0
        14 to 50: 1
        over 50: 0
White females in household
        to age 14: 1
        14 to 50: 2
        over 50: 0
Male black slaves
        to age 14: 1
        14 to 50: 1
        over 50: 0
Female black slaves
        to age 14: 0
        14 to 50: 1
        over 50: 0
Total members in household: 7

François Bernier[45]
Canadian
Catholic
Farmer
White males in household
        to age 14: 0
        14 to 50: 1
        over 50: 0
White females in household
        to age 14: 0
        14 to 50: 1
        over 50: 0
Total members in household: 2

44. Likely the widow of François Bernier, who died in 1794.
45. Son of Widow Bernier; see also Ekberg, *Colonial Ste. Genevieve,* 116.
46. Probably the widow of Charles Bellemard (see ibid., 63).

Widow Belmar[46]
   Creole
   Catholic
   Farmer
   White males in household
      to age 14: 1
      14 to 50: 1
      over 50: 0
   White females in household
      to age 14: 4
      14 to 50: 1
      over 50: 0
   Total members in household: 7

Louis Lacombe[47]
   Canadian
   Catholic
   Farmer
   White males in household
      to age 14: 0
      14 to 50: 1
      over 50: 0
   White females in household
      to age 14: 0
      14 to 50: 2
      over 50: 0
   Total members in household: 3

Nicolas Lacombe
   Creole
   Catholic
   Farmer
   White males in household
      to age 14: 0
      14 to 50: 1
      over 50: 0
   White females in household
      to age 14: 0
      14 to 50: 1
      over 50: 0
   Total members in household: 2

47. He married in 1787 the *métisse* Marie Tirard, widow of Joseph Joubert; see also ibid., 441.

Jérôme Métis*
  Creole
  Catholic
  Farmer
  White males in household
      to age 14: 0
      14 to 50: 1
      over 50: 0
  White females in household
      to age 14: 0
      14 to 50: 1
      over 50: 0
  Total members in household: 2

Charles Aimé[48]
  Creole
  Catholic
  Farmer
  White males in household
      to age 14: 0
      14 to 50: 3
      over 50: 0
  White females in household
      to age 14: 0
      14 to 50: 1
      over 50: 0
  Total members in household: 4

Jean [John] Bives
  American
  Catholic
  Farmer
  White males in household
      to age 14: 0
      14 to 50: 1
      over 50: 0
  Total members in household: 1

François Portugais
  Portugese
  Catholic

48. Charles was married to an Osage woman, Marie-Anne Anouacou (see ibid., 114–16, 223).

Farmer
White males in household
      to age 14: 0
      14 to 50: 1
      over 50: 0
Total members in household: 1

Louis Julien
   Canadian
   Catholic
   Farmer
   White males in household
      to age 14: 0
      14 to 50: 1
      over 50: 0
   Total members in household: 1

François Lacroix[49]
   Canadian
   Catholic
   Farmer
   White males in household
      to age 14: 0
      14 to 50: 0
      over 50: 1
   Total members in household: 1

Joseph Pérodot[50]
   Creole
   Catholic
   Farmer
   White males in household
      to age 14: 5
      14 to 50: 1
      over 50: 0
   White females in household
      to age 14: 0
      14 to 50: 1
      over 50: 0
   Total members in household: 7

49. His first wife was Marguerite, daughter of André and Marguerite Gouvereau, and following her death he married Marie Tirard, widow of Louis Lacombe.
   50. Married in Ste. Genevieve in 1787 Marie-Louise, daughter of André Deguire.

Joseph Montmirel
    Canadian
    Catholic
    Farmer
    White males in household
        to age 14: 1
        14 to 50: 1
        over 50: 0
    Total members in household: 2

Jacob Weiser
    German
    Protestant
    Mill worker
    White males in household
        to age 14: 0
        14 to 50: 1
        over 50: 0
    Total members in household: 1

David Montgomery
    American
    Protestant
    Blacksmith
    White males in household
        to age 14: 0
        14 to 50: 1
        over 50: 0
    Total members in household: 1

At the Saline and Environs

[It is to be noted that in the outlying communities at the Saline and Bois Brûlé newcomers to the region (mostly Americans) predominated.][51]

Monsieur Henry Peyroux [de la Courdrenière][52]
    French

51. Michael K. Trimble, Teresita Majewski, Michael J. O'Brien, and Anna L. Price, "Frontier Colonization of the Saline Creek Valley," in *French Colonial Archeology: The Illinois Country and the Western Great Lakes,* ed. John A. Walthall (Urbana: University of Illinois Press, 1991), 165–88.

52. Peyroux was commandant at Ste. Genevieve 1787–1794 and at New Madrid 1799–1804. Some of his official correspondence may be seen above, document no. 3.

Catholic
Captain in the infantry
White males in household
      to age 14: 0
      14 to 50: 1
      over 50: 0
White females in household
      to age 14: 0
      14 to 50: 1
      over 50: 0
Male black slaves
      to age 14: 2
      14 to 50: 0
      over 50: 1
Female black slaves
      to age 14: 3
      14 to 50: 1
      over 50: 1
Total members in household: 10

Monsieur Gensack[53]
  French
  Catholic
  Interpreter
  White males in household
      to age 14: 0
      14 to 50: 1
      over 50: 0
  Total members in household: 1

Monsieur [Joseph] Barbier[54]
  French
  Catholic
  Farmer
  White males in household
      to age 14: 0
      14 to 50: 1
      over 50: 0
  Total members in household: 1

53. Gensack seems to have functioned for a short while as de Luzières's scribe and interpreter.
54. Concerning Barbier, see above, chap. 7.

Maurice
    Canadian
    Catholic
    Day laborer
    White males in household
            to age 14: 0
            14 to 50: 1
            over 50: 0
    Total members in household: 1

Baptiste Richet
    Canadian
    Catholic
    Day laborer
    White males in household
            to age 14: 0
            14 to 50: 1
            over 50: 0
    Total members in household: 1

Hypolite Bolon[55]
    Creole
    Catholic
    Indian interpreter
    White males in household
            to age 14: 2
            14 to 50: 2
            over 50: 0
    White females in household
            to age 14: 2
            14 to 50: 0
            over 50: 0
    Total members in household: 6

Gabriel Bolon
    Creole
    Catholic

55. Hypolite and his brother, Gabriel, were of French-Canadian ancestry and both knew Indian languages and moved easily between white and red worlds. Hypolite's children were by a Delaware Indian woman. Hypolite evidently served as de Luzières's intermediary with the Indian tribes (Delaware and Shawnee) who lived in the New Bourbon District. Hypolite's children were by a Delaware Indian woman (see Ekberg, *Colonial Ste. Genevieve*, 118).

Hunter
White males in household
      to age 14: 0
      14 to 50: 1
      over 50: 0
Total members in household: 1

Richard Ferrell
American
Anglican
Salt maker
White males in household
      to age 14: 2
      14 to 50: 4
      over 50: 0
White females in household
      to age 14: 1
      14 to 50: 1
      over 50: 0
Total members in household: 8

James Ferrell*
American
Anglican
Salt maker
White males in household
      to age 14: 1
      14 to 50: 3
      over 50: 0
White females in household
      to age 14: 0
      14 to 50: 1
      over 50: 0
Total members in household: 5

Eleizer Parker[56]
American
Anglican
Farmer
White males in household
      to age 14: 0
      14 to 50: 4

56. Concerning the Parker family, see above, Part 1, chap. 7.

over 50: 0
Total members in household: 4

Alexander McLehil (McNeill)
  American
  Anglican
  Blacksmith
  White males in household
      to age 14: 2
      14 to 50: 3
      over 50: 0
  White females in household
      to age 14: 0
      14 to 50: 1
      over 50: 1
  Total members in household: 7

George Johnson
  American
  Anglican
  Iron monger
  White males in household
      to age 14: 0
      14 to 50: 2
      over 50: 0
  White females in household
      to age 14: 1
      14 to 50: 0
      over 50: 0
  Total members in household: 3

Joseph Scott
  American
  Anglican
  Iron monger
  White males in household
      to age 14: 0
      14 to 50: 1
      over 50: 0
  Total members in household: 1

Nathaniel Johnson
  American
  Anglican

Day laborer
White males in household
     to age 14: 0
     14 to 50: 1
     over 50: 0
Total members in household: 1

Nicolas Johnston
  Scot
  Anglican
  Blacksmith
  White males in household
       to age 14: 0
       14 to 50: 2
       over 50: 0
  Total members in household: 2

Daniel Meredith*57
  American
  Anglican
  Armorer
  White males in household
       to age 14: 1
       14 to 50: 2
       over 50: 0
  White females in household
       to age 14: 1
       14 to 50: 1
       over 50: 0
  Total members in household: 5

Frederick Custer
  American
  Anglican
  Salt maker
  White males in household
       to age 14: 0
       14 to 50: 4
       over 50: 0
  White females in household
       to age 14: 0

57. Coming from the Pittsburgh area, he may have encountered de Luzières there in the early 1790s.

14 to 50: 1
over 50: 3
Total members in household: 8

Andrew Cork
American
Anabaptist [i.e., Baptist]
Salt maker
White males in household
        to age 14: 0
        14 to 50: 4
        over 50: 0
White females in household
        to age 14: 0
        14 to 50: 1
        over 50: 0
Total members in household: 5

Henry Smith
American
Anabaptist
Carpenter
White males in household
        to age 14: 0
        14 to 50: 1
        over 50: 0
Total members in household: 1

James Thompson*
American
Anglican
Farmer
White males in household
        to age 14: 0
        14 to 50: 1
        over 50: 0
Total members in household: 1

William Cauhen (Coen)
American
Anglican
Salt maker
White males in household
        to age 14: 0

14 to 50: 7
over 50: 0
White females in household
to age 14: 0
14 to 50: 1
over 50: 0
Total members in household: 8

William Haley*
American
Anglican
Cooper
White males in household
to age 14: 0
14 to 50: 2
over 50: 0
Total members in household: 2

Jeremy Perrell*58
American
Anglican
Salt maker
White males in household
to age 14: 0
14 to 50: 6
over 50: 0
White females in household
to age 14: 2
14 to 50: 2
over 50:
Total members in household: 10

Joseph Donahough*
Irish
Anglican
Salt maker
White males in household
to age 14: 0
14 to 50: 5
over 50: 0
White females in household

58. Perelle served as de Luzières's police officer at the Saline.

to age 14: 3
14 to 50: 2
over 50:
Total members in household: 10

Callordin
American
Anglican
Farmer
White males in household
to age 14: 2
14 to 50: 2
over 50: 0
White females in household
to age 14: 0
14 to 50: 2
over 50: 0
Total members in household: 6

Joseph Duggan
American
Presbyterian
Salt maker
White males in household
to age 14: 0
14 to 50: 4
over 50: 0
White females in household
to age 14: 0
14 to 50: 1
over 50: 0
Total members in household: 5

Monsieur Samuel
American
Presbyterian
Farmer
White males in household
to age 14: 0
14 to 50: 2
over 50: 0
White females in household
to age 14: 1

14 to 50: 2
over 50: 0
Male black slaves
    to age 14: 3
    14 to 50: 2
    over 50: 0
Female black slaves
    to age 14: 0
    14 to 50: 1
    over 50: 0
Total members in household: 11

Jean-Marie Le Grand
    Canadian
    Catholic
    Farmer
    White males in household
        to age 14: 0
        14 to 50: 2
        over 50: 0
    Total members in household: 2

Stroder [William]*
    American
    Presbyterian
    Farmer
    White males in household
        to age 14: 0
        14 to 50: 2
        over 50: 0
    White females in household
        to age 14: 1
        14 to 50: 1
        over 50: 0
    Total members in household: 4

Daily Plame
    American
    Presbyterian
    Farmer
    White males in household
        to age 14: 2
        14 to 50: 3
        over 50: 0

White females in household
       to age 14: 1
       14 to 50: 1
       over 50: 0
Total members in household: 7

Monsieur De James* (Gimes)
  American
  Catholic
  Farmer
  White males in household
       to age 14: 0
       14 to 50: 1
       over 50: 0
  White females in household
       to age 14: 0
       14 to 50: 1
       over 50: 0
  Male black slaves
       to age 14: 2
       14 to 50: 1
       over 50: 0
  Total members in household: 5

Monsieur Haley, father
  American
  Catholic
  Farmer
  White males in household
       to age 14: 1
       14 to 50: 0
       over 50: 1
  White females in household
       to age 14: 0
       14 to 50: 0
       over 50: 1
  Total members in household: 3

William Haley*
  American
  Catholic
  Farmer
  White males in household
       to age 14: 1

       14 to 50: 2
       over 50: 0
White females in household
       to age 14: 1
       14 to 50: 2
       over 50: 0
Total members in household: 6

John Audrey
   American
   Presbyterian
   Cooper
   White males in household
       to age 14: 1
       14 to 50: 2
       over 50: 0
   White females in household
       to age 14: 1
       14 to 50: 2
       over 50: 0
   Total members in household: 6

Human Davis
   American
   Anglican
   Day laborer
   White males in household
       to age 14: 0
       14 to 50: 1
       over 50: 0
   Total members in household: 1

James Havens
   American
   Anglican
   Day laborer
   White males in household
       to age 14: 0
       14 to 50: 1
       over 50: 0
   White females in household
       to age 14: 0
       14 to 50: 1
       over 50: 0

Total members in household: 2
James Graham
   American
   Anglican
   Day laborer
   White males in household
        to age 14: 0
        14 to 50: 1
        over 50: 0
   Total members in household: 1

James McNeal
   American
   Anglican
   Day laborer
   White males in household
        to age 14: 0
        14 to 50: 1
        over 50: 0
   White females in household
        to age 14: 0
        14 to 50: 1
        over 50: 0
   Total members in household: 2

John Duval*
   American
   Anglican
   Day laborer
   White males in household
        to age 14: 0
        14 to 50: 1
        over 50: 0
   Total members in household: 1

Hine
   American
   Anglican
   Salt maker
   White males in household
        to age 14: 0
        14 to 50: 1
        over 50: 0
   Total members in household: 1

James Duval
    American
    Anglican
    Salt maker
    White males in household
            to age 14: 0
            14 to 50: 1
            over 50: 0
    Total members in household: 1

At Bois Brûlé

James Newson*
    American
    Anglican
    Farmer
    White males in household
            to age 14: 2
            14 to 50: 3
            over 50: 0
    White females in household
            to age 14: 0
            14 to 50: 1
            over 50: 0
    Male black slaves
            to age 14: 2
            14 to 50: 1
            over 50: 0
    Female black slaves
            to age 14: 0
            14 to 50: 2
            over 50: 0
    Total members in household: 11

William Hastone [Ashton?]
    American
    Anglican
    Farmer
    White males in household
            to age 14: 4
            14 to 50: 1
            over 50: 0

White females in household
     to age 14: 0
     14 to 50: 2
     over 50: 0
Total members in household: 7

Joseph Boise [Boice]*
  Irish
  Methodist
  Farmer
  White males in household
     to age 14: 2
     14 to 50: 1
     over 50: 0
  White females in household
     to age 14: 2
     14 to 50: 1
     over 50: 0
  Total members in household: 6

David Clark*
  American
  Anabaptist
  Farmer
  White males in household
     to age 14: 0
     14 to 50: 2
     over 50: 0
  White females in household
     to age 14: 0
     14 to 50: 1
     over 50: 0
  Total members in household: 3

Francis Clark*[59]
  Irish

59. On August 28, 1796, the Abbé Paul de St. Pierre, Ste. Genevieve's curate, formally married Francis Clark and his wife, Charité Costard (or Costar or Custard), who had previously been married "according to the American custom (apparently by a justice of the peace)," and the same day the priest baptized Charité and two of the couple's children, Marie and Anne. See Ste. Genevieve Parish Records (microfilm, Missouri State Historical Society, Columbia), Book B, Marriages, 36; ibid., Book C, Baptisms, 69.

Anglican
Farmer
White males in household
      to age 14: 2
      14 to 50: 3
      over 50: 0
White females in household
      to age 14: 2
      14 to 50: 1
      over 50: 0
Total members in household: 8

John Burget
American
Presbyterian
Farmer
White males in household
      to age 14: 2
      14 to 50: 1
      over 50: 0
White females in household
      to age 14: 1
      14 to 50: 1
      over 50: 0
Male black slaves
      to age 14: 1
      14 to 50: 0
      over 50: 0
Female black slaves
      to age 14: 1
      14 to 50: 1
      over 50: 0
Total members in household: 8

Michael Burns*
Irish
Catholic
Farmer
White males in household
      to age 14: 1
      14 to 50: 4
      over 50: 0
White females in household
      to age 14: 3

14 to 50: 1
over 50: 1
Total members in household: 10

Benjamin Walker*
American
Anglican
Farmer
White males in household
    to age 14: 1
    14 to 50: 1
    over 50: 0
White females in household
    to age 14: 0
    14 to 50: 1
    over 50: 0
Total members in household: 3

Barnhart[60]
American
Anglican
Hunter
White males in household
    to age 14: 1
    14 to 50: 1
    over 50: 0
White females in household
    to age 14: 0
    14 to 50: 1
    over 50: 0
Total members in household: 3

Barna Burne
American
Catholic
Farmer
White males in household
    to age 14: 1
    14 to 50: 1
    over 50: 0

60. A Christopher Barnhart was living at Bois Brûlé in 1803 (Houck, *History of Missouri*, 1:381).

White females in household
  to age 14: 0
  14 to 50: 1
  over 50: 0
Total members in household: 3

Macloughlin*
  American
  Anglican
  Wheelwright
  White males in household
    to age 14: 0
    14 to 50: 1
    over 50: 0
  Total members in household: 1

McLanahan[61]
  American
  Anglican
  Farmer
  White males in household
    to age 14: 0
    14 to 50: 1
    over 50: 0
  White females in household
    to age 14: 0
    14 to 50: 1
    over 50: 0
  Total members in household: 2

Jones
  American
  Anglican
  Farmer
  White males in household
    to age 14: 0
    14 to 50: 1
    over 50: 0
  Total members in household: 1

Peller

61. John W. McClenahan, a native of Virginia, settled at Bois Brûlé in 1796 (ibid., 381).

American
Anglican
Farmer
White males in household
      to age 14: 0
      14 to 50: 1
      over 50: 0
Total members in household: 1

Total Heads of Households
New Bourbon: 38
The Saline: 41
Bois Brûlé: 14
Total: 93

Aggregate Tabulations (done by author)
White males
    to age 14: 64
    14 to 50: 158 (This group eligible for service in the district militia.)
    over 50: 9
White females
    to age 14: 49
    14 to 50: 69
    over 50: 7
Male slaves
    to age 14: 34
    14 to 50: 21
    over 50: 3
Female slaves
    to age 14: 18
    14 to 50: 23
    over 50: 4
Plus two free black women described below.
Grand Total: 459

Free Mulattoes and Blacks
There are only two free negresses, Lisette and Rose. The first is 45 years old and lives in the village of New Bourbon, and the second is between 58 and 60 years old and lives at the Saline. They comport themselves well, cultivating the soil and raising animals.[62]

62. Lisette and Rose were common names for female slaves, and it is impossible to determine who had earlier owned these women or how they achieved their freedom.

No. 28

Louis Lorimier, commandant at Cape Girardeau, was nominally the Spanish government's intermediary with the resident Indian tribes in Spanish Illinois. But the most important of these tribes—the Shawnees, Delawares, and Ottawas—resided in de Luzières's New Bourbon District, and he had an interpreter, Hypolite Bolon, to help him communicate with these Indians.[63] Amos Stoddard, who passed through the region in 1804, remarked that "about twenty miles up this [i.e., Apple] creek, and near to it, are three villages of Indians, one of Delawares, and two of Shawnees, which were erected about the year 1794."[64] De Luzières's rough enumeration of these Indians, along with his commentary on them, are rare source materials from that time and place and are of inestimable value to historians and ethnographers. Notice de Luzières's remarks on the fur trade and his obvious interest in the military potential of these tribes as allies in defending Spanish Illinois.

Indians of Various Tribes

Schavanoons (Shawnees), Mis (Miamis), and Walawas (Ottawas)
   70 families
   180 individuals able to bear arms
Their village is situated on the left side of the Rivière à la Pomme, about four leagues from the [Mississippi] river.
Abenakis, commonly called Loups, some previously settled here and some recently arrived from the United States
   120 families
   225 individuals able to bear arms
Their village is situated on the left side of the Rivière à la Pomme, about two leagues above the preceding village.
   190 total number of families
   405 total number of individuals able to bear arms

Observations on the character of these Indians, their involvement in the fur trade, and how to maintain their friendship and trust and keep them more loyal than ever to the government
   1. These diverse Indian tribes are rather civilized and cause very little trouble. They cultivate enough maize to supply part of their subsistence. Until

---

63. See above, note 54.
64. Amos Stoddard, *Sketches, Historical and Descriptive of Louisiana* (Philadelphia: Mathew Carey, 1812), 215.

now they have been very loyal to the government and disposed to ally with the whites for the common defense of the country in all circumstances when the interests of the king [Charles IV of Spain] demand it.

2. These various tribes trade their peltries at New Madrid, Cape Girardeau, Ste. Genevieve, New Bourbon, and St. Louis. Regarding this commerce I notice that it seems to be convenient and necessary to grant an exclusive trading privilege when it is conducted in distant regions with barbarous and uncivilized tribes, that is to say, the tribes that inhabit the upper Mississippi and Missouri valleys. Experience has shown that competition provoked by rivalry will always produce the most baleful results, both for the private parties engaged in this unlicensed commerce and for the health of this commerce in general. Moreover, it has been concluded that the interests of the king and the majority of the inhabitants of the region require, for several years, the concentration of the commercial (and other) relations with the distant and uncivilized tribes in the hands of a small number of persons who are in a position to make the sacrifices and investments and are able to contain them and master them [capables de les contenir et de leurs en imposer]. But I disagree. I am persuaded that the fur trade with the diverse tribes mentioned in the present report [i.e., those located along nearby Apple Creek] must remain free and should in no way be managed with an exclusive privilege. The Indians who reside at the gates of our settlements, who are sufficiently civilized so that there is no need to travel to their villages or their hunting camps, bring their own pelts to the various settlements noted above, and to habitants whom they trust, and exchange them for trade goods and other things they need. For these habitants peltries are precious resources for facilitating payment on merchandise brought up from New Orleans.

3. Although in general these diverse Indian tribes may be rather docile and loyal to the government, one cannot avoid the indispensable necessity of providing them from time to time with gifts—blankets, fabrics, shirts, [alcoholic] beverages, tobacco, powder and lead. When these Indians are on the move (which they frequently are) and stop over, it's customary for the local commandant to furnish them with vittles. In addition to the fact that they consider these gifts very important, many of these Indians are in need—the elderly, the lame, and those suffering from chronic illnesses. Moreover, a large number of them have been encouraged by our government to immigrate from the United States in recent times, and many more are expected. And since they've been rewarded with generous gifts for settling on this side [of the Mississippi River], they naturally expect the same treatment here. Given these considerations, and in view of the large number of Indian tribes situated in this district, I cannot but ask that such gifts be sent to this post each year. Further-

more, I must be authorized (as I've already requested) to supply the king with an accounting of the vittles necessary for those Indians who pass through, and sojourn, here.

No. 29

Despite all of his setbacks in the four years since he had arrived in Spanish Illinois, de Luzières remained an optimist about the potential of the region. A died-in-the-wool monarchist, he was nevertheless a reformer and he believed in the power of government to advance the economy and improve society in general. He was of that generation of educated men in France who had imbibed the single most powerful idea of the European Enlightenment—that rational and effective government could make life better for mankind here on earth. Monarchists like de Luzières and Anne-Robert-Jacques Turgot (enlightened minister of Louis XV), as well as republicans like Thomas Jefferson and Thomas Paine, could believe in this proposition, and de Luzières even uses Jefferson's key word from the Declaration of Independence, "happiness (bonheur)," as the touchstone for government's role in human society. Although a traditional Roman Catholic, de Luzières surely did not believe that monarchical government justified itself simply as being ordained by God. De Luzières wanted to see an activist government, and most especially wanted to see the Spanish royal governor in New Orleans acting on behalf of the New Bourbon District in the manner that de Luzières prescribed.

Observations on the character, attributes and professions of the white residents of the New Bourbon District

1. The old residents of this post, who are all Canadians or Creoles born in the Illinois Country, are generally peaceable, honest, industrious, hospitable, courageous, brave, punctilious in fulfilling their obligations, good navigators of the [Mississippi] river, good subjects of His Majesty and loyal to his government.

2. The new residents of said post are immigrants either from France or the United States of America. The first are all royalists much like the Creoles, and they are absolutely loyal to His Majesty and his government. As for the second, Monsieur [François II] Vallé, my predecessor before the partitioning of his district, was determined, as I will continue to be, to accept only solid folks with resources, or skilled farmers and useful artisans, with their families. Almost all of these are discontent with the regime in the United States. I hope that these émigré residents will continue to behave themselves and remain faithful to His Majesty and loyal to his government. I hope to succeed over

time in making them lose their spirit and habit of chicanery, with which they have been infected in America. I also propose to monitor them very closely, so that if any of these émigrés misbehave and act contrary to the interests, views or intentions of the government I would be able, in conformity with royal orders, to expel them from the colony [i.e., Upper Louisiana]. Please consider, however, that this immigration [of Americans], which I have effectively promoted for the past eighteen months with the permission and approval of the government, is advantageous. Both in this district and in that of Ste. Genevieve it has provided skilled farmers and also able masons, blacksmiths, brewers, turners, carpenters, cabinet makers, weavers, cobblers, and other useful artisans that we are lacking. I can only express my deeply felt wishes that Monsieur [Moses] Austin—an expert in mineralogy, director of lead mines in Virginia, and also a high level manufacturer with this mineral—brings to fruition the project he has conceived. When this is completed, I have strongly urged him to come hither and establish a similar manufacture at our lead mines. He proposes to exploit these mines more systematically and profitably in the concession he's received [from Carondelet], using skilled workers that he's brought over from Europe.[65]

3. The majority of the habitants are increasingly devoted to exploitation of the soil and to agriculture. I spare neither cares nor initiatives to assist them in that wise course of action, assuring them that cultivation is the true and lasting richness of all countries.[66] This is especially true when the country, like this one, is suitable for the production of the most precious of all things, i.e. spring and winter wheat, rye, barley, oats, maize, cotton, English and French potatoes, peas, and other vegetables in general, all kinds of hay and forage from meadows (both natural and man-made), hemp, flax, and fruits of all kinds—apples, pears, peaches, apricots, plums, grapes. Progress in agriculture cannot but proceed in a most tangible and satisfactory fashion when the grist and saw mills being built at Ste. Genevieve, New Bourbon, and New Madrid are completed, which will surely be before next [1798] summer.

4. Some habitants are working successfully at the Saline and other places when it's not the season for agriculture. They also work at the lead mines, which like salt springs, are abundant in this region.

5. No individual at this post [i.e., New Bourbon] devotes himself exclusively to the commerce that may be properly called the fur trade. There are also

65. For more on the Austin–de Luzières connection, see above, Part 1, chaps. 6 and 7.
66. In this passage, de Luzières was mouthing standard economic doctrine of such eighteenth-century French physiocrats as Jacques Turgot, royal finance minister 1774–1776. See Douglas Dakin, *Turgot and the Ancien Régime in France* (London: Methuen, 1939).

no merchants' shops. The wealthiest habitants bring up their goods directly from New Orleans, and the others go and buy them from the merchants in Ste. Genevieve. Those habitants wealthy enough to bring the goods from the said city [i.e., New Orleans] for their own needs also import goods for trade with the Indians, bartering with them, as I have already noted, for peltries that are taken in exchange.

Observations on the means to improve agriculture quickly and effectively in the districts of New Bourbon and Ste. Genevieve, providing various advantages to the inhabitants

1. I have already observed that no doubt one of the quickest and most effective means of promoting agriculture in this region is the completion of grist and saw mills, which are being built at Ste. Genevieve, New Bourbon, and New Madrid. In fact, when farmers become certain that they can either sell all the grain they have produced or can have it milled into fine, high quality, marketable flour—which until now, they have been able to do this only with horse mills, which can scarcely provide for half the habitants—they will hustle to increase grain production. This will provide abundant subsistence in this district but will also provide for exports of good flour to the lower colony [i.e., New Orleans]. Sawmills will promote this precious commerce by providing abundant timber at the lowest prices that will supply wood and planks required for construction of barges, bateaux, and lighters [*chalands*]. This cannot be done now because of the extreme expense of having these materials sawn with human muscle power [*à bras d'hommes*].

2. A second important means to promote agriculture, as well as promoting the export and transport of produce, would be for the government to recruit from the United States of America five or six good workers for constructing barges, lighters, and other vessels, which are still lacking here in Upper Louisiana [i.e., Spanish Illinois]. I should think that this could easily be done under the following conditions. 1) Provide for the expenses, which could be considerable, of transporting them here with their families, belongings, and tools. 2) Negotiate a moderate and reasonable price per [linear] foot of barge or lighter, for which they would agree to provide vessels for the habitants. 3) Assure and guarantee them [the American workers] that when they are not engaged working for said habitants they will be employed by the government for the same wages building barges and other vessels in accordance with the dimensions, proportions, and models provided. The advantages that will result from such an initiative are obvious, both for the habitants of [Spanish] Illinois and for the royal service and the government, which is often short of river vessels and which pays exorbitantly for them when they are needed.

3. A third, equally valuable, means to encourage farmers and workers in this district would be for the government to purchase and send annually to Ste. Genevieve and New Bourbon a number of plow shares (French and English), spades, hoes, pickaxes, shovels, scythes, sickles, axes (French and English), nails of various sizes, and finally a supply of pig iron. Iron necessary for making agriculture equipment is often lacking, and while the price is usually forty sols per livre it has now has jumped to fifty or sixty.[67] The enumerated tools could be transported free of charge on the royal galleys and other vessels that ply the river and could be delivered to the commandants at the various settlements. They would be authorized to distribute the tools and iron wares to the habitants needing them, who would pay only the cost price. Payment could be made in lead or other products such as flour, maize, sow bellies, and peas at the going market values. The government requires these products every year in any case and must pay very dearly for them.

4. A fourth way to promote [agriculture], which would assure the farmers of New Bourbon a firm and lasting prosperity, concerns the vast and fertile Point Basse. This is adjacent to the [Mississippi] river below the inhabited hills of the two settlements and contains 6,000 arpents [5,100 acres] of the most fertile land that I've ever seen. Unfortunately, this land is frequently submerged because of the flooding river. The loss of crops of all varieties caused by this disastrous situation has been incalculable. This scourge of food shortages has necessarily been succeeded by something even worse— the spite of illnesses caused by the putrid and unhealthy exhalations coming from the stagnant and foul waters, which disappear only slowly through evaporation. Nearly all the residents of the two settlements have been afflicted with illnesses that have occasioned an epidemic.[68] The sure method, therefore, to cultivate this rich district while protecting it against such frequent disasters would be to erect levées [digues] to prevent the overflowing of the river. My personal reconnaissances indicate that this could be practically done. The habitants are quite ready to work themselves, and at their own expense, to construct a solid and convenient levée along the river, each landowner being responsible for the extent of his property fronting the river. But because this levée would not be sufficient a levée must also be erected from the river to the hills parallel to Aux Vases Creek, which is where the flooding is worst. This would be beyond their [the habitants] means and capacities. Perhaps the government could cover the expense of this second levée? It would not be terribly costly, not more than 2,000 pi-

67. We saw above (chap. 5) how damnably difficult it was for de Luzières and his associates to get the iron components needed for their proposed gristmills.

68. Concerning malaria in Spanish Illinois, see Ekberg, *Colonial Ste. Genevieve,* chap. 8.

astres.[69] Since this levée would be located on lands belonging to the royal domain, it seems natural and fair that the government should shoulder the expense, since it is always inclined and disposed to encourage and protect new settlements with aid and favors. This is especially true when a project such as this one combines two benefits: securing forever abundant harvests in this district, which is recognized as the richest and most fertile in Upper Louisiana, and providing effectively for the well-being of the human population by preventing in the future the causes of the frequent and inevitable diseases [caused by flooding].

5. Concerning these diseases, I notice that, all things being equal, they are always more frequent in the new settlements, where land-clearing is constantly being done, as is the case here.[70] Moreover, medicines are very rare, and often nonexistent, at this far end of the universe. I've witnessed during the five years I've lived here that lacking these medicines illnesses tend to worsen and become prolonged.[71] Even this year, several ill persons have died for lack of medications appropriate to cure them. I'm also convinced that this mortality would have been even worse if it had not been for the conscientious work of the able and honest Doctor [Walter] Fenwick, an excellent doctor/surgeon, whom I'm trying to get settled in this district. But independently of this doctor it's very much to be desired that the government send for Ste. Genevieve and New Bourbon a box of remedies and medications each year, until the time that this region is populated enough to attract druggists and apothecaries.

6. Furthermore, I noticed when I arrived in [Spanish] Illinois in 1792 that this region lacked midwives, trained in the art of lying-in. I worked hard to get Madame Lacaisse, an able midwife from Gallipolis, to come and set up here. She settled at St. Louis in 1793, where she has since practiced her profession to the public's satisfaction. The Baron de Carondelet held out some hope that in time she would be provided with an annual salary. I asked him eighteen months ago to follow through on his good intentions on behalf of Dame Lacaisse, who was in need of help.[72] I also noted that she had begun to instruct young women in midwifery so that they could practice in various areas of Upper Louisiana. The governor general [Carondelet] responded in a

69. It is interesting to note that recently the U.S. Army Corps of Engineers has built, at the cost of some $50 million, a levée to protect historic Ste. Genevieve and environs.

70. It would also have been true that the new settlements had more newly arrived settlers who may not have gone through the "seasoning" process that eventually provided some resistance to malarial fevers.

71. The one medicine that was at least occasionally available in Spanish Illinois was quinine, which came in the form of "Jesuit bark," bark from the South American cinchona tree.

72. Concerning Dame Lacaisse, see above, chap. 4.

letter of September 15, 1796, that if the said dame [La Caisse] would send him a memorandum drafted in Spanish he foresaw little difficulty in getting her a salary of thirty piastres a month. She sent the memorandum, but shortages at the treasury because of the war prevented this from being effected. As soon as this obstacle disappears, it would be very desirable for the welfare of humanity that the promised salary should be commenced retroactive to January 1, 1797, which would be an equitable reckoning.

7. As soon as I arrived in Ste. Genevieve the lack of public education available to young folks caught my attention. I therefore engaged Monsieur [Augustin-Charles] Frémont de Laurières, a refugée [from the French Revolution] Breton gentleman, who is very honest and well educated, to serve as a teacher.[73] He has now been at work for about two years with success that pleases the residents of Ste. Genevieve and New Bourbon. He has been using a rational plan of education of which I sent a copy some time ago to the Baron de Carondelet, who not only approved the plan but authorized me (by the letter of September 15, 1796) to inform Sieur Frémont that in a short while he would receive a small government pension to encourage him to maintain that institution [i.e., school], which is so precious for instructing the youth. With the zeal, both vigorous and conscientious, with which Sieur Frémont is pursuing the education of young folks, I think he is certainly worthy of receiving immediately the annual pay that I was told to promise him. If this were only twenty piastres per month, it would at least be sufficient to provide him with the means to import from abroad all the text books required to teach his pupils English and French, as well as to pay for rent, heat, and lighting for his public school.

8. I'm proposing these various means of support all the more confidently because I've already used them to enrich and populate a vast area that had been a desert. I've implemented them in the larger [i.e., larger than New Bourbon] district of the department of French Hainault, which I administered for more than thirty years. If one wishes to obtain similarly good results as employed in the center of Europe, where communications were easy and where the things necessary for farming were inexpensive, it's obvious that similar means of support are infinitely more urgent and necessary in the upper part of this colony [Upper Louisiana]. We're far from the metropole [New Orleans], and materials of the first order of importance usually sell for exorbitant prices.

9. Finally, let me remark that the methods I've proposed above to encourage agriculture in [Spanish] Illinois, to markedly stimulate progress, and to

73. Concerning Frémon de Laurières and his proposal to improve education in the region, see Ernest R. Liljegren, "Frontier Education in Spanish Louisiana," *Missouri Historical Review* 35 (1941): 345–72. No evidence exists that de Laurières ever received a government stipend as an educator.

promote the export of all manner of goods and foodstuffs would redound not only to the particular benefit of the local farmers. For, in effectively contributing to soon making this one of the principal and most abundant graineries in the entire colony, they will also contribute to assure the government's ability to provide for all its needs all the time right in the heart of the colony. And this could be done without being forced, as we must be at present, to have recourse to our natural enemy [the United States]. This is always difficult, onerous, expensive, and sometimes indeed impossible, as when circumstances of war obstruct certain routes and communications beyond our frontiers, blocking or impeding the flow of provisions.

Lastly, I will observe that from every possible perspective it would be infinitely advantageous for the general well-being of the residents of [Spanish] Illinois to keep Monsieur Zénon Trudeau as commander-in-chief [i.e., lieutenant governor in St. Louis]. This important observation is dictated not only by my close friendship and intimate relationship to him, but yet more by my confidence that the deep and extensive knowledge of local affairs he has acquired—on the resources, the connections, and the diverse interests of Upper Louisiana during the six years that he's been here—can only provide him with an advantageous position from which to provide for the security and defense of this frontier and for the well-being of the mass of residents. They bless his administration every day and have complete confidence in him. Monsieur Commandant General [Carondelet] knows better than anyone, by his own personal experience, how valuable it is to keep such leaders so that they can continue to govern in the direction they've so wisely chosen, with the approval and agreement of the public.

Observations on the abuses that impede progress and prevent the complete fulfilment of happiness in Illinois, with suggestions about the means to abolish them and insure that they do not multiply

1. The majority of all farming in the villages of [Spanish] Illinois is conducted in vast fields that are enclosed in common by the habitants, who have more or less extensive holdings.[74] These enclosed fields could be spared present drawbacks if they were kept up during the entire year, if livestock were kept out of these fields, which are devoted to grain production, during all seasons. Now, on the contrary, these fields are in poor shape all year long, for they are wide open and accessible to all manner of animals from the time of the maize harvest [September] until the following April. Naturally, it's

---

74. Concerning open-field cultivation in the Illinois Country, see Carl J. Ekberg, *French Roots in the Illinois Country: The Mississippi Frontier in Colonial Times* (Urbana: University of Illinois Press, 1998).

understood that the continuation of such a vicious system of fences and fields makes it absolutely impossible to promote the valuable and profitable cultivation of winter wheat, English potatoes, turnips [*rabiolles*], carrots, and other late-harvest crops. It's also impossible to develop managed meadows [*prairies artificiels*], for from the end of September to the following April they would be absolutely devastated and destroyed by the livestock. Moreover, one is forced to cultivate only maize and spring wheat, which is lower quality than winter wheat and which produces only seven or eight minots per arpent while winter wheat, well-cultivated, could produce thirty or forty.

The way to remedy these problems and promote cultivation of winter wheat and other valuable crops would be to issue an ordinance commanding that the fences around the common fields be kept in good repair for the entire year, and to prohibit all pasturing of animals on them unless individual habitants who wish to do this fence their own plots solidly on all four sides. Moreover, we're not lacking for other vacant land close to the villages that could be used for livestock pasturage. Such an ordinance would not only promote more systematic and productive cultivation of the fields, it would also encourage the habitants to develop both natural and man-made meadows. These are very rare in [Spanish] Illinois, but they could provide close-at-hand healthier and more abundant fodder for the livestock. This same ordinance could require the habitants of the said villages [Ste. Genevieve and New Bourbon] to select close-at-hand a large area, similarly to what is done so advantageously in Europe, for pasturing their livestock and common flocks; these could be taken out to pasture in the morning and brought back in the evening. This would not be prohibitively expensive, would not exceed what is paid to the beadle in each parish, and could be equitably distributed among the habitants prorated on the basis of the number of each individual's animals. Such a system would result in further assorted advantages, for example having at hand each morning and evening the milk cows and being able to monitor the wants and needs of the beef cattle. While, in the actual state of affairs, I know a large number of habitants, each owning twenty-five milk cows, who often lack milk for their morning coffee and who make neither butter nor cheese because of the simple obstacle of bringing in their milk cows on a regular basis. I've also verified that most all of the habitants of this area waste about half the value of their cattle (reckoned in the number of days that their slaves spend looking for them when the animals are to hell-and-gone in the woods) during the six time periods when these beasts are indispensable for farm work: 1) During wheat sowing in the spring 2) during maize sowing 3) during plowing 4) during wheat harvest 5) during hay gathering in the woods 6) and during maize harvest. To these very serious drawbacks associated with the free-grazing of livestock in the woods is added the loss of a great number, especially horses, calves, and bulls who run off, are stolen, or are eaten by wolves.

2. It cannot be denied that—even with such fertility of soil, which is as good as can be found in any country whatsoever and which is suitable for all manner of crops, and even with governmental encouragements to increase prosperity—all this would be useless and worthless if farmers cannot cultivate their fields, orchards, and gardens (as well as controlling their livestock) with perfect confidence and security. For livestock, harvests, fruits, and vegetables cannot be continually, even daily, prey for thiefs and brigands, which is nevertheless the vextious situation for Ste. Genevieve's and New Bourbon's habitants today. My five years of residency at these two places has permitted me to verify and to see with my own eyes the daily disorders and thefts in the fields, woods, gardens, orchards, and stables, and to become assured that slaves are committing most of the thefts. It's only too obvious that these sorts of folks are naturally inclined to thievery, brigandage, and troublemaking. But what contributes to their excesses in this region is the extreme and counterproductive freedom they enjoy, and of which they take advantage. Neither law nor order are observed with them. Furthermore, the slaves are virtually always armed; they run about freely almost every night; they frequently hold dances at night, after which they cause big trouble.[75] It is very rare that any of them caught en flagrante delicto are given exemplary punishment, sufficiently severe to put a stop to things. Upper Louisiana, no more than the lower colony, has any overseers or bosses capable of managing, overseeing, and punishing them in their quarters. I understand that this region was first settled by habitants from Canada, where there are no slaves. At first there weren't many, and there was little inclination rigorously to enforce policing ordinances regarding them. I further believe that their masters' lack of severity and exactitude in overseeing them is a consequence of the benevolence and kindness that generally characterizes the Creoles of the upper part of this colony. But today the number of slaves has dramatically increased, the increase is accelerating, and the disorders they cause continues to be excessive. I believe that it is urgent and necessary to rectify this situation effectively.

Shortly after returning to [Spanish] Illinois [from New Orleans] in August 1793 in order to settle down here, I was forcefully struck by the daily disorders caused by the slaves, their impunity, and the absolute failure to enforce the policy regulations intended to control them. I spoke about this with Monsieur Zénon Trudeau, and he told me that he had experienced [when he assumed

75. The issue of black slaves carrying firearms arose on several occasions in colonial Ste. Genevieve (see Ekberg, *Colonial Ste. Genevieve*, 185, 210, 237, 348–49).

command of Spanish Illinois in 1792] the same astonishment and that he had already taken note of his observations in this regard. He felt, as I do, that there was an urgent necessity to rectify these disorders. Therefore, we got together and drafted a memorandum concerning a proposed regulation that we planned to send to the governor general, suggesting that he proceed with it and have it printed. But the hostile and critical circumstances that successively intervened persuaded us to postpone this proposal and wait for quieter times. If the governor general thinks that the present time is appropriate to proceed with this regulation, which would end the disorders and establish sufficient control over the slaves to prevent them from future indulgences, we, after receiving your response, could rush a copy of this proposal to you.

I must, however, state that despite the postponement of this proposal for a general regulation Monsieur Zénon Trudeau and Monsieur [François] Vallé have not even brought forth any regional regulations in an attempt to remedy the worst excesses in their respective districts. But I will observe on this subject that here in Upper Louisiana, like in many French provinces where regional regulations and edicts have little impact, only those decreed by the supreme authority, and especially those that are printed up, make a real impression and are effective. Besides, it's less the amount and multiplicity of regulations that remedy disorders but rather there punctilious enforcement. To achieve this desirable goal, it would suffice that in each outpost the commandant would have at his disposition three or four soldiers—honest, intelligent, and energetic—who would be specifically charged with enforcing police regulations and maintaining good order. These men should receive double wages, which wouldn't cost very much and which would produce excellent results.

I acknowledge that some offenses are committed by white vagabonds and unruly subjects, and especially by Indians who are settled at Ste. Genevieve, even right in the village itself. But the same regulation that I'm proposing would also specify the rigor of punishments to which white thieves would be subjected. This, in conjunction with the oversight that would be meticulously employed to assure its enforcement, would effectively serve to make it work.

As for the Indians, it would be useful to hand down some higher orders [i.e., from the governor general], notifying them that the government doesn't want them living in the settlements, nor too close by, except to grant them land in areas that they chose sufficient for their settlement. Moreover, there's only the small tribe of Peorias who are at issue, and they already seem to have the intention of leaving the village of Ste. Genevieve in order to settle in the woods. As soon as Monsieur Vallé receives an order about this situation, it would be easy to persuade them [the Peorias] to go ahead and make their move.

3. There's yet another sort of abuse here in Upper Louisiana, whose impact is very prejudicial to its well-being and which could at any time produce very injurious and disastrous results. I'm speaking of the fires in the fields, woods, and meadows close to the outposts and the settled areas. These occur after the harvest, and sometimes even before it is completed. During the autumn and winter these fires are carelessly lit and take off without any particular useful reason. This often occurs through negligence by the numerous smokers in this region—whites, as well as Indians and slaves—who light up their pipes every where they work. They habitually put them down without making sure they're extinguished, so that fires, whipped by the impetuous winds that are common in this area, spread into the dry brush and trees. Before you know it, vast areas are quickly ravaged, burning vegetation, young trees and fences, and even subjecting houses to the greatest danger. I have often witnessed this, and even experienced it myself. It's easy to understand that independently of the danger to which this common, even daily, abuse exposes wooden structures, as well as the fences, it is necessarily hugely prejudicial in other ways: first in the fields, where all the autumn grains and plantings are exposed to be roasted and totally ravaged. It's the same in the meadows where the grasses are burned down to their roots and can no longer provide any pasture for livestock, which obliges them to wander off great distances in search of fodder. They get lost and often perish in the woods. Fires destroy young trees and the seedlings of those that have been cut, and this new growth is very important to preserve and encourage in proximity to the settlements in this region. This is particularly true in a region where all construction is done in wood, where the fencing is very extensive, where wood is required for heat at the salt springs, at the forges and at the lead smelting furnaces. For coal mines have not yet been discovered, at least around Ste. Genevieve and New Bourbon, that could help supply part of the energy needs. Finally, if this abuse continues future generations will experience great difficulty having these essential resources [wood products] available.

It's claimed that these fires assist in the hunting of wild animals, but because none, or very few, live near the settlements the fires are useless. But, supposing that they do help in taking a few deer, this small advantage in no way compensates for the incalculable damages occasioned by these fires.

It seems to me that this abuse could be forestalled and prevented with the regulation I proposed above, i.e. to prohibit all persons from starting any fires, unless absolutely necessary, in the fields, the woods, and the meadows within a radius of five leagues [approx. fourteen miles] from any village or inhabited area. Or, minimally, require that any fire lit out of necessity be attended and not left until it is entirely extinguished. Violators would be subject to an appropriate fine that would go to the informer [*dénonciateur*], which would be in addition to the cost of the damages the fire may have caused. I've been repeatedly assured that in earlier times these fires were prohibited by the commandants and that they were far less frequent.

4. Another abuse equally prejudicial to the conservation of wood and which, if it continues, will contribute more than any other to its scarcity is the vicious method by which whites, as well as slaves, get their firewood. They cut a large tree but take only the smaller branches from higher up, leaving and wasting more than three-quarters of each tree. Soon, this will mean that village residents will be forced to range out long distances in order to find their firewood. Moreover, it is notorious that all the woods located near the villages are strewn with the trunks of these abandoned trees, although they're not rotted and are still suitable for firewood. It strikes me that it would easy and simple to remedy this abuse with the regulations I've proposed. This would prohibit any person from cutting any tree not located on his own property, i.e. in the woods and on the lands of the royal domain, for the purpose of heating his house, boiling off salt or smelting lead before harvesting and utilizing all the tree trunks previously felled that are located in the environs of the villages and settlements. Violators would be subject to a fine, part of which would go to the informer. Furthermore, all persons would be prohibited, with the same penalties, during the time that mature trees are being harvested and utilized, from cutting any other trees in the woods and within the royal domain to use for heating or the other purposes noted above. First, all the trees already felled would have to be used up.

5. Another obstacle that obviously stands in the way of increasing livestock in this region (which is ideal for raising large numbers of animals and using them advantageously in commerce) is the incredible abundance of wolves. Each year, they devour three-quarters of the swine and young calves and lambs, not only out in the woods but even in the villages and settlements themselves. I have seen successfully employed in France and close to my estate of Luzières [in the province of Hainault], where this sort of voracious animal used to be numerous, a method for killing some of them and chasing the others away. This consisted of rendezvousing at a designated place just before dawn during several successive Sundays the village habitants who were the best shots. The men were formed up in a chain to hunt down the animals with the help of dogs, and the government agreed to pay three or four hundred francs to the hunter who after one year had killed the largest number of wolves during these general roundups and hunts. I believe that it would be possible to employ usefully the same method here. It would simply require that the government agree to provide a bounty of thirty piastres to the man who killed the largest number of wolves during the course of the year.

Information on the military forces of New Bourbon and on what would be required in this new command post in order to put it in a good defensive posture

1. Based on the enumeration of population given above, there are in this post of New Bourbon and its dependencies, 157 white habitants able to bear arms—that is, 132 militia men on foot and 25 cavalry. These added to those from Ste. Genevieve, the closest neighboring outpost, would create a total force of 266 foot and 60 cavalry.

2. The enumeration also shows that in the District of New Bourbon there are 405 Indians able to bear arms. All of these are very loyal to the government and well disposed to do for the defense of the colony whatever the commandants [of New Bourbon and Ste. Genevieve] prescribe for them.

3. One could also assemble, among the best and most docile of the slaves in the districts of Ste. Genevieve and New Bourbon, a company of about 120 men able to bear arms. They could be used while being commanded by two or three masters.

4. I have requested a battle flag from His Majesty [Carlos IV] in order to demonstrate to the public that this is a command [i.e., military] outpost. I am here reiterating this request.

5. It is equally necessary to send up a drum to facilitate assembling the militia and to proclaim the hour of retreat to the habitants, and especially the slaves.

6. Because some of the habitants don't have any fusils, it would be good to send me about the forty lacking. I could hold these at my place and pass them out when required to those who don't have any.

7. It is equally necessary that I be provided with powder, balls, and gun flints, proportionate to the number of habitants. These I would distribute whenever it should be necessary to assemble and arm them, which happens rather often when Indians, foreigners [i.e., Americans], and vagabonds steal horses, commit other disorders and must be put down.

8. It would also be suitable and proper that I should be sent an artillery train of several canons of sufficient caliber that the Indians, who fear only this one weapon, can be controlled.

9. It would also be good to have in this outpost, sooner rather than later, at least four soldiers along with a non-commissioned officer. These men could back up my operations in implementing the police regulations and help maintain good order. They are also indispensably necessary to guard the bad guys [*malfaiteurs*] and others who may be incarcerated, perhaps for violating the regulations or perhaps for indebtedness. From this it follows that it will be equally imperative to have a solid jail for securely holding such prisoners.

10. When I was in New Orleans in [April and May] 1793, I asked the then governor general [Carondelet] to send more troops to [Spanish] Illinois to secure the frontier here and also to increase the amount of hard currency in circulation, for there was very little of it indeed. He assured me that he planned to do so, and he was only waiting for the return of peace in order to implement the plan. He even intimated that he was seriously considering sending two or three companies [of Spanish regulars] to be distributed between Ste. Genevieve and New Bourbon. Because circumstances suggest that there should always be a greater number of troops in Upper Louisiana than there are at present, I have reason to presume that when the increase in troop levels is implemented the post of New Bourbon will receive as its share about sixty men. Near by, there's a nice elevated location appropriate for the construction of a fort. It's all the more advantageous because that location commands and dominates the [Mississippi] river and the road that leads from the foreign side [i.e., the Northwest Territory of the United States] over here. But, while waiting for serious and detailed initiatives for this fort's construction, a small building could be built right on the same spot to serve as provisional lodging for the non-commissioned officer and the four soldiers that I have earnestly requested be sent to this post. This small building could also serve as a jail, and eventually as a guardhouse. These initial buildings, with their circumferential wooden palisade, wouldn't cost very much. This is especially true because the land on which they would be built belongs to me, and I would convey it free of charge to His Majesty as a place to erect the proposed fort.

Observations concerning the advantages of having two salaried couriers, working full time, in each outpost of Upper Louisiana

I can't think of a better way to finish this analysis than to propose having two salaried, mounted couriers, working full time, in each outpost: New Madrid, Cape Girardeau, New Bourbon, Ste. Genevieve, and St. Louis. This would bring together three precious advantages: 1) It would speed up the delivery of packages, dispatches, and orders of the government. 2) The mounted couriers would be specifically charged with providing constant intelligence about good order in the posts, as well as making sure that police regulations are enforced. In the past, something similar was done with good success in France with the mounted constabulary [la maréchaussée]. 3) Finally, they would help post commandants in fulfilling their responsibilities—dispatching orders, executing commands, and gathering local, timely intelligence.

I presume that for the sum of twenty piastres per month as salaries for each of these horsemen, who would combine all the necessary qualities for satisfactorily fulfilling all the diverse functions proposed, could easily be found and selected from among the local habitants.

I am further persuaded that the total expenditures for this proposal would not much exceed the current costs of employing couriers in the various posts.

With a salary of twenty piastres per month for each of these horsemen, they would be required to: 1) furnish good horses, fully equipped, and always ready to move out. 2) equip themselves with fusils, sabers, and pistols. 3) supply for themselves powder, shot, and gunflints. 4) carry and deliver to the respective post commandants and their neighbors letters, packages, and dispatches. 5) keep a lookout, day and night, with an eye to maintaining good order, and to make sure that police regulations are enforced in their respective outposts. 6) receive every evening the orders of their respective commandants and report to them every morning any disorders or other infractions they may observe; implement the special orders given them by the commandants in the service of the king and the public; and accompany the commandants on all the inspection tours conducted in their respective districts relevant to the royal service and the public. It would be useful to authorize these mounted royal couriers to wear the same uniforms, consisting of blue pants and jacket, with red collar, cuffs and lining, yellow buttons, white braided epaulettes, round hat with a red cockade. They should be given the rank of brigadier of cavalry, which would correspond to sergeant of infantry.

The creation of this service would be infinitely advantageous from every possible perspective: It would evidently be inexpensive, since the costs of outpost couriers would be saved; it would assure speedy delivery of governmental correspondence, and it could effectively help to maintain good order in the various outposts mentioned above. If adopted, I guarantee that in supporting the general police regulation, which is outlined in my preceding remarks, no other region will be better administered and less subject to abuses than that of Upper Louisiana.

Done at New Bourbon in [Spanish] Illinois, December 1, 1797.

delassus De Luzieres

No. 30

This letter, dated nine days after de Luzières's "New Bourbon Census" and "Observations on the Inhabitants," was in fact the cover letter for those documents. The use of "sauvages" and "indiens" in the same document is very unusual. This may have been due to the influence of Monsieur Gensack (or Jensack), who was serving as de Luzières's scribe in late 1797. Jensack seems to disappear as suddenly as he appeared, and was never appointed royal interpreter by the Spanish regime in Louisiana as de Luzières suggested.

De Luzières to Gayoso de Lemos   PC, Leg. 214
New Bourbon, December 20, 1797

Monsieur and very respectable governor and friend:

I have the honor of addressing to you the memoir for which you asked, containing the state of the population at my post. This is followed by observations on the manners, characteristics, and occupations of the inhabitants of all colors; on what might be done for them to increase their prosperity; on what abuses may be eliminated to increase their happiness; and on what can be done in the said post to put it in condition so that it may be defended.

I have differed sending you this work, which is the fruit of my observations and reflections during the five years that I've been living in the Illinois, because I wished to be assured that all honest and sensible persons, interested in the well-being of this region, were in agreement with it. I'll not conceal from you that before submitting this work in final form I made a special trip to St. Louis to submit it to my friend, Zénon Trudeau (except for the section dealing with him personally), and that he has expressed approval with its entire contents. . . .

I cannot insist strongly enough about getting gifts sent to my post for the Indians [*sauvages*]. They are very numerous, both those who have been here awhile and those recently arrived from the United States, whom the [Spanish] government has invited to come here and settle. In addition to the fact that it would be inconsistent to have attracted the Indians [*indiens*] here and then not welcome them, if they are not pleased with the gifts and foodstuffs they ask of me, and that are indispensable to them as they pass by and stay over here, I would absolutely be obliged to resign my post. . . .

Another recommendation . . . that I wish very much you would implement concerns Monsieur Jensack, an unfortunate refugee from St. Domingue, a young man well-born and very well raised in France. He is very well educated and has a perfect knowledge of English. Indeed, he has helped me put the enclosed memoir in final form. Messieurs [Carlos] Howard and Zénon Trudeau agree that he should be appointed royal interpreter at Ste. Genevieve, where he already provides a precious service by serving ad interim without pay. . . .

Your very humble and very obedient and affectionate servant,

De Lassus de Luzières

No. 31

Kaskaskia was becoming increasingly Americanized toward the end of the eighteenth century but still contained a large francophone population, including some newcomers from Canada like Pierre Ménard. Kaskaskia became ter-

ritorial capital of Illinois in 1808 and the first state capital in 1818. During the territorial period the Edgar-Morrison faction was one of the most important political groups in Illinois. Americans were flooding into Spanish Illinois in the late colonial period as Spanish authorities decided to risk the danger of letting in Protestants who might also be subversive republicans at heart. Walter Fenwick, son of Joseph Fenwick, was killed in a duel in 1811, the vicious habit of dueling having been brought to the region by American frontiersmen.

De Luzières to Governor Gayoso　　　　　PC, Leg. 215A
New Bourbon, March 19, 1798

Monsieur, distinguished governor and friend:

The letter of September 23 [1797] with which you've honored me only arrived a few days ago via New Madrid. . . .

In the future we'll be getting news more promptly and more regularly from the United States because a postal route has just been established between Philadelphia and Kaskaskia. This village is located on the other side [of the Mississippi], just across from New Bourbon, and we have dined there at the homes of John Edgar, Robert Morrison, Pierre Ménard, and others. . . .

Regarding the immigrants from the United States of America who are arriving to settle in our area, I can assure you, my respectable governor, that I have a deep knowledge of these sorts of men. The nearly 100,000 livres [roughly $20,000, a huge sum in that day and age] it cost me during the three years [1790–1803] that I lived unhappily among them wasn't spent without my having come to know intimately their ways of living and thinking. However, no general rule exists without exceptions. Since their immigration [to Spanish Louisiana] is now not only permitted but promoted, encouraged, and protected by the government, Monsieur Vallé and I have agreed scrupulously to admit only solid folks from well-to-do families, or skilled farmers and useful artisans; also, all those disgruntled with the government, especially with the taxes in the United States. Vallé and I also agree that this immigration is already stimulating distinct and beneficial improvements in agriculture, handicrafts, and industry. I have no doubt that Messieurs Zénon Trudeau [lieutenant governor in St. Louis], Delassus, my son [commandant at New Madrid], and Lorimier [commandant at Cape Girardeau] are experiencing the same successes and advantages in their respective districts. . . .

I have not yet received the commission of doctor-surgeon for the posts of Ste. Geneviève and New Bourbon. I requested this for the skilled and able Doctor Walter Fenwick, who, along with his numerous family, is a very good Catholic. This commission will replace the one sent to me in 1793 for Sieur Le Moine, surgeon of Gallipolis on the Ohio, who persistently rejected my requests for him to come and settle in the Illinois.

Monsieur and distinguished governor, your very humble and very obedient servant, Delassus de Luzières

No. 32

Likely the slave, Benjamin, whom de Luzières was purchasing with this bill-of-sale came from Kentucky with his late owner, Robert Brewster. Brewster does not appear on de Luzières's 1797 enumeration of New Bourbon, which means that he had only recently immigrated to Spanish Illinois. The phrase defining Benjamin as "absolute property" is unusual and represents a hardening of views about chattel slavery as the turn of the nineteenth century approached, for the traditional Roman-Catholic-Creole view of slaves in the Illinois Country certainly granted them the possession of their own souls, as well as certain other rights defined by the Code Noir. According to de Luzières's 1797 census of New Bourbon (see above document no. 27), he owned eight black slaves (four males and four females) at that time.

Slave Purchase
Ste. Genevieve Civil Records, Slaves, Bills of Sale, no. 14, microfilm Missouri Historical Society, St. Louis.
Ste. Genevieve, February 2, 1799

Before me, Don François Vallé, captain and civil and military commander of the post of Ste. Genevieve of the Illinois, appeared Monsieur Gimes [James] Dunn, resident of Kentucky. He, party of the first part, is one of the executors named in the will of the late Sieur Robert Brouster [Brewster], resident of New Bourbon, who died in Kentucky. Also appearing, party of the second part, was Don Pierre-Charles Dehault De Lassus De Luzières, Grand Cross Chevalier in the Royal Order of St. Michel, captain and civil and military commandant of the post of New Bourbon. The said Sieur Dunn in his capacity as executor of the will of the said late Brouster has deemed it advantageous for the heirs named in the will, who are not here and who are residents of Ireland in Europe, to sell now for a reasonable price a mulatto slave named Benjamin, about fifteen and one-half years old, who belonged to the said deceased Brouster.

We declare to have sold and conveyed to the said Sieur Delassus De Luzières the said mulatto slave named Benjamin to own and to use as his absolute property [en toute propriété], for himself and his heirs, from this day forward forever for the sum of 350 piastres, of which 40 are being paid now in cash. The remainder of 310 piastres will be paid within a period of eighteen months, starting today. The said Monsieur De Lassus de Luzières accepts these terms of sale and pledges to provide as guarantor, as additional security for the said payment, Sieur Paschal Detchemendy, also present, who has promised to guarantee on behalf of the said Sieur de Lassus de Luzières the sum of 310 piastres, payable within eighteen months. And to secure and guarantee this payment the said Sieur delassus De Luzières herewith obligates himself, both to the said Sieur Dunn and to the said Sieur Paschal Detchemendy, his person and his possessions, as well as the mulatto slave Benjamin. And to facilitate payment of the said sum of 310 piastres within eighteen months the said Sieur delassus De Luzières agrees to deliver and remit here to the said Gimes Dunn the said sum payable within eighteenth months to him; or with his [Dunn's] orders to the bearer to whom he has given the note made to him here. Furthermore, the said Sieur Dunn herewith acknowledges to have received the payment of 40 piastres cash stipulated above.

Done and agreed to at Ste. Genevieve on February 2, 1799, at 5:00 in the afternoon. The said sieurs Dunn, Delassus De Luzières and Paschal Detchemendy have signed in the presence of sieurs Frémon de Laurière and Jean-Baptiste Pratte, our witnesses, who have also signed along with us the said commandant.

Signatures: Pre delassus De Luzières, James Dunn, Frémon De Lauriere, P Detchemendy, Frcois Vallé, Pratte

No. 33

This narrative (written in the third person) of de Luzières's experiences in America is basically accurate, with one notable exception. He did not move with his family from the Pittsburgh area to Spanish Illinois in 1793–1794 to seek the protection of his son, Carlos Delassus, for Carlos did not become commandant at New Madrid until 1796. His move was motivated by the grand scheme for commercial wealth that he had dreamt up with his colleagues, Pierre Audrain and Bartholémé Tardiveau. De Luzières thought it best not to go into that issue when he addressed the U.S. Congress. No evidence exists that anyone in Congress took de Luzières's petition seriously, or even bothered to look at it.

PC, Leg. 216B
Memorial addressed by Pierre-Charles Dehault De Luzières to the honorable members of the Congress of the United States of America

Don Pierre-Charles Dehault De Luzières, chevalier and captain, civil and military commandant for His Catholic Majesty the King of Spain [Carlos IV] of the post of New Bourbon and its dependencies, located in the western part of Illinois on the right bank of the Mississippi River has the honor of informing you of the following: When he decided to emigrate from the kingdom of France, and having seen a prospectus for real estate sales at Scioto on the right bank of the Ohio River, he decided to purchase from the Scioto Company 2,000 acres of land. Accordingly, he paid to the representatives of this company in Paris 6,000 livres tournois,[76] plus the cost of the title work, on June 19, 1790.

His original plan was to send a representative to reconnoiter the area and take possession of the property. However, representatives of the Scioto Company assured him and the men who were hauling his furniture and possessions (however extensive they might be) that once they were delivered to one of the Company's freighters in the port of Le Havre de Grace he would have no freight to pay from this port all the way to Scioto.... He therefore decided to go to Scioto himself with his wife, several of his children, plus eight servants and *engagés.* Accordingly, he embarked with all of his furniture and possessions at Le Havre de Grace on August 24, 1790, on the ship *Citoyens de Paris.*

But when the supplicant arrived at Philadelphia in America [October 15], Sieur Millet, captain of the ship, refused to let him disembark and refused to unload his possessions until he had paid 2,532 livres tournois for his passengers and 627 livres tournois for his possessions. During his layover in Philadelphia, he was required to pay 1,365 livres tournois and 15 sous for storage, food and lodging for his family, servants and *engagés.* Despite the protestations made by the supplicant, in concert with other *émigrés* headed for Scioto, he was forced to pay 4,050 livres tournois for transportation and freight from Philadelphia to Buffalo Creek on the Ohio. Arriving at Washington [an American fort built in 1789 near present-day Cincinnati], the supplicant learned that no preparations had been made to welcome the *émigrés* at Buffalo Creek and get them embarked for Scioto. Colonel Franks, one of the commissaires of the Scioto Company, had assured them that this would be done. The supplicant therefore decided to remain at Washington with his family and some other folks where he remained for close to two months at a cost of 1,460 livres tournois.

In February 1791, concluding that there was not the least hope of obtaining the lands at Scioto that had been sold to him by the Company, he decided to proceed to Pittsburgh. The high cost of transport from Buffalo Creek up the Ohio to Pittsburgh, plus the expense of renting a house there, amounted to 5,325 livres tournois. Following these setbacks, which were so costly and prejudicial, the supplicant again protested to the Company. To these diverse and

76. In the Illinois Country during the late eighteenth century, the French livre was valued at one-fifth of a Spanish piastre, whose value was the same as the American dollar. Therefore, in very, very rough terms the livre was worth 20 cents.

unexpected expenses must be added the loss of his *engagés*. Not getting settled on the land that the supplicant had acquired at Scioto, and therefore not being employed in the work they were supposed to have, they've freed themselves and deserted, which amounts to a loss of at least 2,500 livres tournois. In that situation, so burdensome and deplorable for an honest family that had immigrated and had its hopes dashed, there remained little else for the supplicant to do other than purchase a plantation on the Monongahela near Pittsburgh and have a house built at great expense. This was done with funds that came from selling part of his silverware and finest possessions. The supplicant lost the rest of his fortune that he had left behind in France because of the French Revolution. He had hoped to use this to support himself on the plantation he had purchased, but he was forced to sell it at a big loss of at least 17,000 livres tournois. In 1793 he had moved on to Louisiana, where one of his sons, a former officer in the Walloon guards in Spain, had risen to the rank of lieutenant colonel in the fixed regiment of Louisiana. He was commandant at New Madrid on the Mississippi River close to the mouth of the Ohio, and the supplicant hoped to find with him safety, succor and relief from his misery.

The supplicant settled at New Bourbon in the Illinois Country close to Ste. Genevieve and in 1797 he became commandant of this new settlement. In 1792 the Scioto Company was dissolved and its principal members went bankrupt. Several émigrés had purchased land from the company. Among these were the marquis de Marnesia[77] and the supplicant, who wrote to Congress to inform it about their frightful situation and the manner in which they had been so shamefully defrauded. They also asked Congress to indemnify them with lands on the Illinois River in proportion to the quantities that they purchased from the Scioto Company. Congress appointed some commissioners, and conferences were held with the marquis de Marnesia. He was led to believe that Congress viewed the case favorably and would deal compassionately with it. But the Marquis de Marnesia, who was to pursue the issue, returned to Europe.

The supplicant has since learned that the Congress continues to view with compassion and fairness the case of immigrants who had purchased land

77. Claude-François Adrien, marquis de Lezay-Marnesia (1735–1800), was elected to the States General from the Jura region in 1789 and joined the Third Estate (as did Lafayette) at the time of the Tennis Court Oath in June, thereby becoming a member of the National Assembly. Disenchanted with the course of the Revolution he left for America and wound up in the Ohio River valley where he must have met de Luzières. See Moreau-Zanelli, *Gallipolis,* passim; also "Prospects for the Gallipolis Settlement: French Diplomatic Dispatches," edited and translated by Phillip J. Wolfe and Warren J. Wolfe, in *Ohio History* 103 (Winter–Spring 1994): 41–56.

from the Scioto Company and has indemnified them with lands on the Ohio River. Notably, Sieur Gervais has obtained 4,000 acres facing Sandy Creek [across the Ohio from present-day Ashland, Kentucky]. The supplicant believes it's reasonable that he should share in this beneficence of Congress and hopes to obtain a like quantity of 4,000 acres of land. His total expenses for the price he paid for land at Scioto, as well as for his expenses stemming from the total collapse of that initiative, amount to 40,859 livres 15 sous.[78] If, as he hopes, the supplicant received this equitable indemnity of 4,000 acres, he requests that Congress give him this land on the Illinois River close to its entrance into the Mississippi, above the village of Cahokia, in the area of the grottoes of Pelissa (Piasa or Paillissa).[79] This land lends itself to improvement, and the supplicant wants it for his older son [Jacques-Marcellin], who wishes to settle there.

The supplicant flatters himself to think that the Congress will render him justice and grant his request. It's well known that residents along the American side of the Mississippi own land on the Spanish side—without difficulty, inconvenience, or obstacles—as those residing on the Spanish side own land on the American side. Finally, the supplicant wishes to add, with faith and honesty, that while he himself lived with his family for more than three years in the United States close to Pittsburgh, he always conducted himself in irreproachable fashion. He is even persuaded that if need be generals Ste. Claire and Gipson, Colonel Moÿland, Sergeants Neville and Hoara, who know him well, would vouch for his conduct, probity, and honesty.

For these reasons, the supplicant confidently rests his case with you, Honorable Members, in requesting that he be granted, for himself and his heirs, in full ownership as an indemnity based on the considerations detailed above, the quantity of 4,000 acres of land on the left bank of the Illinois River close to its entrance into the Mississippi, in the area known as the grottoes of Palissa [sic], The location could be selected by Colonel Moulin, commandant of Cahokia, who could then authorize the said supplicant to forthwith have the 4,000 acres surveyed.

Done at New Bourbon in the Illinois, March 29, 1799, and signed by Dehault de Lassus de Luzières.

78. This would have been roughly $8,000. See above, n. 75.
79. The Piasa or Piasa Bird was a mythological creature painted by prehistoric Indians on a cliff above the Mississippi River in present-day Jersey County near Elsah, Illinois. See David J. Costa, "Culture-Hero and Trickster Stories," in Brian Swann, ed., *Algonquian Spirit: Contemporary Translations of the Algonquian Literatures of North America* (Lincoln: University of Nebraska Press, 2005), 297; Finiels, *Account of Upper Louisiana*, 76, 83.

No. 34

This avowal to take an oath of loyalty to King Carlos IV of Spain, drafted by an unknown person, was signed by John Matthews. "Legitimate" for his woman presumably means that John and Nancy had been officially married. As governor general of Spanish Louisiana, Manuel Gayoso de Lemos demanded that all immigrants to Spanish Illinois be Roman Catholics. His predecessor, Luis-Hector de Carondelet, had been more lenient, as evidenced by the many Protestants of various denominations that appear on de Luzières's 1797 enumeration of the population of New Bourbon (printed above). De Luzières as commandant of the New Bourbon District received Matthews's oath. Matthews did in fact apply for a land grant with the intendent general of Louisiana, Ramón de Lopéz y Angulo, and this grant was eventually confirmed by the U.S. Land Office (see the next document). The headwaters of the St. Francis River are in St. Francois County, Missouri, about thirty-five miles west of Ste. Genevieve.

Ste. Genevieve Civil Records, Official Documents, nos. 83, 84
October 17, 1800

John Matthews, farmer from North Carolina, and a woman named Nancy, a boy and a girl, four horses, eight head of cattle, twenty-five pigs, and assorted household and farming implements.

I the undersigned certify that I am prepared to take an oath of loyalty to His Catholic Majesty [i.e., King Carlos IV of Spain], that my woman [or wife] is legitimate, as are my above-mentioned children, and that the above-mentioned animals belong to us. I further certify that my family members profess the Roman Catholic and Apostolic religion.

Done at New Bourbon, October 17, 1800
John Matthews

In view of the declaration given above, and after having duly received the oath from the said John Matthews, we have accepted him as a resident of our district [of New Bourbon] and permitted him to settle in this district at the Forks of the St. Francis River. He has permission to seek out there unclaimed land from the royal domain and ask that it be granted to him by the intendant of the province [of Louisiana] so that he may establish his farmstead there.

Done at New Bourbon, October 17, 1800
P^re [Pierre] Delassus De Luzières

No. 35

Notice that Matthews submitted his request for a land grant just three days after he had taken his loyalty oath to King Carlos IV, as seen in the preceding document. On January 7, 1806, Matthews requested comfirmation from the U.S. Land Office of 1,070 square arpents (approx. 910 acres) on the "Waters of St. François," which he claimed to have been working since 1802. He was granted 640 acres, one square mile. His neighbor, William Dillon, received the same acreage (See American state papers: documents, legislative and executive, of the Congress of the United States, Public Lands. *[Washington: Gales and Seaton, 1832–1861], 3, 308–9). Thomas Madden was assistant for the Ste. Genevieve–New Bourbon region to Antoine Soulard, surveyor general of Spanish Upper Louisiana.*

Ste. Genevieve Civil Records, Concessions, no. 66
John Matthews Concession
October 20, 1800

To Monseignor Ramón de Lopéz y Angulo
Intendant General of Louisiana
   John Matthews humbly begs the honor of informing you that he has been admitted as a resident of New Bourbon, that he has a family and animals, and that he wishes to settle down and develop a farm. He has found an appropriate tract of land containing 600 square arpents [approx. 510 acres] situated on the north branch of the St. Francis River contiguous on the north to the lands of Sieur William Dillon. Accordingly, the supplicant puts this issue in your hands.

Monseignor:
   Regarding that it should please you to grant him the above-mentioned land consisting of 600 square arpents for him and his heirs in full ownership in order to cultivate the land and raise a large number of animals—it has been granted to no one, which the surveyor of this district [Thomas Madden], as well as the closest neighbors, can certify. The supplicant prays unceasingly for your long life.
      Done at New Bourbon, October 20, 1800
         John Matthews

   The undersigned civil and military commandant of the outpost and district of New Bourbon certifies to Monseignor, the intendant of this province [Louisiana], that the contents of the present request are sincere and truthful, that the supplicant is an honest man and a good farmer, that he has a numerous family and a very large number of animals, and that he is well suited advantageously to exploit and increase the value of the concession that he requests and where he wished to establish his farmstead. The real estate in question is vacant, being claimed by no one, and is part of the royal domain. We have been assured of this by Sieur [Thomas] Madden, surveyor of this district, as well as the two closest neighbors, who are willing to provide depositions if the supplicant asks for them.

Done at New Bourbon, October 25, 1800

    Pre [Pierre] Delassus De Luzières

No. 36

The spring of 1804 was a time of special bitterness for de Luzières. Most inhabitants of Spanish Illinois would have preferred not to become citizens of the young, expansionary American republic. But after what had occurred in France during the republican phase of the Revolution—i.e., the bloody Terror (1793–1794)—no one in all Louisiana was more royalist and less republican than de Luzières. He seems to have been slow in recognizing that he was destined to die an American citizen, but by April 1804 he was forced to recognize that that indeed would be his bitter fate. And, of course, Captain Amos Stoddard, the new American commandant of Upper Louisiana, immediately extinguished the New Bourbon District, depriving de Luzières of any authority he had had. De Luzières's son, De Lassus, soon departed St. Louis for Spanish Florida and continued to serve in the royal Spanish army until 1811.[80]

Archives of the Missouri Historical Society, Delassus-St. Vrain Collection
De Luzières to Don Charles Dehault De Lassus, colonel in the armies of His Catholic Majesty, former lieutenant governor of Upper Louisiana at St. Louis
New Bourbon, April 10, 1804

In accordance with the order and instructions addressed to me by His Catholic Majesty's commissioners, as well as by you yourself, to render to the United States of America the post and district of New Bourbon, I thought that it was indispensible for me to draft an exact inventory of all the titles, acts, procedures, and other current papers located in the archives of the said post. . . .

It is not without pain and regret that I understand that this will be my last official correspondence with you. I will nevertheless continue to pray to God that he will always keep you in his holy and tender care.

    Pierre Delassus De Luzières

80. Robert R. Archibald, "Honor and Family: The Career of Lt. Gov. Carlos de Hault de Lassus," *Gateway Heritage* 12, no. 4 (Spring 1992): 32–41.

Index

Abenaki Indians, 136, 138, 143, 161, 199. *See also* Delaware Indians

Adet, Pierre-Auguste, French minister to U.S.: sends General Collot to reconnoiter Mississippi Valley, 27, 154

Agriculture: in Illinois Country, 9, 44–45, 75, 108, 116–17, 120–22, 149, 164, 202–3

Aimé, Charles: farmer on 1797 New Bourbon census, 178

Allen, Thomas: wanted for rape, 92–93

American Revolution, 14, 21, 26, 32, 33, 53, 61, 62, 75, 82, 91, 138, 166n30

Americans: character of, 33, 35, 36, 45, 58, 94–99; de Luzières recruits, 2, 73–83, 150–52; killed by Shawnees, 47–48; at New Madrid, 74; Pinckney's Treaty and, 95–99; at Ste. Genevieve, 102; settle in Spanish Illinois, 74, 76, 82, 84, 88–89, 108, 157–58, 217, 223–25; threaten Spanish Illinois, 3, 61–63, 86, 129–30, 138, 140

Anopheles mosquitoes: carry malaria, 143

Anse à la Graisse: early name of New Madrid, 74, 135, 150, 151

Apple Creek: boundary of Ste. Genevieve district, 84, 86; Indian tribes located along, 85, 200

Apples: commerce in, 34, 56, 87, 94, 151, 162, 202

Aranda, Pedro Pablo de: Spanish statesman comments about the U.S., 33

Architecture: of riverboats, 54; in Ste. Genevieve, 51, 60

Arkansas Post, 70, 122

Arras, bishopric of, 9

Auction sales, 97, 110–11

Audrain, Pierre: associate of de Luzières, 1, 26–28, 35–50; moves to Detroit, 66–67, 159; resident of Pittsburgh, 26, 31, 158

Audrey, John: cooper at Saline, 191

Austin Moses: moves to Spanish Illinois, 80, 159, 292; visits de Luzières household, 80–81, 100, 158

Barbier, Joseph: farmer at the Saline, 181; fights with Americans, 94–96; ships apples to New Orleans, 94

Barlow, Joel: sells real estate in Paris, 1, 14–16, 21

Barnhart: hunter at Bois Brûlé, 196

Bastille, fortress of, 11

Bateaux. See Riverboats

Belmar, Widow: head-of-household on 1797 New Bourbon census, 176–77

Bernier, François: farmer on 1797 New Bourbon census, 176

Bernier, Widow: head-of-household on 1797 New Bourbon census, 176

Big Field (*Grand Champ*), 51, 94, 112

Bives, John: farmer on 1797 New Bourbon census, 178

Black Code (*Code Noir*), 218

Blacks: fertility among, 88; as free persons, 109, 161–62, 198; in New Bourbon, 83, 87–88, 164–98 passim; in New Orleans, 42; as slaves, 71, 85–88, 157–58, 161, 163; work on de Luzières house, 51, 83

Bois Brûlé, 125; census of, 180, 193–98; division of New Bourbon District, 81, 87, 89–93

Boise (Boyce?), Joseph: farmer at Bois Brûlé, 194

227